THE ART OF INVISIBILITY

Also by Kevin Mitnick

Ghost in the Wires: My Adventures as the World's Most Famous Hacker (with William L. Simon)

The Art of Intrusion: The Real Stories Behind the Exploits of Hackers, Intruders, and Deceivers (with William L. Simon)

The Art of Deception: Controlling the Human Element of Security (with William L. Simon)

THE ART OF INVISIBILITY

The World's Most Famous Hacker Teaches You How to Be Safe in the Age of Big Brother and Big Data

KEVIN MITNICK
with Robert Vamosi

Foreword by Mikko Hypponen

Little, Brown and Company
New York Boston London

Little, Brown and Company
Hachette Book Group
1290 Avenue of the Americas, New York, NY 10104
littlebrown.com

First Edition: February 2017

Little, Brown and Company is a division of Hachette Book Group, Inc. The Little, Brown name and logo are trademarks of Hachette Book Group, Inc.

The publisher is not responsible for websites (or their content) that are not owned by the publisher.

The Hachette Speakers Bureau provides a wide range of authors for speaking events. To find out more, go to hachettespeakersbureau.com or call (866) 376-6591.

Library of Congress Cataloging-in-Publication Data
Names: Mitnick, Kevin D. (Kevin David), author. | Vamosi, Robert, author.
Title: The art of invisibility : the world's most famous hacker teaches you how to be safe in the age of big brother and big data / Kevin Mitnick with Robert Vamosi.
Description: First edition. | New York: Little, Brown and Company, [2017] | Includes bibliographical references and index.
Identifiers: LCCN 2016024302 | ISBN 978-0-316-38050-8 (hc) / 978-0-316-55454-1 (int'l pb)
Subjects: LCSH: Internet—Security measures. | Computer security. | Data protection. | Privacy, Right of.
Classification: LCC TK5105.875.I57 M58 2017 | DDC 005.8—dc23 LC record available at https://lccn.loc.gov/2016024302

10 9 8 7 6 5 4 3 2 1

LSC-C

Printed in the United States of America

To my loving mother, Shelly Jaffe,
and my grandmother Reba Vartanian

Contents

Foreword by Mikko Hypponen

A couple of months ago, I met up with an old friend who I hadn't seen since high school. We went for a cup of coffee to catch up on what each of us had been doing for the past decades. He told me about his work of distributing and supporting various types of modern medical devices, and I explained how I've spent the last twenty-five years working with Internet security and privacy. My friend let out a chuckle when I mentioned online privacy. "That sounds all fine and dandy," he said, "but I'm not really worried. After all, I'm not a criminal, and I'm not doing anything bad. I don't care if somebody looks at what I'm doing online."

Listening to my old friend, and his explanation on why privacy does not matter to him, I was saddened. I was saddened because I've heard these arguments before, many times. I hear them from people who think they have nothing to hide. I hear them from people who think only criminals need to protect themselves. I hear them from people who think only terrorists use encryption. I hear them from people who think we don't need to protect our rights. But we do need to protect our rights. And privacy does not just affect our rights, it *is* a human right. In fact, privacy is recognized as a fundamental human right in the 1948 United Nations Universal Declaration of Human Rights.

If our privacy needed protection in 1948, it surely needs it much more today. After all, we are the first generation in human history that can be monitored at such a precise level. We can be monitored digitally throughout our lives. Almost all of our communications can be seen one way or another. We even carry small tracking devices on us all the time—we just don't call them tracking devices, we call them smartphones.

Online monitoring can see what books we buy and what news articles we read—even which parts of the articles are most interesting to us. It can see where we travel and who we travel with. And online monitoring knows if you are sick, or sad, or horny. Much of the monitoring that is done today compiles this data to make money. Companies that offer free services somehow convert those free services into billions of dollars of revenue—nicely illustrating just how valuable it is to profile Internet users in mass scale. However, there's also more targeted monitoring: the kind of monitoring done by government agencies, domestic or foreign.

Digital communication has made it possible for governments to do bulk surveillance. But it has also enabled us to protect ourselves better. We can protect ourselves with tools like encryption, by storing our data in safe ways, and by following basic principles of operations security (OPSEC). We just need a guide on how to do it right.

Well, the guide you need is right here in your hands. I'm really happy Kevin took the time to write down his knowledge on the art of invisibility. After all, he knows a thing or two about staying invisible. This is a great resource. Read it and use the knowledge to your advantage. Protect yourself and protect your rights.

Back at the cafeteria, after I had finished coffee with my old friend, we parted ways. I wished him well, but I still sometimes think about his words: "I don't care if somebody looks at what I'm doing online." You might not have anything to hide, my friend. But you have everything to protect.

Mikko Hypponen is the chief research officer of F-Secure. He's the only living person who has spoken at both DEF CON and TED conferences.

THE ART OF INVISIBILITY

INTRODUCTION

Time to Disappear

Almost two years to the day after Edward Joseph Snowden, a contractor for Booz Allen Hamilton, first disclosed his cache of secret material taken from the National Security Agency (NSA), HBO comedian John Oliver went to Times Square in New York City to survey people at random for a segment of his show on privacy and surveillance. His questions were clear. Who is Edward Snowden? What did he do?[1]

In the interview clips Oliver aired, no one seemed to know. Even when people said they recalled the name, they couldn't say exactly what Snowden had done (or why). After becoming a contractor for the NSA, Edward Snowden copied thousands of top secret and classified documents that he subsequently gave to reporters so they could make them public around the world. Oliver could have ended his show's segment about surveillance on a depressing note—after years of media coverage, no one in America really seemed to care about domestic spying by the government—but the comedian chose another tack. He flew to Russia, where Snowden now lives in exile, for a one-on-one interview.[2]

The first question Oliver put to Snowden in Moscow was: What did you hope to accomplish? Snowden answered that he wanted to show the world what the NSA was doing—collecting data on almost everyone. When Oliver showed him the interviews from Times Square, in which one person after another professed not to know who Snowden was, his response was, "Well, you can't have everyone well informed."

Why aren't we more informed when it comes to the privacy issues that Snowden and others have raised? Why don't we seem to care that a government agency is wiretapping our phone calls, our e-mails, and even our text messages? Probably because the NSA, by and large, doesn't directly affect the lives of most of us—at least not in a tangible way, as an intrusion that we can *feel*.

But as Oliver also discovered in Times Square that day, Americans do care about privacy when it hits home. In addition to asking questions about Snowden, he asked general questions about privacy. For example, when he asked how they felt about a secret (but made-up) government program that records images of naked people whenever the images are sent over the Internet, the response among New Yorkers was also universal—except this time everyone opposed it, emphatically. One person even admitted to having recently sent such a photo.

Everyone interviewed in the Times Square segment agreed that people in the United States should be able to share anything—even a photo of a penis—privately over the Internet. Which was Snowden's basic point.

It turns out that the fake government program that records naked pictures is less far-fetched than you might imagine. As Snowden explained to Oliver in their interview, because companies like Google have servers physically located all over the world, even a simple message (perhaps including nudity) between a husband and wife within the same US city might first bounce off a foreign server. Since that data leaves the United States, even for a nanosecond, the NSA could, thanks to the Patriot Act, collect and archive that text or e-mail (including the indecent photo) because it technically entered the United States from a foreign source at the moment when it was captured. Snowden's point: average Americans are being caught up in a post-9/11 dragnet that was initially designed to stop foreign terrorists but that now spies on practically everyone.

You would think, given the constant news about data breaches and surveillance campaigns by the government, that we'd be much more outraged. You would think that given how fast this happened—in just a handful of years—we'd be reeling from the shock and marching in the streets. Actually, the opposite is true. Many of us, even many readers of this book, now accept to at least some degree the fact that everything we do—all our phone calls, our texts, our e-mails, our social media—can be seen by others.

And that's disappointing.

Perhaps you have broken no laws. You live what you think is an average and quiet life, and you feel you are unnoticed among the crowds of others online today. Trust me: even you are not invisible. At least not yet.

I enjoy magic, and some might argue that sleight of hand is necessary for computer hacking. One popular magic trick is to make an object invisible. The secret, however, is that the object does not physically disappear or actually become invisible. The object always remains in the background, behind a curtain, up a sleeve, in a pocket, whether we can see it or not.

The same is true of the many personal details about each and every one of us that are currently being collected and stored, often without our noticing. Most of us simply don't know how easy it is for others to view these details about us or even where to look. And because *we* don't see this information, we might believe that we are invisible to our exes, our parents, our schools, our bosses, and even our governments.

The problem is that if you know where to look, all that information is available to just about anyone.

Whenever I speak before large crowds—no matter the size of the room—I usually have one person who challenges me on this fact. After one such event I was challenged by a very skeptical reporter.

I remember we were seated at a private table in a hotel bar in a large US city when the reporter said she'd never been a victim of a data breach. Given her youth, she said she had relatively few assets to her name, hence few records. She never put personal details into any of her stories or her personal social media—she kept it professional. She considered herself invisible. So I asked her for permission to find her Social Security number and any other personal details online. Reluctantly she agreed.

With her seated nearby I logged in to a site, one that is reserved for private investigators. I qualify as the latter through my work investigating hacking incidents globally. I already knew her name, so I asked where she lived. This I could have found on the Internet as well, on another site, if she hadn't told me.

In a couple of minutes I knew her Social Security number, her city of birth, and even her mother's maiden name. I also knew all the places she'd ever called home and all the phone numbers she'd ever used. Staring at the screen, with a surprised look on her face, she confirmed that all the information was more or less true.

The site I used is restricted to vetted companies or individuals. It charges a low fee per month plus additional costs for any information lookups, and from time to time it will audit me to find out whether I have a legitimate purpose for conducting a particular search.

But similar information about anyone can be found for a small lookup fee. And it's perfectly legal.

Have you ever filled out an online form, submitted information to a school or organization that puts its information online, or had a legal case posted to the Internet? If so, you have volunteered personal information to a third party that may do with the information what it pleases. Chances are that some—if not all—of that data is now online and available to companies that make it their business to collect every bit of personal information off the Internet. The Privacy Rights Clearinghouse lists more than 130 companies that collect personal information (whether or not it's accurate) about you.[3]

And then there's the data that you don't volunteer online but that is nonetheless being harvested by corporations and governments—information about whom we e-mail, text, and call; what we search for online; what we buy, either in a brick-and-mortar or an online store; and where we travel, on foot or by car. The volume of data collected about each and every one of us is growing exponentially each day.

You may think you don't need to worry about this. Trust me: you do. I hope that by the end of this book you will be both well-informed and prepared enough to do something about it.

The fact is that we live with an illusion of privacy, and we probably have been living this way for decades.

At a certain point, we might find ourselves uncomfortable with how much access our government, our employers, our bosses, our teachers, and our parents have into our personal lives. But since that access has been gained gradually, since we've embraced each small digital convenience without resisting its impact on our privacy, it becomes increasingly hard to turn back the clock. Besides, who among us wants to give up our toys?

The danger of living within a digital surveillance state isn't so much that the data is being collected (there's little we can do about that) but *what is done with the data* once it is collected.

Imagine what an overzealous prosecutor could do with the large dossier of raw data points available on you, perhaps going back several years. Data today, sometimes collected out of context, will live forever. Even US Supreme Court justice Stephen Breyer agrees that it is "difficult for anyone to know, in advance, just when a particular set of statements might later appear (to a prosecutor) to be relevant to some such investigation."[4] In other words, a picture of you drunk that someone posted on Facebook might be the least of your concerns.

You may think you have nothing to hide, but do you know that for sure? In a well-argued opinion piece in *Wired,* respected security researcher Moxie Marlinspike points out that something as simple as being in possession of a small lobster is actually a federal crime in the United States.[5] "It doesn't matter if you bought it at a grocery store, if someone else gave it to you, if it's dead or alive, if you found it after it died of natural causes, or even if you killed it while acting in self-defense. You can go to jail because of a lobster."[6] The point here is there are many minor, unenforced laws that you could be breaking without knowing it. Except now there's a data trail to prove it just a few taps away, available to any person who wants it.

Privacy is complex. It is not a one-size-fits-all proposition. We all have different reasons for sharing some information about ourselves freely with strangers and keeping other parts of our lives private. Maybe you simply don't want your significant other reading your personal stuff. Maybe you don't want your employer to know about your private life. Or maybe you really do fear that a government agency is spying on you.

These are very different scenarios, so no one recommendation offered here is going to fit them all. Because we hold complicated and therefore very different attitudes toward privacy, I'll guide you through what's important—what's happening today with surreptitious data collection—and let you decide what works for your own life.

If anything, this book will make you aware of ways to be private within the digital world and offer solutions that you may or may not choose to adopt. Since privacy is a personal choice, degrees of invisibility, too, will vary by individual.

In this book I'll make the case that each and every one of us is being watched, at home and out in the world—as you walk down the street, sit at a café, or drive down the highway. Your computer, your phone, your car, your home alarm system, even your refrigerator are all potential points of access into your private life.

The good news is, in addition to scaring you, I'm also going to show you what to do about the lack of privacy—a situation that has become the norm.

In this book, you'll learn how to:

- encrypt and send a secure e-mail
- protect your data with good password management
- hide your true IP address from places you visit
- obscure your computer from being tracked
- defend your anonymity
- and much more

Now, get ready to master the art of invisibility.

CHAPTER ONE

Your Password Can Be Cracked!

Jennifer Lawrence was having a rough Labor Day weekend. The Academy Award winner was one of several celebrities who woke one morning in 2014 to find that their most private pictures—many of which showed them in the nude—were being splashed about on the Internet.

Take a moment to mentally scan all the images that are currently stored on your computer, phone, and e-mail. Sure, many of them are perfectly benign. You'd be fine with the whole world seeing the sunsets, the cute family snapshots, maybe even the jokey bad-hair-day selfie. But would you be comfortable sharing each and every one of them? How would you feel if they suddenly all appeared online? Maybe not all our personal photos are salacious, but they're still records of private moments. We should be able to decide whether, when, and how to share them, yet with cloud services the choice may not always be ours.

The Jennifer Lawrence story dominated the slow Labor Day weekend news cycle in 2014. It was part of an event called theFappening, a huge leak of nude and nearly nude photographs of Rihanna, Kate Upton, Kaley Cuoco, Adrianne Curry, and almost three hundred other celebrities, most of them women, whose cell-phone images had somehow been remotely accessed and shared. While some people were, predictably, interested in seeing these photos, for many the incident was an unsettling reminder that the same thing could have happened to them.

So how did someone get access to those private images of Jennifer Lawrence and others?

Since all the celebrities used iPhones, early speculation centered on a massive data breach affecting Apple's iCloud service, a cloud-storage option for iPhone users. As your physical device runs out of memory, your photos, new files, music, and games are instead stored on a server at Apple, usually for a small monthly fee. Google offers a similar service for Android.

Apple, which almost never comments in the media on security issues, denied any fault on their end. The company issued a statement calling the incident a "very targeted attack on user names, passwords, and security questions" and added that "none of the cases we have investigated has resulted from any breach in any of Apple's systems including iCloud or Find my iPhone."[1]

The photos first started appearing on a hacker forum well known for posting compromised photos.[2] Within that forum you can find active discussions of the digital forensic tools used for surreptitiously obtaining such photos. Researchers, investigators, and law enforcement use these tools to access data from devices or the cloud, usually following a crime. And of course the tools have other uses as well.

One of the tools openly discussed on the forum, Elcomsoft Phone Password Breaker, or EPPB, is intended to enable law enforcement and government agencies to access iCloud accounts and is sold publicly. It is just one of many tools out there, but it appears to be the most popular on the forum. EPPB requires that users have the target's iCloud username and password information first. For people using this forum, however, obtaining iCloud usernames and passwords is not a problem. It so happened that over that holiday weekend in 2014, someone posted to a popular online code repository (Github) a tool called iBrute, a password-hacking mechanism specifically designed for acquiring iCloud credentials from just about anyone.

Using iBrute and EPPB together, someone could impersonate a victim and download a full backup of that victim's cloud-stored iPhone data onto another device. This capability is useful when you upgrade your phone, for example. It is also valuable to an attacker, who then can see everything you've ever done on your mobile device. This yields much more information than just logging in to a victim's iCloud account.

Jonathan Zdziarski, a forensics consultant and security researcher, told *Wired* that his examination of the leaked photos from Kate Upton, for example, was consistent with the use of iBrute and EPPB. Having access to a restored iPhone backup gives an attacker lots of personal information that might later be useful for blackmail.[3]

In October 2016, Ryan Collins, a thirty-six-year-old from Lancaster, Pennsylvania, was sentenced to eighteen months in prison for "unauthorized access to a protected computer to obtain information" related to the hack. He was charged with illegal access to over one hundred Apple and Google e-mail accounts.[4]

To protect your iCloud and other online accounts, you must set a strong password. That's obvious. Yet in my experience as a penetration tester (pen tester)—someone who is paid to hack into computer networks and find vulnerabilities—I find that many people, even executives at large corporations, are lazy when it comes to passwords. Consider that the CEO of Sony Entertainment, Michael Lynton, used "sonyml3" as his domain account password. It's no wonder his e-mails were hacked and spread across the Internet since the attackers had administrative access to most everything within the company.

Beyond your work-related passwords are those passwords that protect your most personal accounts. Choosing a hard-to-guess password won't prevent hacking tools such as oclHashcat (a password-cracking tool that leverages graphics processing units—or GPUs—for high-speed cracking) from possibly cracking your password, but it will make the process slow enough to encourage an attacker to move on to an easier target.

It's a fair guess that some of the passwords exposed during the July 2015 Ashley Madison hack are certainly being used elsewhere, including on bank accounts and even work computers. From the lists of 11 million Ashley Madison passwords posted online, the most common were "123456," "12345," "password," "DEFAULT," "123456789," "qwerty," "12345678," "abc123," and "1234567."[5] If you see one of your own passwords here, chances are you are vulnerable to a data breach, as these common terms are included in most password-cracking tool kits available online. You can always check the site www.haveibeenpwned.com to see if your account has been compromised in the past.

In the twenty-first century, we can do better. And I mean *much* better, with longer and much more complex configurations of letters and numbers. That may sound hard, but I will show you both an automatic and a manual way to do this.

The easiest approach is to forgo the creation of your own passwords and simply automate the process. There are several digital password managers out there. Not only do they store your passwords within a locked vault and allow one-click access when you need them, they also generate new and really strong, unique passwords for each site when you need them.

Be aware, though, of two problems with this approach. One is that password managers use one master password for access. If someone happens to infect your computer with malware that steals the password database and your master password through keylogging—when the malware records every keystroke you make—it's game over. That person will then have access to all your passwords. During my pen-testing engagements, I sometimes replace the password manager with a modified version that transmits the master password to us (when the password manager is open-source). This is done after we gain admin access to the client's network. We then go after all the privileged passwords. In other words, we will use password managers as a back door to get the keys to the kingdom.

The other problem is kind of obvious: If you lose the master password, you lose all your passwords. Ultimately, this is okay, as you can always perform a password reset on each site, but that would be a huge hassle if you have a lot of accounts.

Despite these flaws, the following tips should be more than adequate to keep your passwords secure.

First, strong passphrases, not passwords, should be long—at least twenty to twenty-five characters. Random characters—ek5iogh#skf&skd—work best. Unfortunately the human mind has trouble remembering random sequences. So use a password manager. Using a password manager is far better than choosing your own. I prefer open-source password managers like Password Safe and KeePass that only store data locally on your computer.

Another important rule for good passwords is never use the same password for two different accounts. That's hard. Today we have passwords on just about everything. So have a password manager generate and store strong, unique passwords for you.

Even if you have a strong password, technology can still be used to defeat you. There are password-guessing programs such as John the Ripper, a free open-source program that anyone can download and that works within configuration parameters set by the user.[6] For example, a user might specify how many characters to try, whether to use special symbols, whether to include foreign language sets, and so on. John the Ripper and other password hackers are able to permute the password letters using rule sets that are extremely effective at cracking passwords. This simply means it tries every possible combination of numbers, letters, and symbols within the parameters until it is successful at cracking your password. Fortunately, most of us aren't up against nation-states with virtually unlimited time and resources. More likely we're up against a spouse, a relative, or someone we really pissed off who, when faced with a twenty-five-character password, won't have the time or resources to successfully crack it.

Let's say you want to create your passwords the old-fashioned way and that you've chosen some really strong passwords. Guess what? It's okay to write them down. Just don't write "Bank of America: 4the1sttimein4ever*." That would be too obvious. Instead replace the name of your bank (for example) with something cryptic, such as "Cookie Jar" (because some people once hid their money in cookie jars) and follow it with "4the1st." Notice I didn't complete the phrase. You don't need to. You know the rest of the phrase. But someone else might not.

Anyone finding this printed-out list of incomplete passwords should be sufficiently confused—at least at first. Interesting story: I was at a friend's house—a very well-known Microsoft employee—and during dinner we were discussing the security of passwords with his wife and child. At one point my friend's wife got up and went to the refrigerator. She had written down all her passwords on a single piece of paper and stuck it to the appliance's door with a magnet. My friend just shook his head, and I grinned widely. Writing down passwords might not be a perfect solution, but neither is forgetting that rarely used strong password.

Some websites—such as your banking website—lock out users after several failed password attempts, usually three. Many sites, however, still do not do this. But even if a site does lock a person out after three failed attempts, that isn't how the bad guys use John the Ripper or oclHashcat. (Incidentally, oclHashcat distributes the hacking process over multiple GPUs and is much more powerful than John the Ripper.) Also, hackers don't actually try every single possible password on a live site.

Let's say there has been a data breach, and included within the data dump are usernames and passwords. But the passwords retrieved from the data breach are mere gibberish.

How does that help anyone break into your account?

Whenever you type in a password, whether it is to unlock your laptop or an online service—that password is put through a one-way algorithm known as a hash function. It is not the same as encryption. Encryption is two-way: you can encrypt and decrypt as long as you have a key. A hash is a fingerprint representing a particular string of characters. In theory, one-way algorithms can't be reversed—or at least not easily.

What is stored in the password database on your traditional PC, your mobile device, or your cloud account is not MaryHadALittleLamb123$ but its hash value, which is a sequence of numbers and letters. The sequence is a token that represents your password.[7]

It is the password hashes, not the passwords themselves, that are stored in the protected memory of our computers and can be obtained from a compromise of targeted systems or leaked in data breaches. Once an attacker has obtained these password hashes, the hacker can use a variety of publicly available tools, such as John the Ripper or oclHashcat, to crack the hashes and obtain the actual password, either through brute force (trying every possible alphanumeric combination) or trying each word in a word list, such as a dictionary. Options available in John the Ripper and oclHashcat allow the attacker to modify the words tried against numerous rule sets, for example the rule set called leetspeak—a system for replacing letters with numbers, as in "k3v1n m17n1ck." This rule will change all passwords to various leetspeak permutations. Using these methods to crack passwords is much more effective than simple brute force. The simplest and most common passwords are easily cracked first, then more complex passwords are cracked over time. The length of time it takes depends on several factors. Using a password-cracking tool together with your breached username and hashed password, hackers may be able to access one or more of your accounts by trying that password on additional sites connected to your e-mail address or other identifier.

In general, the more characters in your password, the longer it will take password-guessing programs such as John the Ripper to run through all the possible variations. As computer processors get faster, the length of time it takes to calculate all the possible six-character and even eight-character passwords is becoming a lot shorter, too. That's why I recommend using passwords of twenty-five characters or more.

After you create strong passwords—and many of them—never give them out. That seems painfully obvious, but surveys in London and other major cities show that people have traded their passwords in exchange for something as trivial as a pen or a piece of chocolate.[8]

A friend of mine once shared his Netflix password with a girlfriend. It made sense at the time. There was the immediate gratification of letting her choose a movie for them to watch together. But trapped within Netflix's recommended-movie section were all his "because you watched..." movies, including movies he had watched with past girlfriends. *The Sisterhood of the Traveling Pants,* for instance, is not a film he would have ordered himself, and his girlfriend knew this.

Of course, everyone has exes. You might even be suspicious if you dated someone who didn't. But no girlfriend wants to be confronted with evidence of those who have gone before her.

If you password-protect your online services, you should also password-protect your individual devices. Most of us have laptops, and many of us still have desktops. You may be home alone now, but what about those dinner guests coming later? Why take a chance that one of them could access your files, photos, and games just by sitting at your desk and moving the mouse? Another Netflix cautionary tale: back in the days when Netflix primarily sent out

DVDs, I knew a couple who got pranked. During a party at their house, they'd left their browser open to their Netflix account. Afterward, the couple found that all sorts of raunchy B- and C-list movies had been added to their queue—but only after they'd received more than one of these films in the mail.

It's even more important to protect yourself with passwords at the office. Think of all those times you're called away from your desk into an impromptu meeting. Someone could walk by your desk and see the spreadsheet for the next quarter's budget. Or all the e-mails sitting in your inbox. Or worse, unless you have a password-protected screen saver that kicks in after a few seconds of inactivity, whenever you're away from your desk for an extended period—out to lunch or at a long meeting—someone could sit down and write an e-mail and send it as you. Or even alter the next quarter's budget.

There are creative new methods to preventing this, like screen-locking software that uses Bluetooth to verify if you are near your computer. In other words, if you go to the bathroom and your mobile phone goes out of Bluetooth range of the computer, the screen is immediately locked. There are also versions that use a Bluetooth device like a wristband or smartwatch and will do the same thing.

Creating passwords to protect online accounts and services is one thing, but it's not going to help you if someone gains physical possession of your device, especially if you've left those online accounts open. So if you password-protect only one set of devices, it should be your mobile devices, because these are the most vulnerable to getting lost or stolen. Yet *Consumer Reports* found that 34 percent of Americans don't protect their mobile devices with any security measures at all, such as locking the screen with a simple four-digit PIN.[9]

In 2014 a Martinez, California, police officer confessed to stealing nude photos from the cell phone of a DUI suspect, a clear violation of the Fourth Amendment, which is part of the Constitution's Bill of

Rights.[10] Specifically, the Fourth Amendment prohibits unreasonable searches and seizures without a warrant issued by a judge and supported by probable cause—law enforcement officers have to state why they want access to your phone, for instance.

If you haven't already password-protected your mobile device, take a moment now and do so. Seriously.

There are three common ways to lock your phone—whether it's an Android or iOS or something else. The most familiar is a passcode—a sequence of numbers that you enter in a specific order to unlock your phone. Don't settle for the number of digits the phone recommends. Go into your settings and manually configure the passcode to be stronger—seven digits if you want (like an old phone number from your childhood.) Certainly use more than just four.

Some mobile devices allow you to choose a text-based passcode, such as the examples we created on page 15. Again, choose at least seven characters. Modern mobile devices display both number and letter keys on the same screen, making it easier to switch back and forth between them.

Another lock option is visual. Since 2008, Android phones have been equipped with something called Android lock patterns (ALPs). Nine dots appear on the screen, and you connect them in any order you want; that connecting sequence becomes your passcode. You might think this ingenious and that the sheer range of possible combinations makes your sequence unbreakable. But at the PasswordsCon conference in 2015, researchers reported that—human nature being what it is—participants in a study availed themselves of just a few possible patterns out of the 140,704 possible combinations on ALP.[11] And what were those predictable patterns? Often the first letter of the user's name. The study also found that people tended to use the dots in the middle and not in the remote four corners. Consider that the next time you set an ALP.

Finally there's the biometric lock. Apple, Samsung, and other popular manufacturers currently allow customers the option of using a fingerprint scanner to unlock their phones. Be aware that these are not foolproof. After the release of Touch ID, researchers—perhaps expecting Apple to have improved upon the current crop of fingerprint scanners already on the market—were surprised to find that several old methods of defeating fingerprint scanners still work on the iPhone. These include capturing a fingerprint off of a clean surface using baby powder and clear adhesive tape.

Other phones use the built-in camera for facial recognition of the owner. This, too, can be defeated by holding up a high-resolution photograph of the owner in front of the camera.

In general, biometrics by themselves are vulnerable to attacks. Ideally biometrics should be used as just one authenticating factor. Swipe your fingertip or smile for the camera, then enter a PIN or passcode. That should keep your mobile device secure.

What if you created a strong password but didn't write it down? Password resets are a godsend when you absolutely can't access an infrequently used account. But they can also be low-hanging fruit for would-be attackers. Using the clues we leave in the form of social media profiles all over the Internet, hackers can gain access to our e-mail—and other services—simply by resetting our passwords.

One attack that has been in the press involves obtaining the target's last four digits of his or her credit card number, and then using that as proof of identity when calling in to a service provider to change the authorized e-mail address. That way, the attacker can reset the password on his or her own without the legitimate owner knowing.

Back in 2008 a student at the University of Tennessee, David Kernell, decided to see whether he could access then vice presidential candidate Sarah Palin's personal Yahoo e-mail account.[12] Kernell could have guessed various passwords, but access to the account might have been locked after a few failed tries. Instead he used the password reset function, a process he later described as "easy."[13]

I'm sure we've all received strange e-mails from friends and associates containing links to porn sites in foreign countries only to learn later that our friends' e-mail accounts had been taken over. These e-mail takeovers often occur because the passwords guarding the accounts are not strong. Either someone learned the password—through a data breach—or the attacker used the password reset function.

When first setting up an account such as an e-mail or even a bank account, you may have been asked what are usually labeled as security questions. Typically there are three of them. Often there are drop-down menus listing suggested questions, so you can choose which ones you want to answer. Usually they are really obvious.

Where were you born? Where did you go to high school? Or college? And the old favorite, your mother's maiden name, which apparently has been in use as a security question since at least 1882.[14] As I'll discuss below, companies can and do scan the Internet and collect personal information that makes answering these basic security questions a piece of cake. A person can spend a few minutes on the Internet and have a good chance of being able to answer all the security questions of a given individual.

Only recently have these security questions improved somewhat. For example, "What is the state where your brother-in-law was born?" is pretty distinct, though answering these "good" questions correctly can carry its own risks, which I'll get to in a minute. But many so-called security questions are still too easy, such as "What is your father's hometown?"

In general, when setting these security questions, try to avoid the most obvious suggestions available from the drop-down menu. Even if the site includes only basic security questions, be creative. No one says you have to provide straightforward answers. You can be clever about it. For example, as far as your streaming video service is concerned, maybe tutti-frutti is your new favorite color. Who would guess that? It is a color, right? What you provide as the answer becomes the "correct" answer to that security question.

Whenever you do provide creative answers, be sure to write down both the question and the answer and put them in a safe place (or simply use a password manager to store your questions and answers). There may be a later occasion when you need to talk to technical support, and a representative might ask you one of the security questions. Have a binder handy or keep a card in your wallet (or memorize and consistently use the same set of responses) to help you remember that "In a hospital" is the correct answer to the question "Where were you born?" This simple obfuscation would thwart someone who later did their Internet research on you and tried a more reasonable response, such as "Columbus, Ohio."

There are additional privacy risks in answering very specific security questions honestly: you are giving out more personal information than is already out there. For example, the honest answer to "What state was your brother-in-law born in?" can then be sold by the site you gave that answer to and perhaps combined with other information or used to fill in missing information. For example, from the brother-in-law answer one can infer that you are or were married and that your partner, or your ex, has a sibling who is either a man or married to a man born in the state you provided. That's a lot of additional information from a simple answer. On the other hand, if you don't have a brother-in-law, go ahead and answer the question creatively, perhaps by answering "Puerto Rico." That should confuse anyone trying to build a profile on you. The more red herrings you provide, the more you become invisible online.

When answering these relatively uncommon questions, always consider how valuable the site is to you. For example, you might trust your bank to have this additional personal information but not your streaming video service. Also consider what the site's privacy policy might be: look for language that says or suggests that it might sell the information it collects to third parties.

The password reset for Sarah Palin's Yahoo e-mail account required her birth date, zip code, and the answer to the security question "Where did you meet your husband?" Palin's birth date and zip code could easily be found online (at the time, Palin was the governor of Alaska). The security question took a bit more work, but the answer to it, too, was accessible to Kernell. Palin gave many interviews in which she stated repeatedly that her husband was her high school sweetheart. That, it turns out, was the correct answer to her security question: "High school."

By guessing the answer to Palin's security question, Kernell was able to reset her Yahoo Mail password to one that he controlled. This allowed him to see all her personal Yahoo e-mails. A screenshot of her inbox was posted on a hacker website. Palin herself was locked out of her e-mail until she reset the password.[15]

What Kernell did was illegal, a violation of the Computer Fraud and Abuse Act. Specifically, he was found guilty on two counts: anticipatory obstruction of justice by destruction of records, a felony, and gaining unauthorized access to a computer, a misdemeanor. He was sentenced in 2010 to one year and one day in prison plus three years of supervised release.[16]

If your e-mail account has been taken over, as Palin's was, first you will need to change your password using (yes, you guessed it) the password reset option. Make this new password a stronger password, as I suggested above. Second, check the Sent box to see exactly what was sent in your name. You might see a spam message that was sent to multiple parties, even your entire contacts list. Now you know why your friends have been sending you spam for all these years—someone hacked their e-mail accounts.

Also check to see whether anyone has added himself to your

account. Earlier we talked about mail forwarding with regard to multiple e-mail accounts. Well, an attacker who gains access to your e-mail service could also have all your e-mail forwarded to his account. You would still see your e-mail normally, but the attacker would see it as well. If someone has added himself to your account, delete this forwarding e-mail address immediately.

Passwords and PINs are part of the security solution, but we've just seen that these can be guessed. Even better than complex passwords are two-factor authentication methods. In fact, in response to Jennifer Lawrence and other celebrities having their nude photos plastered over the Internet, Apple instituted two-factor authentication, or 2FA, for its iCloud services.

What is 2FA?

When attempting to authenticate a user, sites or applications look for at least two of three things. Typically these are something you have, something you know, and something you are. Something you have can be a magnetic stripe or chip-embedded credit or debit card. Something you know is often a PIN or an answer to a security question. And something you are encompasses biometrics—fingerprint scanning, facial recognition, voice recognition, and so on. The more of these you have, the surer you can be that the user is who she says she is.

If this sounds like new technology, it's not. For more than forty years most of us have been performing 2FA without realizing it.

Whenever you use an ATM, you perform 2FA. How is that possible? You have a bank-issued card (that's something you have) and a PIN (that's something you know). When you put them together, the unmanned ATM out on the street knows that you want access to the account identified on the card. In some countries, there are additional means of authentication at ATMs, such as facial recognition and a palm print. This is called multifactor authentication (MFA).

Something similar is possible online. Many financial and health-care institutions, as well as commercial e-mail and social media accounts, allow you to choose 2FA. In this case, the something you know is your password, and the something you have is your cell phone. Using the phone to access these sites is considered "out of band" because the phone is not connected to the computer you are using. But if you have 2FA enabled, an attacker should not be able to access your 2FA-protected accounts without having your mobile device in hand.

Say you use Gmail. To enable 2FA you will be asked to input your cell-phone number on the Gmail site. To verify your identity, Google will then send an SMS code of six digits to your phone. By subsequently inputting that code on the Gmail site, you have just verified that this computer and that cell-phone number are connected.

After that, if someone tries to change the password on your account from a new computer or device, a text message will be sent to your phone. Only when the correct verification code is entered on the website will any change to your account be saved.

There's a wrinkle to that, though. According to researchers at Symantec, if you do send an SMS to confirm your identity, someone who happens to know your cell-phone number can do a bit of social engineering and steal your 2FA-protected password reset code if you are not paying close attention.[17]

Say I want to take over your e-mail account and don't know your password. I do know your cell-phone number because you're easy to find through Google. I can go to the reset page for your e-mail service and request a password reset, which, because you enabled two-factor authentication, will result in an SMS code being sent to your phone. So far, so good, right? Hang on.

A recent attack on a phone used by political activist DeRay Mckesson showed how the bad guys could trick your mobile operator to do a SIM swap.[18] In other words, the attacker could hijack your cellular service and then receive your SMS messages—for example, the SMS code from Google to reset Mckesson's Gmail account that was protected with two-factor authentication. This is much more likely than fooling someone into reading off his or her SMS message with a new password. Although that is still possible, and involves social engineering.

Because I won't see the verification code sent by your e-mail provider to your phone, I'll need to pretend to be someone else in order to get it from you. Just seconds before you receive the actual SMS from, say, Google, I as the attacker can send a one-time SMS, one that says: "Google has detected unusual activity on your account. Please respond with the code sent to your mobile device to stop unauthorized activity."

You will see that yes, indeed, you just got an SMS text from Google containing a legitimate verification code, and so you might, if you are not being careful, simply reply to me in a message and include the code. I would then have less than sixty seconds to enter the verification code. Now I have what I need to enter on the password reset page and, after changing your password, take over your e-mail account. Or any other account.

Since SMS codes are not encrypted and can be obtained in the way I just described, an even more secure 2FA method is to download the Google Authenticator app from Google Play or the iTunes app store for use with an iPhone. This app will generate a unique access code on the app itself each time you want to visit a site that requires 2FA—so there's no SMS to be sent. This app-generated six-digit code is synced with the site's authentication mechanism used to grant access to the site. However, Google Authenticator stores your one-time password seed in the Apple Keychain with a setting for "This Device Only." That means if you back up your iPhone and restore to a *different* device because you are upgrading or replacing a lost phone, your Google Authenticator codes will not be transferred and it's a huge hassle to reset them. It's always a good idea to print out the emergency codes in case you end up switching physical devices. Other apps like 1Password allow you to back up and restore your one-time password seeds so you don't have this problem.

Once you have registered a device, as long as you continue to log in to the site from that device, you will be prompted for a new access code unless you specifically check the box (if available) to trust the computer for thirty days, even if you take your laptop or phone to another location. However, if you use another device—say, you borrow your spouse's computer—then you will be asked for additional authentication. Needless to say, if you're using 2FA, always have your cell phone handy.

Given all these precautions, you might wonder what advice I give to people who are conducting any type of financial transaction online.

For about $100 a year you can get antivirus and firewall protection for up to three computers under your control. The trouble is that when you're surfing the Web, you might load into your browser a banner ad that contains malware. Or maybe you open your e-mail, and one of the e-mails contains malware. One way or another you are going to get your computer infected if it regularly touches the Internet, and your antivirus product may not catch everything that's out there.

So I recommend you spend around $200 to get yourself a Chromebook. I like iPads, but they're expensive. The Chromebook is as close to an easy-to-use tablet as an iPad is, and it costs much less.

My point is that you need to have a secondary device that you use exclusively for financial stuff—perhaps even medical stuff as well. No apps can be installed unless you first register with a Gmail account—this will limit you to opening the browser to surf the Internet.

Then, if you haven't already done so, activate 2FA on the site so that it recognizes the Chromebook. Once you've completed your banking or health-care business, put the Chromebook away until the next time you have to balance your checkbook or arrange a doctor's appointment.

This seems like a hassle. It is. It replaces the convenience of anytime banking with *almost* anytime banking. But the result is that you are far less likely to have someone messing around with your banking and credit information. If you use the Chromebook only for the two or three apps you install, and if you bookmark the banking or health-care websites and visit no others, it is very unlikely that you will have a Trojan or some other form of malware residing on your machine.

So we've established that you need to create strong passwords and not share them. You need to turn on 2FA whenever possible. In the next few chapters we'll look at how common day-to-day interactions can leave digital fingerprints everywhere and what you can do to protect your privacy.

CHAPTER TWO

Who Else Is Reading Your E-mail?

If you're like me, one of the first things you do in the morning is check your e-mail. And, if you're like me, you also wonder who else has read your e-mail. That's not a paranoid concern. If you use a Web-based e-mail service such as Gmail or Outlook 365, the answer is kind of obvious and frightening.

Even if you delete an e-mail the moment you read it on your computer or mobile phone, that doesn't necessarily erase the content. There's still a copy of it somewhere. Web mail is cloud-based, so in order to be able to access it from any device anywhere, at any time, there have to be redundant copies. If you use Gmail, for example, a copy of every e-mail sent and received through your Gmail account is retained on various servers worldwide at Google. This is also true if you use e-mail systems provided by Yahoo, Apple, AT&T, Comcast, Microsoft, or even your workplace. Any e-mails you send can also be inspected, at any time, by the hosting company. Allegedly this is to filter out malware, but the reality is that third parties can and do access our e-mails for other, more sinister and self-serving, reasons.

* * *

In principle, most of us would never stand for anyone except the intended recipient reading our mail. There are laws protecting printed mail delivered through the US Postal Service, and laws protecting stored content such as e-mail. Yet in practice, we usually know and probably accept that there's a certain trade-off involved in the ease of communication e-mail affords. We know that Yahoo (among others) offers a free Web-mail service, and we know that Yahoo makes the majority of its money from advertising. Perhaps we've not realized exactly how the two might be connected and how that might affect our privacy.

One day, Stuart Diamond, a resident of Northern California, did. He realized that the ads he saw in the upper-right-hand corner of his Yahoo Mail client were not random; they were based on the contents of the e-mails he had been sending and receiving. For example, if I mentioned in an e-mail an upcoming speaking trip to Dubai, the ads I might see in my e-mail account would suggest airlines, hotels, and things to do while in the United Arab Emirates.

This practice is usually carefully spelled out in the terms of service that most of us agreed to but probably never read. Nobody wants to see ads that have nothing to do with our individual interests, right? And as long as the e-mail travels between Yahoo account holders, it seems reasonable that the company would be able to scan the contents of those e-mails in order to target ads to us and maybe block malware and spam, which is unwanted e-mail.

However, Diamond, along with David Sutton, also from Northern California, began to notice that the contents of e-mails sent to and received from addresses *outside* Yahoo also influenced the ad selection presented to them. That suggested that the company was intercepting and reading *all* their e-mail, not just those sent to and from its own servers.

Based on the patterns they observed, the two filed a class-action lawsuit in 2012 against Yahoo on behalf of its 275 million account holders, citing concerns around what is essentially equivalent to illegal wiretapping by the company.

Did that end the scanning? No.

In a class-action suit, there is a period of discovery and response from both parties. In this case that initial phase lasted nearly three years. In June of 2015, a judge in San Jose, California, ruled that the men had sufficient grounds for their class-action suit to proceed and that people who sent or received Yahoo Mail since October 2, 2011, when the men filed their initial request, could join in the lawsuit under the Stored Communications Act. Additionally, a class of non–Yahoo Mail account holders living in California may also sue under that state's Invasion of Privacy Act. That case is still pending.

In defending itself against another e-mail-scanning lawsuit, this one filed early in 2014, Google accidentally published information about its e-mail scanning process in a court hearing, then quickly attempted and failed to have that information redacted or removed. The case involved the question of precisely what was scanned or read by Google. According to the plaintiffs in the case, which included several large media companies, including the owners of *USA Today,* Google realized at some point that by scanning only the contents of the inbox, they were missing a lot of potentially useful content. This suit alleged that Google shifted from scanning only archived e-mail, which resides on the Google server, to scanning all Gmail still in transit, whether it was sent from an iPhone or a laptop while the user was sitting in Starbucks.

Sometimes companies have even tried to secretly scan e-mails for their own purposes. One well-known instance of this happened at Microsoft, which suffered a huge backlash when it revealed that it had scanned the inbox of a Hotmail user who was suspected of having pirated a copy of the company's software. As a result of this disclosure, Microsoft has said it will let law enforcement handle such investigations in the future.

These practices aren't limited to your private e-mail. If you send e-mail through your work network, your company's IT department may also be scanning and archiving your communications. It is up to the IT staff or their managers whether to let any flagged e-mail pass through their servers and networks or involve law enforcement. This includes e-mails that contain trade secrets or questionable material such as pornography. It also includes scanning e-mail for malware. If your IT staff is scanning and archiving your e-mails, they should remind you each time you log in what their policy is—although most companies do not.

While most of us may tolerate having our e-mails scanned for malware, and perhaps some of us tolerate scanning for advertising purposes, the idea of third parties reading our correspondence and acting on specific contents found within specific e-mails is downright disturbing. (Except, of course, when it comes to child pornography.[1])

So whenever you write an e-mail, no matter how inconsequential, and even if you delete it from your inbox, remember that there's an excellent chance that a copy of those words and images will be scanned and will live on—maybe not forever, but for a good long while. (Some companies may have short retention policies, but it's safe to assume that most companies keep e-mail for a long time.)

Now that you know the government and corporations are reading your e-mails, the least you can do is make it much harder for them to do so.

Most web-based e-mail services use encryption when the e-mail is in transit. However, when some services transmit mail between Mail Transfer Agents (MTAs), they may not be using encryption, thus your message is in the open. For example, within the workplace a boss may have access to the company e-mail system. To become invisible you will need to encrypt your messages—that is, lock them so that only the recipients can unlock and read them. What is encryption? It is a code.

A very simple encryption example—a Caesar cipher, say—substitutes each letter for another one a certain number of positions away in the alphabet. If that number is 2, for example, then using a Caesar cipher, *a* becomes *c, c* becomes *e, z* becomes *b,* and so forth. Using this offset-by-two encryption scheme, "Kevin Mitnick" becomes "Mgxkp Okvpkem."[2]

Most encryption systems used today are, of course, much stronger than any basic Caesar cipher. Therefore they should be much harder to break. One thing that's true about all forms of encryption is that they require a key, which is used as a password to lock and open the encrypted message. Symmetrical encryption means that the same key is used both to lock and unlock the encrypted message. Symmetrical keys are hard to share, however, when two parties are unknown to each other or physically far apart, as they are on the Internet.

Most e-mail encryption actually uses what's called asymmetrical encryption. That means I generate two keys: a private key that stays on my device, which I never share, and a public key that I post freely on the Internet. The two keys are different yet mathematically related.

For example: Bob wants to send Alice a secure e-mail. He finds Alice's public key on the Internet or obtains it directly from Alice, and when sending a message to her encrypts the message with her key. This message will stay encrypted until Alice—and only Alice—uses a passphrase to unlock her private key and unlock the encrypted message.

So how would encrypting the contents of your e-mail work?

The most popular method of e-mail encryption is PGP, which stands for "Pretty Good Privacy." It is not free. It is a product of the Symantec Corporation. But its creator, Phil Zimmermann, also authored an open-source version, OpenPGP, which is free. And a third option, GPG (GNU Privacy Guard), created by Werner Koch, is also free. The good news is that all three are interoperational. That means that no matter which version of PGP you use, the basic functions are the same.

When Edward Snowden first decided to disclose the sensitive data he'd copied from the NSA, he needed the assistance of like-minded people scattered around the world. Paradoxically, he needed to get off the grid while still remaining active on the Internet. He needed to become invisible.

Even if you don't have state secrets to share, you might be interested in keeping your e-mails private. Snowden's experience and that of others illustrate that it isn't easy to do that, but it is possible, with proper diligence.

Snowden used his personal account through a company called Lavabit to communicate with others. But e-mail is not point-to-point, meaning that a single e-mail might hit several servers around the world before landing in the intended recipient's inbox. Snowden knew that whatever he wrote could be read by anyone who intercepted the e-mail anywhere along its journey.

So he had to perform a complicated maneuver to establish a truly secure, anonymous, and fully encrypted means of communication with privacy advocate and filmmaker Laura Poitras, who had recently finished a documentary about the lives of whistle-blowers. Snowden wanted to establish an encrypted exchange with Poitras, except only a few people knew her public key. She didn't make her public key very public.

To find her public key, Snowden had to reach out to a third party, Micah Lee of the Electronic Frontier Foundation, a group that supports privacy online. Lee's public key was available online and, according to the account published on the *Intercept,* an online publication, he had Poitras's public key, but he first needed to check to see if she would permit him to share it. She would.[3]

At this point neither Lee nor Poitras had any idea who wanted her public key; they only knew that someone did. Snowden had used a different account, not his personal e-mail account, to reach out. But if you don't use PGP often, you may forget to include your PGP key on important e-mails now and again, and that is what happened to Snowden. He had forgotten to include his own public key so Lee could reply.

With no secure way to contact this mystery person, Lee was left with no choice but to send a plain-text, unencrypted e-mail back to Snowden asking for his public key, which he provided.

Once again Lee, a trusted third party, had to be brought into the situation. I can tell you from personal experience that it is very important to verify the identity of the person with whom you are having a secure conversation, preferably through a mutual friend—and make sure you are communicating with that friend and not someone else in disguise.

I know how important this is because I've been the poser before, in a situation where it worked to my advantage that the other party didn't question my real identity or the public key I sent. I once wanted to communicate with Neill Clift, a graduate student in organic chemistry at the University of Leeds, in England, who was very skilled at finding security vulnerabilities in the Digital Equipment Corporation's VMS operating system. I wanted Clift to send me all the security holes that he'd reported to DEC. For that I needed him to think that I actually worked for DEC.

I started by posing as someone named Dave Hutchins and sending Clift a spoofed message from him. I had previously called Clift pretending to be Derrell Piper from VMS engineering, so I (posing as Hutchins) wrote in my e-mail that Piper wanted to exchange e-mails with Clift about a project. In going through DEC's e-mail system, I already knew that Clift and the real Piper had previously e-mailed each other, so this new request wouldn't sound all that odd. I then sent an e-mail spoofing Piper's real e-mail address.

To further convince Clift this was all on the up-and-up, I even suggested that he use PGP encryption so that someone like Kevin Mitnick wouldn't be able to read the e-mails. Soon Clift and "Piper" were exchanging public keys and encrypting communications—communications that I, as Piper, could read. Clift's mistake was in not questioning the identity of Piper himself. Similarly, when you receive an unsolicited phone call from your bank asking for your Social Security number or account information, you should always hang up and call the bank yourself—you never know who is on the other side of the phone call or e-mail.

Given the importance of the secrets they were about to share, Snowden and Poitras could not use their regular e-mail addresses. Why not? Their personal e-mail accounts contained unique associations—such as specific interests, lists of contacts—that could identify each of them. Instead Snowden and Poitras decided to create new e-mail addresses.

The only problem was, how would they know each other's new e-mail addresses? In other words, if both parties were totally anonymous, how would they know who was who and whom they could trust? How could Snowden, for example, rule out the possibility that the NSA or someone else wasn't posing as Poitras's new e-mail account? Public keys are long, so you can't just pick up a secure phone and read out the characters to the other person. You need a secure e-mail exchange.

By enlisting Micah Lee once again, both Snowden and Poitras could anchor their trust in someone when setting up their new and anonymous e-mail accounts. Poitras first shared her new public key with Lee. But PGP encryption keys themselves are rather long (not quite pi length, but they are long), and, again, what if someone were watching his e-mail account as well? So Lee did not use the actual key but instead a forty-character abbreviation (or a fingerprint) of Poitras's public key. This he posted to a public site—Twitter.

Sometimes in order to become invisible you have to use the visible.

Now Snowden could anonymously view Lee's tweet and compare the shortened key to the message he received. If the two didn't match, Snowden would know not to trust the e-mail. The message might have been compromised. Or he might be talking instead to the NSA.

In this case, the two matched.

Now several orders removed from who they were online—and where they were in the world—Snowden and Poitras were almost ready to begin their secure anonymous e-mail communication. Snowden finally sent Poitras an encrypted e-mail identifying himself only as "Citizenfour." This signature became the title of her Academy Award–winning documentary about his privacy rights campaign.

That might seem like the end—now they could communicate securely via encrypted e-mail—but it wasn't. It was just the beginning.

In the wake of the 2015 terrorist attacks in Paris, there was discussion from various governments about building in back doors or other ways for those in government to decrypt encrypted e-mail, text, and phone messages—ostensibly from foreign terrorists. This would, of course, defeat the purpose of encryption. But governments actually don't need to see the encrypted contents of your e-mail to know whom you are communicating with and how often, as we will see.

As I mentioned before, the purpose of encryption is to encode your message so that only someone with the correct key can later decode it. Both the strength of the mathematical operation and the length of the encryption key determine how easy it is for someone without a key to crack your code.

Encryption algorithms in use today are public. You want that.[4] Be afraid of encryption algorithms that are proprietary and not public. Public algorithms have been vetted for weakness—meaning people have been purposely trying to break them. Whenever one of the public algorithms becomes weak or is cracked, it is retired, and newer, stronger algorithms are used instead. The older algorithms still exist, but their use is strongly discouraged.

The keys are (more or less) under your control, and so, as you might guess, their management is very important. If you generate an encryption key, you—and no one else—will have the key stored on your device. If you let a company perform the encryption, say, in the cloud, then that company might also keep the key after he or she shares it with you. The real concern is that this company may also be compelled by court order to share the key with law enforcement or a government agency, with or without a warrant. You will need to read the privacy policy for each service you use for encryption and understand who owns the keys.

When you encrypt a message—an e-mail, text, or phone call—use end-to-end encryption. That means your message stays unreadable until it reaches its intended recipient. With end-to-end encryption, only you and your recipient have the keys to decode the message. Not the telecommunications carrier, website owner, or app developer—the parties that law enforcement or government will ask to turn over information about you. How do you know whether the encryption service you are using is end-to-end encryption? Do a Google search for "end-to-end encryption voice call." If the app or service doesn't use end-to-end encryption, then choose another.

If all this sounds complicated, that's because it is. But there are PGP plug-ins for the Chrome and Firefox Internet browsers that make encryption easier. One is Mailvelope, which neatly handles the public and private encryption keys of PGP. Simply type in a passphrase, which will be used to generate the public and private keys. Then whenever you write a Web-based e-mail, select a recipient, and if the recipient has a public key available, you will then have the option to send that person an encrypted message.[5]

Even if you encrypt your e-mail messages with PGP, a small but information-rich part of your message is still readable by just about anyone. In defending itself from the Snowden revelations, the US government stated repeatedly that it doesn't capture the actual contents of our e-mails, which in this case would be unreadable with PGP encryption. Instead, the government said it collects only the e-mail's metadata.

What is e-mail metadata? It is the information in the To and From fields as well as the IP addresses of the various servers that handle the e-mail from origin to recipient. It also includes the subject line, which can sometimes be very revealing as to the encrypted contents of the message. Metadata, a legacy from the early days of the Internet, is still included on every e-mail sent and received, but modern e-mail readers hide this information from display.[6]

PGP, no matter what "flavor" you use, does not encrypt the metadata—the To and From fields, the subject line, and the time-stamp information. This remains in plain text, whether it is visible to you or not. Third parties will still be able to see the metadata of your encrypted message; they'll know that on such-and-such a date you sent an e-mail to someone, that two days later you sent another e-mail to that same person, and so on.

That might sound okay, since the third parties are not actually reading the content, and you probably don't care about the mechanics of how those e-mails traveled—the various server addresses and the time stamps—but you'd be surprised by how much can be learned from the e-mail path and the frequency of e-mails alone.

Back in the '90s, before I went on the run from the FBI, I performed what I called a metadata analysis on various phone records. I began this process by hacking into PacTel Cellular, a cellular provider in Los Angeles, to obtain the call detail records (CDRs) of anyone who called an informant whom the FBI was using to obtain information about my activities.

CDRs are very much like the metadata I'm talking about here; they show the time a phone call was made, the number dialed, the length of the call, and the number of times a particular number was called—all very useful information.

By searching through the calls that were being placed through PacTel Cellular to the informant's landline, I was able to obtain a list of the cell-phone numbers of the people who called him. Upon analysis of the callers' billing records, I was able to identify those callers as members of the FBI's white-collar crime squad, operating out of the Los Angeles office. Sure enough, some of the numbers each individual dialed were internal to the Los Angeles office of the FBI, the US attorney's office, and other government offices. Some of those calls were quite long. And quite frequent.

Whenever they moved the informant to a new safe house, I was able to obtain the landline number of the safe house because the agents would call it after trying to reach the informant on his pager. Once I had the landline number for the informant, I was also able to obtain the physical address through social engineering—that is, by pretending to be someone at Pacific Bell, the company that provided the service at the safe house.

Social engineering is a hacking technique that uses manipulation, deception, and influence to get a human target to comply with a request. Often people are tricked into giving up sensitive information. In this case, I knew the internal numbers at the phone company, and I pretended to be a field technician who spoke the correct terminology and lingo, which was instrumental in obtaining sensitive information.

So while recording the metadata in an e-mail is not the same as capturing the actual content, it is nonetheless intrusive from a privacy perspective.

If you look at the metadata from any recent e-mail you'll see the IP addresses of the servers that passed your e-mail around the world before it reached its target. Each server—like each person who accesses the Internet—has a unique IP address, a numerical value that is calculated using the country where you are located and who your Internet provider is. Blocks of IP addresses are set aside for various countries, and each provider has its own sub-block, and this is further subdivided by type of service—dial-up, cable, or mobile. If you purchased a static IP address it will be associated with your subscriber account and home address, otherwise your external IP address will be generated from a pool of addresses assigned to your Internet service provider. For example, a sender—someone sending you an email—might have the IP address 27.126.148.104, which is located in Victoria, Australia.

Or it could be 175.45.176.0, which is one of North Korea's IP addresses. If it is the latter, then your e-mail account might be flagged for government review. Someone in the US government might want to know why you're communicating with someone from North Korea, even if the subject line reads "Happy Birthday."

By itself, you still might not think the server address is very interesting. But the frequency of contact can tell you a lot. Additionally, if you identify each element—the sender and the receiver and their locations—you can start to infer what's really going on. For example, the metadata associated with phone calls—the duration, the time of day they're made, and so on—can tell you a lot about a person's mental health. A 10:00 p.m. call to a domestic violence hotline lasting ten minutes or a midnight call from the Brooklyn Bridge to a suicide prevention hotline lasting twenty minutes can be very revealing. An app developed at Dartmouth College matches patterns of stress, depression, and loneliness in user data. This user activity has also been correlated with student grades.[7]

Still don't see the danger in having your e-mail metadata exposed? A program created at MIT called Immersion will visually map the relationships between the senders and receivers of all the e-mail you have stored in your e-mail account just by using the metadata. The tool is a way to visually quantify who matters to you most. The program even includes a sliding time scale, so you can see how the people you know rise and fall in importance to you over time. Although you might think you understand your relationships, seeing them graphically represented can be a sobering experience. You might not realize how often you e-mail someone you don't really know or how little you e-mail someone you know very well. With the Immersion tool you can choose whether to upload the data, and you can also delete the information once it has been graphed.[8]

According to Snowden, our e-mail, text, and phone metadata is being collected by the NSA and other agencies. But the government can't collect metadata from everyone—or can it? Technically, no. However, there's been a sharp rise in "legal" collection since 2001.

Authorized under the US Foreign Intelligence Surveillance Act of 1978 (FISA), the US Foreign Intelligence Surveillance Court (known as FISC, or the FISA Court) oversees all requests for surveillance warrants against foreign individuals within the United States. On the surface it seems reasonable that a court order would stand between law enforcement and an individual. The reality is somewhat different. In 2012 alone, 1,856 requests were presented, and 1,856 requests were approved, suggesting that the process today is largely a rubber-stamp approval operation for the US government.[9] After the FISA Court grants a request, law enforcement can compel private corporations to turn over all their data on you—that is, if they haven't already done so.

To become truly invisible in the digital world you will need to do more than encrypt your messages. You will need to:

Remove your true IP address: This is your point of connection to the Internet, your fingerprint. It can show where you are (down to your physical address) and what provider you use.

Obscure your hardware and software: When you connect to a website online, a snapshot of the hardware and software you're using may be collected by the site. There are tricks that can be used to find out if you have particular software installed, such as Adobe Flash. The browser software tells a website what operating system you're using, what version of that operating system you have, and sometimes what other software you have running on your desktop at the time.

Defend your anonymity: Attribution online is hard. Proving that you were at the keyboard when an event occurred is difficult. However, if you walk in front of a camera before going online at Starbucks, or if you just bought a latte at Starbucks with your credit card, these actions can be linked to your online presence a few moments later.

As we've learned, every time you connect to the Internet, there's an IP address associated with that connection.[10] This is problematic if you're trying to be invisible online: you might change your name (or not give it at all), but your IP address will still reveal where you are in the world, what provider you use, and the identity of the person paying for the Internet service (which may or may not be you). All these pieces of information are included within the e-mail metadata and can later be used to identify you uniquely. Any communication, whether it's e-mail or not, can be used to identify you based on the Internal Protocol (IP) address that's assigned to the router you are using while you are at home, work, or a friend's place.

IP addresses in e-mails can of course be forged. Someone might use a proxy address—not his or her real IP address but someone else's—

so that an e-mail appears to originate from another location. A proxy is like a foreign-language translator—you speak to the translator, and the translator speaks to the foreign-language speaker—only the message remains exactly the same. The point here is that someone might use a proxy from China or even Germany to evade detection on an e-mail that really comes from North Korea.

Instead of hosting your own proxy, you can use a service known as an anonymous remailer, which will mask your e-mail's IP address for you. An anonymous remailer simply changes the e-mail address of the sender before sending the message to its intended recipient. The recipient can respond via the remailer. That's the simplest version.

There are also variations. Some type I and type II remailers do not allow you to respond to e-mails; they are simply one-way correspondence. Type III, or Mixminion, remailers do offer a full suite of services: responding, forwarding, and encryption. You will need to find out which service your remailer supplies if you choose this method of anonymous correspondence.

One way to mask your IP address is to use the onion router (Tor), which is what Snowden and Poitras did.

Developed by the US Naval Research Laboratory in 2004 as a way for military personnel to conduct searches without exposing their physical locations, the Tor open-source program has since been expanded. Tor is designed to be used by people living in harsh regimes as a way to avoid censorship of popular media and services and to prevent anyone from tracking what search terms they use. Tor remains free and can be used by anyone, anywhere—even you.

How does Tor work? It upends the usual model for accessing a website.

Usually when you go online you open an Internet browser and type in the name of the site you want to visit. A request goes out to that site, and milliseconds later a response comes back to your browser with the website page. The website knows—based on the IP address—who the service provider is, and sometimes even where in the world you are located, based on where the service provider is located or the latency of the hops from your device to the site. For example, if your device says it is in the United States, but the time and number of hops your request takes to reach its destination suggest you are somewhere else in the world, some sites—gaming sites, in particular—will detect that as possible fraud.

When you use Tor, the direct line between you and your target website is obscured by additional nodes, and every ten seconds the chain of nodes connecting you to whatever site you are looking at changes without disruption to you. The various nodes that connect you to a site are like layers within an onion. In other words, if someone were to backtrack from the destination website and try to find you, they'd be unable to because the path would be constantly changing. Unless your entry point and your exit point become associated somehow, your connection is considered anonymous.

When you use Tor, your request to open a page—say, mitnick security.com—is not sent directly to that server but first to another Tor node. And just to make things even more complicated, that node then passes the request to another node, which finally connects to mitnicksecurity.com. So there's an entry node, a node in the middle, and an exit node. If I were to look at who was visiting my company site, I would only see the IP address and information from the exit node, the last in the chain, and not the first, your entry node. You can configure Tor so it uses exit nodes in a particular country, such as Spain, or even a specific exit node, perhaps in Honolulu.

To use Tor you will need the modified Firefox browser from the Tor site (torproject.org). Always look for legitimate Tor browsers for your operating system from the Tor project website. Do not use a third-party site. For Android operating systems, Orbot is a legitimate free Tor app from Google Play that both encrypts your traffic and obscures your IP address.[11] On iOS devices (iPad, iPhone), install the Onion Browser, a legitimate app from the iTunes app store.

You might be thinking, why doesn't someone just build an e-mail server within Tor? Someone did. Tor Mail was a service hosted on a site accessible only to Tor browsers. However, the FBI seized that server in an unrelated case and therefore gained access to all the encrypted e-mail stored on Tor Mail. This is a cautionary tale showing that even when you think your information is safe, foolproof, it probably isn't.[12]

Although Tor uses a special network, you can still access the Internet from it, but the pages are much slower to load. However, in addition to allowing you to surf the searchable Internet, Tor gives you access to a world of sites that are not ordinarily searchable—what's called the Dark Web. These are sites that don't resolve to common names such as Google.com and instead end with the .onion extension. Some of these hidden sites offer, sell, or provide items and services that may be illegal. Some of them are legitimate sites maintained by people in oppressed parts of the world.

It should be noted, however, that there are several weaknesses with Tor:

- You have no control over the exit nodes, which may be under the control of government or law enforcement[13]
- You can still be profiled and possibly identified[14]
- Tor is very slow

That being said, if you still decide to use Tor you should not run it in the same physical device that you use for browsing. In other words, have a laptop for browsing the Web and a separate device for Tor (for instance, a Raspberry Pi minicomputer running Tor software). The idea here is that if somebody is able to compromise your laptop they still won't be able to peel off your Tor transport layer as it is running on a separate physical box.[15]

In the case of Snowden and Poitras, as I said, simply connecting to each other over encrypted e-mail wasn't good enough. After Poitras created a new public key for her anonymous e-mail account, she could have sent it to Snowden's previous e-mail address, but if someone were watching that account, then her new identity would be exposed. A very basic rule is that you have to keep your anonymous accounts completely separate from anything that could relate back to your true identity.

To be invisible you will need to start with a clean slate for each new secure contact you make. Legacy e-mail accounts might be connected in various ways to other parts of your life—friends, hobbies, work. To communicate in secrecy, you will need to create new e-mail accounts using Tor so that the IP address setting up the account is not associated with your real identity in any way.

Creating anonymous e-mail addresses is challenging but possible.

There are private e-mail services you can use. Since you will leave a trail if you pay for those services, you're actually better off using a free Web service. A minor hassle: Gmail, Microsoft, Yahoo, and others require you to supply a phone number to verify your identify. Obviously you can't use your real cell-phone number, since it may be connected to your real name and real address. You might be able to set up a Skype phone number if it supports voice authentication instead of SMS authentication; however, you will still need an existing e-mail account and a prepaid gift card to set up a Skype number.[16] If you think using a prepaid cell phone in and of itself will protect your anonymity, you're wrong. If you've ever used a prepaid phone to make calls associated with your real identity, it's child's play to discover who you are.

Instead you'll want to use a disposable phone. Some people think of burner phones as devices used only by terrorists, pimps, and drug dealers, but there are plenty of perfectly legitimate uses for them. For example, a business reporter, after having her garbage gone through by private investigators hired by Hewlett-Packard, who was eager to find out who might be leaking critical board-of-directors information, switched over to burner phones so that the private investigators would have a harder time identifying her calls. After that experience she only spoke to her source on that burner phone.[17]

Similarly, a woman who is avoiding an abusive ex might gain a little peace of mind by using a phone that doesn't require a contract or, for that matter, a Google or an Apple account. A burner phone typically has few or very limited Internet capabilities. Burner phones mostly provide voice, text, and e-mail service, and that's about all some people need. You, however, should also get data because you can tether this burner phone to your laptop and use it to surf the Internet. (On page 117 I tell you how to change the media access control—MAC—address on your laptop so that each time you tether with a burner phone it appears to be new device.)

However, purchasing a burner phone anonymously will be tricky. Actions taken in the real world can be used to identify you in the virtual world. Sure, I could walk into Walmart and pay cash for a burner phone and one hundred minutes of airtime. Who would know? Well, lots of people would.

First, how did I get to Walmart? Did I take an Uber car? Did I take a taxi? These records can all be subpoenaed.

I could drive my own car, but law enforcement uses automatic license plate recognition technology (ALPR) in large public parking lots to look for missing and stolen vehicles as well as people on whom there are outstanding warrants. The ALPR records can be subpoenaed.

Even if I walked to Walmart, once I entered the store my face would be visible on several security cameras within the store itself, and that video can be subpoenaed.

Okay, so let's say I send someone else to the store—someone I don't know, maybe a homeless person I hired on the spot. That person walks in and buys the phone and several data refill cards with cash. That would be the safest approach. Maybe you arrange to meet this person later away from the store. This would help physically distance yourself from the actual sales transaction. In this case the weakest link could still be the person you sent—how trustworthy is he? If you pay him more than the value of the phone, he will probably be happy to deliver the phone as promised.

Activation of the prepaid phone requires either calling the mobile operator's customer service department or activating it on the provider's website. To avoid being recorded for "quality assurance," it's safer to activate over the Web. Using Tor over an open wireless network after you've changed your MAC address should be the minimum safeguards. You should make up all the subscriber information you enter on the website. For your address, just Google the address of a major hotel and use that. Make up a birth date and PIN that you'll remember in case you need to contact customer service in the future.

There are e-mail services that don't require verification, and if you don't need to worry about authorities, Skype numbers work well for Google account registration and similar stuff, but for the sake of illustration, let's say that after using Tor to randomize your IP address, and after creating a Gmail account that has nothing to do with your real phone number, Google sends your phone a verification code or a voice call. Now you have a Gmail account that is virtually untraceable.

So we have an anonymous e-mail address established using familiar and common services. We can produce reasonably secure e-mails whose IP address—thanks to Tor—is anonymous (although you don't have control over the exit nodes) and whose contents, thanks to PGP, can't be read except by the intended recipient.

Note that to keep this account anonymous you can only access the account from within Tor so that your IP address will never be associated with it. Further, you should never perform any Internet searches while logged in to that anonymous Gmail account; you might inadvertently search for something that is related to your true identity. Even searching for weather information could reveal your location.[18]

As you can see, becoming invisible and keeping yourself invisible require tremendous discipline and perpetual diligence. But it is worth it in order to be invisible.

The most important takeaways are: first, be aware of all the ways that someone can identify you even if you undertake some but not all of the precautions I've described. And if you do undertake all these precautions, know that you need to perform due diligence every time you use your anonymous accounts. No exceptions.

It's also worth reiterating that end-to-end encryption — keeping your message unreadable and secure until it reaches the recipient as opposed to simply encrypting it — is very important. End-to-end encryption can be used for other purposes, such as encrypted phone calls and instant messaging, which we'll discuss in the next two chapters.

CHAPTER THREE

Wiretapping 101

You spend countless hours on your cell phone every day, chatting, texting, surfing the Internet. But do you actually know how your cell phone works?

Cellular service, which we use on our mobile devices, is wireless and relies upon cellular towers, or base stations. To maintain connectivity, cell phones continually send out tiny beacons to the tower or towers physically closest to them. The signal response to those beacons from the towers translates into the number of "bars" you have—no bars, no signal.

To protect the identity of the user somewhat, these beacons from your cell phone use what is known as international mobile subscriber identity, or IMSI, a unique number assigned to your SIM card. This was originally from the time when cellular networks needed to know when you were on their towers and when you were roaming (using other carriers' cell towers). The first part of the IMSI code uniquely identifies the mobile network operator, and the remaining part identifies your mobile phone to that network operator.

Law enforcement has created devices that pretend to be cellular base stations. These are designed to intercept voice and text messages.

In the United States, law enforcement and intelligence agencies also use other devices to catch IMSIs (see page 225). The IMSI is captured instantly, in less than a second, and without warning. Typically IMSI catchers are used at large rallies, allowing law enforcement to later identify who was in attendance, particularly if those individuals were actively calling others to join in.

Devices like these can also be used by commuting services and apps to create traffic reports. Here the actual account number, or IMSI, doesn't matter, only how fast your cell phone moves from tower to tower or geographic region to geographic region. The amount of time it takes a cell phone to come and go from each tower determines the traffic status: red, yellow, or green.[1]

Your mobile device connects to a series of cellular towers whenever it's powered up. The closest tower actually handles your call, text, or Internet session. As you move around, your phone pings the nearest tower and, if necessary, your call moves from tower to tower, all the while maintaining consistency. The other nearby towers are all on standby, so that if you move from point A to point B and another tower comes into range for a better signal, then the handoff is smooth and you shouldn't experience a dropped call.

Suffice it to say that your mobile device emits a unique sequence that is logged on a number of individual cellular towers. So anyone looking at the logs of a specific tower would see the temporary mobile subscriber identity (TMSI) of all the people in the general area at any given moment, whether they made calls or not. Law enforcement can and does request this information from cellular carriers, including the back-end account identities of specific holders.

Ordinarily, if you look at just one cell tower's log, the data might only show that someone was passing through and that his or her device contacted a specific cell tower as a standby. If a call was made or if data was exchanged, there would also be a record of that call and its duration.

Data from multiple cell-tower logs, however, can be used to geographically pinpoint a user. Most mobile devices ping three or more towers at a time. Using logs from those cell towers, someone can triangulate, based on the relative strength of each ping, a fairly exact location of the phone's user. So the phone you carry around every day is essentially a tracking device.

How can you avoid being tracked?

Signing a contract with a cell-phone carrier requires a name, address, and a Social Security number. Additionally, there's a credit check to make sure you can pay your monthly bill. You can't avoid this if you go with a commercial carrier.

A burner phone seems like a reasonable option. A prepaid cell phone, perhaps one that you replace frequently (say, weekly or even monthly), avoids leaving much of a trail. Your TMSI will show up on cell tower logs, then disappear. If you purchased the phone discreetly, it won't be traceable back to a subscriber account. Prepaid cell services are still subscriber accounts, so the IMSI will always be assigned to an account. Therefore, a person's anonymity depends on how he or she acquired the burner device.

For the sake of argument, let's assume you have successfully disconnected yourself from the purchase of a burner phone. You followed the steps outlined on page 49 and used a person unrelated to you to purchase the phone for cash. Is the use of that disposable phone untraceable? The short answer is no.

Here's a cautionary tale: one afternoon in 2007, a $500 million container loaded with the drug ecstasy went missing from a port in Melbourne, Australia. The owner of the container, Pat Barbaro, a known drug dealer, reached into his pocket, pulled out one of his twelve cell phones, and dialed the number of a local reporter, Nick McKenzie, who would only know the caller by the name Stan.

Barbaro would later use his other burner phones to text McKenzie, attempting to anonymously obtain information from the investigative reporter about the missing container. As we will see, this didn't work.

Burner phones, despite what many people may think, are not truly anonymous. Under the US Communications Assistance for Law Enforcement Act (CALEA), all IMSIs connected with burner phones are reported, just as those subscribers under contract with major carriers are. In other words, a law enforcement official can spot a burner phone from a log file just as easily as he can spot a registered contract phone. While the IMSI won't identify who owns the phone, patterns of usage might.

In Australia, where CALEA does not exist, law enforcement was still able to keep tabs on Barbaro's many phones using rather traditional methods. For instance, they might have noticed a call made with his personal phone and then a few seconds later seen in the log files another call or text from one of his burner phones in the same cell site. Over time, the fact that these IMSIs more often than not appeared together on the same cell sites might suggest that they belonged to a single individual.

The problem with Barbaro's having many cell phones at his disposal was that no matter which phone he used, personal or burner, so long as he stayed in the same spot, the signal would hit the same cellular tower. The burner-phone calls always appeared next to his registered-phone calls. The registered phone, listed in his name with a carrier, was entirely traceable and helped law enforcement identify him. It established a solid case against him, particularly because this pattern was repeated at other locations. This helped Australian authorities convict Barbaro of orchestrating one of the largest ecstasy shipments in Australia's history.

McKenzie concluded, "Ever since the phone buzzed that day in my pocket, and 'Stan' briefly entered my life, I've been especially conscious about how a person's communications leave a trail, no matter how careful they are."[2]

You could, of course, have only a burner phone. This would mean that you would need to purchase additional minutes anonymously using prepaid cards or Bitcoin from time to time, which you can do by using an open Wi-Fi safely after changing your media access control (MAC) address on your wireless card (see page 117), and being out of any camera view. Or you could, as suggested in the previous chapter, hire a stranger to pay cash at the store to purchase the prepaid phone and several refill cards.[3] This adds cost and perhaps inconvenience, but you would have an anonymous phone.

Although it may seem brand new, cellular technology is more than forty years old, and it, like copper-wire telephone systems, contains legacy technologies that can compromise your privacy.

Each generation of cell-phone technology has offered new features, mostly intended to move more data more efficiently. First-generation phones, or 1G, had the telephone technology available in the 1980s. These early 1G networks and handsets were analog-based, and they used a variety of now discontinued mobile standards. In 1991, the second-generation (2G) digital network was introduced. This 2G network offered two standards: global system for mobile communications (GSM) and code division multiple access (CDMA). It also introduced short message service (SMS), unstructured supplementary services data (USSD), and other simple communications protocols that are still in use today. We're currently in the middle of 4G/LTE and on the way toward 5G.

No matter what generation of technology a given carrier is using (2G, 3G, 4G, or 4G/LTE), there is an underlying international signal protocol known as the signaling system. The signaling system protocol (currently in version 7), among other things, keeps mobile calls connected when you drive along a freeway and switch from cell tower to cell tower. It can also be used for surveillance. Signaling system 7 (SS7) does basically everything necessary to route a call, such as:

- Setting up a new connection for a call
- Tearing down that connection when the call ends
- Billing the appropriate party making the call
- Managing extra features such as call-forwarding, calling party name and number display, three-way calling, and other Intelligent Network (IN) services
- Toll-free (800 and 888) as well as toll (900) calls
- Wireless services, including subscriber identification, carrier, and mobile roaming

Speaking at the Chaos Communication Congress, an annual computer hacker conference held in Berlin, Germany, Tobias Engel, founder of Sternraute, and Karsten Nohl, chief scientist for Security Research Labs, explained that they could not only locate cell-phone callers anywhere in the world, they could also listen in on their phone conversations. And if they couldn't listen in real time, they could record the encrypted calls and texts for later decryption.

In security, you are only as secure as the weakest link. What Engel and Nohl found was that while developed countries in North America and Europe have invested billions in creating relatively secure and private 3G and 4G networks, they must still use signaling system 7 (SS7) as an underlying protocol.

SS7 handles the process for call-establishment, billing, routing, and information-exchange functions. Which means if you can tap into SS7, you can manipulate the call. SS7 allows an attacker to use a small carrier in, say, Nigeria to access calls made in Europe or the

United States. "It's like you secure the front door of the house, but the back door is wide open," said Engel.

The two researchers tested a method in which an attacker uses a phone's call-forwarding function and SS7 to forward a target's outgoing calls to himself before conferencing (three-way calling) in their intended recipient. Once the attacker has established himself, he can listen to all calls made by the targeted individual from any place on earth.

Another strategy would be for the attacker to set up radio antennas to collect all cellular calls and texts within a given area. For any encrypted 3G calls, the attacker could ask SS7 to provide him with the proper decryption key.

"It's all automated, at the push of a button," Nohl said. "It would strike me as a perfect spying capability, to record and decrypt pretty much any network... Any network we have tested, it works."[4] He then enumerated almost every major carrier in North America and Europe, around twenty in all.

Nohl and Engel also found that they could locate any cell-phone user by using an SS7 function called an anytime interrogation query. That is, they could do so until the function was shut down early in 2015. However, since all carriers must track their users in order to provide service, SS7 provides other functions that still allow some remote surveillance. It should be noted that the specific flaws identified by Nohl and Engel have been mostly mitigated by the carriers since their research went public.

You might think that encryption alone would help keep cell-phone calls private. Beginning with 2G, GSM-based phone calls have been encrypted. However, the initial methods used to encrypt calls in 2G were weak and eventually broke down. Unfortunately, the cost of upgrading cellular networks to 3G proved prohibitive for many carriers, so a weakened 2G remained in use until around 2010 or so.

In the summer of 2010, a team of researchers led by Nohl divided all the possible encryption keys used by 2G GSM networks among themselves and crunched the numbers to produce what's called a rainbow table, a list of precomputed keys or passwords. They published the table to show carriers around the world just how insecure 2G encryption using GSM is. Each packet—or unit of data between source and destination—of voice, text, or data sent over 2G GSM could be decrypted in just a few minutes using the published table of keys.[5] This was an extreme example, but the team considered it necessary; when Nohl and others had previously presented their findings to the carriers, their warnings fell on deaf ears. By demonstrating how they could crack 2G GSM encryption, they more or less forced the carriers to make the change.

It is important to note that 2G still exists today, and carriers are considering selling access to their old 2G networks for use in Internet of Things devices (devices other than computers that connect to the Internet, such as your TV and refrigerator), which only need occasional data transmission. If this happens, we will need to make sure the devices themselves have end-to-end encryption because we know that 2G will not provide strong enough encryption by itself.

Of course eavesdropping existed before mobile devices really took off. For Anita Busch, the nightmare started the morning of June 20, 2002, when she awoke to a neighbor's urgent knock on her door. Someone had put a bullet hole in the windshield of her car as it sat in the driveway. Not only that, someone had also left Busch a rose, a dead fish, and a one-word note—"Stop"—on the car's hood.[6] Later she would learn that her phones had been tapped, and not by law enforcement.

The fact that the scene with a bullet hole and a dead fish was reminiscent of a bad Hollywood gangster movie made some sense. Busch, a seasoned reporter, was at the time only a few weeks into a freelance assignment chronicling organized crime's growing influence in Hollywood for the *Los Angeles Times*. She was researching

Steven Seagal and his former business partner, Julius R. Nasso, who had been indicted for conspiring with the New York Mafia to extort money from Seagal.[7]

What followed finding the note on her car was a series of phone messages. The caller apparently wanted to share some information about Seagal. Much later Busch learned that the caller had been hired by Anthony Pellicano, a former high-profile Los Angeles private investigator who at the time Busch's car was tampered with was already suspected by the FBI of illegal wiretapping, bribery, identity theft, and obstruction of justice. Busch's copper-wire phone had been tapped by Pellicano, who knew by eavesdropping on her calls that she was writing a newspaper story about his clients. The fish head on her car was an attempt to warn her off.

Typically wiretapping is only associated with phone calls, but wiretapping laws in the United States can also cover eavesdropping on e-mail and instant messages. For the moment I'll focus on wiretapping's traditional use, in copper-wire landlines.

Landlines are the hardwired phones in your home or business, and wiretapping involves literally tapping into the live wire. Back in the day, phone companies each had physical banks of switches on which they performed a version of wiretapping. What that means is that the phone company had special appliances that the frame techs hooked up to the target phone number on the mainframe in the central office. There is additional wiretapping equipment that dials into this appliance and is used to monitor the target. Today, that way of eavesdropping is retired: phone companies are all required to implement the technical requirements mandated by CALEA.

Although a growing number of people today have shifted to mobile phones, many still retain their landlines for their copper-wire dependability. Others use what's called Voice over Internet Protocol (VoIP) technology, which is telephony over the Internet and usually bundled in the home or office with your cable or Internet service.

Whether it's a physical switch at the phone company or a digital switch, law enforcement does have the ability to eavesdrop on calls.

The 1994 CALEA requires telecommunications manufacturers and carriers to modify their equipment for the purposes of allowing law enforcement to wiretap the line. So under CALEA, any landline call in the United States is theoretically subject to interception. And under CALEA, all law enforcement access requires a Title III warrant. That said, it's still illegal for an ordinary citizen to conduct a wiretap, which is what Anthony Pellicano did to covertly monitor Anita Busch and others. His list of eavesdropping victims happens to include Hollywood celebrities such as Sylvester Stallone, David Carradine, and Kevin Nealon, among others.

His list of wiretap victims also includes my friend Erin Finn, because her ex-boyfriend was obsessed with her and wanted to track her every move. Because her phone line had been tapped, I, too, was monitored when I called her. The coolest part of the saga is that AT&T paid me thousands of dollars as part of a class-action settlement because of Pellicano's wiretapping of my calls to Finn. Which is somewhat ironic, because on another occasion, I was the one doing the tapping. Pellicano's purpose in wiretapping people was perhaps more malicious than mine; he was trying to intimidate witnesses into either not testifying or testifying in a certain way.

Back in the mid-1990s, a wiretap had to be installed by technicians. So Pellicano, or one of his people, had to hire someone who worked at PacBell to tap Busch's and Finn's telephone lines. The technicians were able to set up extensions of the target phones at Pellicano's office, in Beverly Hills. In this case there were no taps done at the junction box, or the terminal at the side of the house or apartment complex, although that is also possible.[8]

As you may recall from reading my previous book *Ghost in the Wires,* I once drove down from my father's apartment in Calabasas to Long Beach to set up a physical wiretap on a phone line used by Kent, a friend of my late brother. There were many questions surrounding my brother's death, from a drug overdose, and I believed he had a part in that death, though I later learned he was not involved. In the utility space within the apartment complex where Kent lived, I used social engineering to pretend to be a line technician calling a particular unit within GTE (General Telephone and Electronics) to find where the cable and pair assigned to Kent's phone were located. It turned out that Kent's phone wires ran through a completely separate apartment building. And so in a second utility space, I was ultimately able to clip my voice-activated microcassette tape recorder to his phone line at the terminal box (the place where phone company technicians connect the lines to each apartment).

After that, anytime Kent made a call, I could record both sides of the conversation without his knowing I was doing so—though I should note that while the recordings were in real time, my listening to them was not. Every day over the next ten days I had to make the sixty-minute drive to Kent's apartment, afterward listening to the retrieved tapes for any mention of my brother. Unfortunately, nothing ever came of it. Years later I learned that my uncle had likely been responsible for my brother's death.

Given how easy it was for Pellicano and me to tap into private phone conversations, you may wonder how you can become invisible with a copper-wire landline phone that is apparently open to surveillance? You can't, without buying special equipment. For the truly paranoid, there are landline phones that will encrypt all your voice conversations over copper wires.[9] These phones do solve the problem of interception of private phone calls, but only if both ends of the call use encryption; otherwise they may be easy to monitor.[10] For the rest of us, there are some basic telephone choices we can make to avoid being eavesdropped on.

The move toward digital telephony has made surveillance easier, not harder. Today, if a tap is necessary on a digital phone line, it can be done remotely. The switching computer simply creates a second, parallel stream of data; no additional monitoring equipment is required. This also makes it much harder to determine whether a given line has been tapped. And in most cases such taps are only discovered by accident.

Shortly after Greece hosted the 2004 Summer Olympics, engineers at Vodafone-Panafon removed some rogue software that had been discovered to be running in the company's cellular network for more than a year. In practice, law enforcement intercepts all voice and text data sent over any cellular network through a remote-controlled system called RES (remote-control equipment subsystem), the digital equivalent of an analog wiretap. When a subject under surveillance makes a mobile call, the RES creates a second data stream that feeds directly to a law enforcement officer.

The rogue software discovered in Greece tapped into Vodafone's RES, meaning that someone other than a legitimate law enforcement officer was listening to conversations conducted over its cellular network; in this case, the wiretapper was interested in government officials. During the Olympics, some countries—such as the United States and Russia—provided their own private communications systems for state-level conversations. Other heads of state and business executives from around the world used the compromised Vodafone system.

An investigation showed that the communications of the Greek prime minister and his wife—as well as those of the mayor of Athens, the Greek European Union commissioner, and the ministries of national defense, foreign affairs, the mercantile marine, and justice—had been monitored during the Olympics. Other intercepted phones belonged to members of civil rights organizations, antiglobalization groups, the ruling New Democracy party, the Hellenic Navy general staff, as well as peace activists and a Greek-American employee at the United States embassy in Athens.[11]

The spying might have continued longer had Vodafone not called in the hardware vendor for its RES system, Ericsson, while investigating a separate complaint—that its text messages were suffering delivery failures at a higher than normal rate. After diagnosing the problem, Ericsson notified Vodafone that it had found rogue software.

Unfortunately, more than a decade afterward, we still don't know who did this. Or why. Or even how common this activity might be. To make matters worse, Vodafone apparently mishandled the investigation.[12] For one thing, key log files covering the event were missing. And instead of letting the rogue program run after discovery—a common practice in computer criminal investigations—Vodafone abruptly removed it from their system, which may have tipped off the perpetrators and allowed them to further cover their tracks.

The Vodafone case is an unsettling reminder of how vulnerable our cell phones are to interception. But there are ways you can still be invisible with a digital phone.

Besides cell phones and old-fashioned landlines, a third telephony option, as I mentioned earlier, is Voice over Internet Protocol (VoIP). VoIP is great for any wireless device that lacks a native means of making a phone call, e.g., an Apple iPod Touch; it's more like surfing the Internet than making a classic phone call. Landlines require copper wire. Mobile phones use cell towers. VoIP is simply transmitting your voice over the Internet—either using wired or wireless Internet services. VoIP also works on mobile devices, such as laptops and tablets, whether or not they have cellular service.

To save money, many homes and offices have switched to the VoIP systems being offered by new service providers and existing cable companies. VoIP uses the same coaxial cable that brings streaming video and high-speed Internet into your home.

The good news is that VoIP phone systems do use encryption; specifically, something called session description protocol security descriptions, or SDES. The bad news is that on its own, SDES is not very secure.

Part of the problem with SDES is the encryption key is not shared over SSL/TLS (a network cryptographic protocol), which is secure. If the vendor doesn't use SSL/TLS, however, then the key is sent in the clear. Instead of asymmetric encryption, it uses symmetric encryption, which means that the key generated by the sender must somehow be passed to the recipient in order for the call to be unscrambled.

Let's say Bob wants to make a call to Alice, who is in China. Bob's SDES-encrypted VoIP phone generates a new key for that call. Somehow Bob has to get that new key to Alice so her VoIP equipment can decrypt his phone call and they can have a conversation. The solution SDES offers is to send the key to Bob's carrier, which then passes it to Alice's carrier, which then shares it with her.

Do you see the flaw? Remember what I said about end-to-end encryption in the previous chapter? The conversation stays secure until the recipient opens it at the other end. But SDES shares the key from Bob to Bob's carrier and, if Alice's carrier is different, the call is encrypted from Alice's carrier to Alice. Whether the gap is significant is debatable. Something like this also happens with Skype and Google Voice. New keys are generated whenever a call is initialized, but those keys are then given over to Microsoft and Google. So much for wanting to have a private conversation.

Fortunately, there are ways to encrypt mobile VoIP from end to end.

Signal, an application from Open Whisper Systems, is a free, open-source VoIP system for mobile phones that provides true end-to-end encryption for both iPhone and Android.[13]

The main advantage of using Signal is that the key management is handled only between the calling parties, not through any third party. That means that, as in SDES, new keys are generated with each call; however, the only copies of the keys are stored on the users' devices. Since CALEA allows access to any record of a specific call, law enforcement would in this case only see the encrypted traffic across the mobile carrier's line, which would be unintelligible. And Open Whisper Systems, the nonprofit organization that makes Signal, does not have the keys, so a warrant would be useless. The keys exist only on the devices at either end of the call. And once the call ends, those session keys are destroyed.

Currently CALEA does not extend to end users or their devices.

You might think that having encryption on your cell phone would drain your battery. It does, but not by much. Signal uses push notifications, as do the apps WhatsApp and Telegram. Thus you only see a call when it is incoming, which cuts down on battery use while you're listening for new calls. The Android and iOS apps also use audio codecs and buffer algorithms native to the mobile network, so again the encryption is not draining a lot of power while you're making a call.

In addition to using end-to-end encryption, Signal also uses perfect forward secrecy (PFS). What is PFS? It's a system that uses a slightly different encryption key for every call, so that even if someone does manage to get hold of your encrypted phone call and the key that was used to encrypt it, your other calls will remain secure. All PFS keys are based on a single original key, but the important thing is that if someone compromises one key, it doesn't mean your potential adversary has access to your further communications.

CHAPTER FOUR

If You Don't Encrypt, You're Unequipped

If someone were to pick up your unlocked cell phone right now, that person could gain access to your e-mail, your Facebook account, and perhaps even your Amazon account. On our mobile devices, we no longer log in individually to services, as we do on our laptops and desktops; we have mobile apps, and, once we're logged in, they remain open. Besides your photos and your music, there are other unique features on your cell phone, such as SMS text messages. These, too, become exposed if someone gains physical access to your unlocked mobile device.

Consider this: in 2009 Daniel Lee of Longview, Washington, was arrested on suspicion of selling drugs.[1] While he was in custody the police went through his non-password-protected cell phone and immediately discovered several drug-related text messages. One such thread was from an individual called Z-Jon.

It read, "I've got a hundred and thirty for the one-sixty I owe you from last night." According to court testimony, the Longview police didn't just read Z-Jon's messages to Lee, they also actively responded, arranging their own drug deal. Posing as Lee, the police sent Z-Jon a text message in reply, asking him if he "needed more." Z-Jon responded,

"Yeah, that would be cool." When Z-Jon (whose real name is Jonathan Roden) showed up for that meeting, the Longview police arrested him for attempted heroin possession.

The police also noticed another thread of text messages on Lee's phone and arrested Shawn Daniel Hinton under similar circumstances.[2]

Both men appealed, and in 2014, with the help of the American Civil Liberties Union, the Washington State Supreme Court overturned Roden's and Hinton's convictions by a lower court, asserting that the police had violated the defendants' expectation of privacy.

The Washington State justices said that had Lee seen the messages from Roden and Hinton first or instructed the police officers to respond by saying "Daniel's not here," that would have changed the fundamentals in both cases. "Text messages can encompass the same intimate subjects as phone calls, sealed letters and other traditional forms of communication that have historically been strongly protected under Washington law," Justice Steven Gonzalez wrote in Hinton's case.[3]

The justices ruled that the expectation of privacy should extend from the paper-letter era into the digital age. In the United States, law enforcement is not permitted to open a physically sealed letter without the recipient's permission. The expectation of privacy is a legal test. It is used to determine whether the privacy protections within the Fourth Amendment to the United States Constitution apply. It remains to be seen how the courts decide future cases and whether they include this legal test.

Text technology—also known as short message service, or SMS—has been around since 1992. Cell phones, even feature phones (i.e., non-smartphones), allow for sending brief text messages. Text messages are not necessarily point-to-point: in other words, the messages do not literally travel from phone to phone. Like an e-mail, the message you type out on your phone is sent unencrypted, in the clear, to a short message service center (SMSC), part of the mobile network designed to store, forward, and deliver the SMS—sometimes hours later.

Native mobile text messages—those initiated from your phone and not an app—pass through an SMSC at the carrier, where they may or may not be not stored. The carriers state they retain texts for only a few days. After that time has expired, the carriers insist that your text messages are stored only on the phones that send and receive them, and the number of messages stored varies by the phone model. Despite these claims, I think all mobile operators in the United States retain text messages regardless of what they tell the public.[4]

There is some doubt surrounding this claim by the carriers. Documents exposed by Edward Snowden suggest a tight relationship between the NSA and at least one of the carriers, AT&T. According to *Wired,* beginning in 2002—shortly after 9/11—the NSA approached AT&T and asked them to begin building secret rooms in some of the carrier's facilities. One was to be located in Bridgeton, Missouri, and another on Folsom Street in downtown San Francisco. Eventually other cities were added, including Seattle, San Jose, Los Angeles, and San Diego. The purpose of these secret rooms was to channel all the Internet, e-mail, and phone traffic through a special filter that would look for keywords. It is unclear whether text messages were included, although it seems reasonable to think they were. It is also unclear whether this practice still exists at AT&T or any other carrier post-Snowden.[5]

One clue suggests that this practice does not continue.

In the 2015 AFC championship game, leading up to Super Bowl XLIX, the New England Patriots ignited controversy with their victory over the Indianapolis Colts, 45–7. At the heart of the controversy was whether the New England team had knowingly underinflated their footballs. The National Football League has strict rules around the proper inflation of its footballs, and after that playoff game it was determined that the balls contributed by the New England team did not meet the criteria. Central to the investigation were text messages sent by the Patriots' star quarterback, Tom Brady.

Publicly Brady denied involvement. Showing investigators the text messages he sent and received before and during the game would have perhaps confirmed this. Unfortunately, the day he met with key investigators, Brady abruptly switched cell phones, discarding the one he had used between November 2014 and approximately March 6, 2015, to a brand-new phone. Brady later told the committee that he had destroyed his original phone and all the data on it, including his stored text messages. As a result Brady received a four-game suspension from the NFL, which was later lifted by court order.[6]

"During the four months that the cell phone was in use, Brady had exchanged nearly 10,000 text messages, none of which can now be retrieved from that device," the league said. "Following the appeal hearing, Mr. Brady's representatives provided a letter from his cellphone carrier confirming that the text messages sent from or received by the destroyed cellphone could no longer be recovered."[7]

So if Tom Brady had a note from his carrier saying that his text messages were all destroyed, and the carriers themselves say they don't retain them, the only way to prolong the life of a text is to back up your mobile device to the cloud. If you use a service from your carrier, or even from Google or Apple, those companies may have access to your text messages. Apparently Tom Brady didn't have time to back up the contents of his old phone to the cloud before his emergency upgrade.

Congress has not addressed the issue of data retention in general and mobile phones in particular. In fact, Congress has debated in recent years whether to require all mobile carriers to archive text messages for up to two years. Australia decided to do this in 2015, so it remains to be seen if this works there.

So how can you keep your text messages private? First of all, don't use the native text messaging service that goes through your wireless carrier. Instead use a third-party app. But which one?

To mask our online identities—to enjoy the Internet anonymously—we will need to trust *some* software and software services. That trust is hard to verify. In general, open-source and nonprofit organizations provide perhaps the most secure software and services because there are literally thousands of eyes poring over the code and flagging anything that looks suspicious or vulnerable. When you use proprietary software, you more or less have to take the vendor's word.

Software reviews, by their nature, can only tell you so much—such as how a particular interface feature works. The reviewers spend a few days with the software and write their impressions. They don't actually use the software, nor can they report on what happens over the long term. They only record their initial impressions.

In addition, reviewers do not tell you whether you can trust the software. They don't vet the security and privacy aspects of the product. And just because a product comes from a well-known brand name doesn't mean it is secure. In fact we should be wary of popular brand names because they may lure us into a false sense of security. You shouldn't take the vendor at its word.

Back in the 1990s, when I needed to encrypt my Windows 95 laptop, I chose a now discontinued utility product from Norton called Norton Diskreet. Peter Norton is a genius. His first computer utility automated the process of undeleting a file. He went on to create a lot of great system utilities back in the 1980s, at a time when few people could understand a command prompt. But then he sold the company to Symantec, and someone else started writing the software in his name.

At the time I acquired Diskreet, a product that is no longer available, 56-bit DES encryption (DES stands for "data encryption standard") was a big deal. It was the strongest encryption you could hope for. To give you some context, today we use AES 256-bit encryption (AES stands for "advanced encryption standard"). Each added bit of encryption adds exponentially more encryption keys and therefore more security. DES 56-bit encryption was considered state-of-the-art secure until it was cracked in 1998.[8]

Anyway, I wanted to see whether the Diskreet program was robust enough to hide my data. I also wanted to challenge the FBI if they ever seized my computer. After purchasing the program I hacked into Symantec and located the program's source code.[9] After I analyzed what it did and how it did it, I discovered that Diskreet only used thirty bits of the 56-bit key—the rest was just padding with zeros.[10] That's even less secure than the forty bits that was allowed to be exported outside the United States.

What that meant in practical terms was that someone—the NSA, law enforcement, or an enemy with a very fast computer—could crack the Diskreet product much more easily than advertised, since it didn't really use 56-bit encryption at all. Yet the company was marketing the product as having 56-bit encryption. I decided to use something else instead.

How would the public know this? They wouldn't.

Although social networks such as Facebook, Snapchat, and Instagram rank at the top when it comes to popularity among teens, text messaging reigns supreme overall, according to data supplied by Niche.com.[11] A recent study found that 87 percent of teenagers text daily, compared to the 61 percent who say they use Facebook, the next most popular choice. Girls send, on average, about 3,952 text messages per month, and boys send closer to 2,815 text messages per month, according to the study.[12]

The good news is that today all the popular messaging apps provide some form of encryption when sending and receiving your texts—that is, they protect what's called "data in motion." The bad news is that not all the encryption being used is strong. In 2014, researcher Paul Jauregui of the security firm Praetorian found that it was possible to circumvent the encryption used by WhatsApp and engage in a man-in-the-middle (MitM) attack, in which the attacker intercepts messages between the victim and his recipient and is able to see every message. "This is the kind of stuff the NSA would love," Jauregui observed.[13] As of this writing, the encryption used in WhatsApp has been updated and uses end-to-end encryption on both iOS and Android devices. And the parent company for WhatsApp, Facebook, has added encryption to its 900 million Messenger users, although it is an opt-in, meaning you have to configure "Secret Conversations" to work.[14]

The worse news is what happens to data that's archived, or "data at rest." Most mobile text apps do not encrypt archived data, either on your device or on a third-party system. Apps such as AIM, BlackBerry Messenger, and Skype all store your messages without encrypting them. That means the service provider can read the content (if it's stored in the cloud) and use it for advertising. It also means that if law enforcement—or criminal hackers—were to gain access to the physical device, they could also read those messages.

Another issue is data retention, which we mentioned above—how long does data at rest stay at rest? If apps such as AIM and Skype archive your messages without encryption, how long do they keep them? Microsoft, which owns Skype, has said that "Skype uses automated scanning within Instant Messages and SMS to (a) identify suspected spam and/or (b) identify URLs that have been previously flagged as spam, fraud, or phishing links." So far this sounds like the anti-malware scanning activity that companies perform on our e-mails. However, the privacy policy goes on to say: "Skype will retain your information for as long as is necessary to: (1) fulfill any of the Purposes (as defined in article 2 of this Privacy Policy) or (2) comply with applicable legislation, regulatory requests and relevant orders from competent courts."[15]

That doesn't sound so good. How long is "as long as is necessary"?

AOL Instant Messenger (AIM) may have been the first instant message service that any of us used. It's been around a long while. Designed for desktop or traditional PCs, AIM originally took the form of a little pop-up window that appeared in the lower right-hand corner of the desktop. Today it is available as a mobile app as well. But in terms of privacy, AIM raises some red flags. First, AIM keeps an archive of all messages sent through its service. And, like Skype, it also scans the contents of those messages. A third concern is that AOL keeps records of the messages in the cloud in case you ever want to access a chat history from any terminal or device different from the one where you had your last session.[16]

Since your AOL chat data is not encrypted and is available from any terminal because it lives in the cloud, it is easy for law enforcement and criminal hackers to get a copy. For example, my AOL account was hacked by a script kiddie whose online handle is Virus—his real name is Michael Nieves.[17] He was able to social-engineer (in other words, get on the phone and sweet-talk) AOL and gain access to their internal customer-database system, called Merlin, which allowed him to change my e-mail address to one associated with a separate account under his control. Once he did that he was able to reset my password and gain access to all my past messages. In 2007 Nieves was charged with four felonies and a misdemeanor for, according to the complaint, hacking into "internal AOL computer networks and databases, including customer billing records, addresses and credit card information."

As the Electronic Frontier Foundation has said, "no logs are good logs." AOL has logs.

* * *

Non-native text apps may say they have encryption, but it might not be good or strong encryption. What should you look for? A text app that provides end-to-end encryption, meaning that no third-party has access to the keys. The keys should exist on each device only. Note, too, if either device is compromised with malware, then using any type of encryption is worthless.

There are three basic "flavors" of text apps:

- Those that provide no encryption at all—meaning that anyone can read your text messages.
- Those that provide encryption, but not from end to end—meaning that the communication can be intercepted by third parties such as the service provider, which has knowledge of the encryption keys.
- Those that provide encryption from end to end—meaning that the communication can't be read by third parties because the keys are stored on the individual devices.

Unfortunately the most popular text-messaging apps—like AIM—are not very private. Even Whisper and Secret may not be totally private. Whisper is used by millions and markets itself as anonymous, but researchers have poked holes in these claims. Whisper tracks its users, while the identities of Secret users are sometimes revealed.

Telegram is another messaging app that offers encryption, and it is considered a popular alternative to WhatsApp. It runs on Android, iOS, and Windows devices. Researchers have, however, found an adversary can compromise Telegram servers and get access to critical data.[18] And researchers have found it easy to retrieve encrypted Telegram messages, even after they have been deleted from the device.[19]

So now that we've eliminated some popular choices, what remains? Plenty. When you're on the app store or Google Play, look for apps that use something called off-the-record messaging, or OTR. It is a higher-standard end-to-end encryption protocol used for text messages, and it can be found in a number of products.[20]

Your ideal text message app should also include perfect forward secrecy (PFS). Remember that this employs a randomly generated session key that is designed to be resilient in the future. That means if one key is compromised, it can't be used to read your future text messages.

There are several apps that use both OTR and PFS.

ChatSecure is a secure text-messaging app that works on both Android and iPhones.[21] It also provides something called certificate pinning. That means it includes a proof-of-identity certificate, which is stored on the device. Upon each contact with the servers at ChatSecure, the certificate within the app on your device is compared with the certificate at the mother ship. If the stored certificate does not match, the session does not continue. Another nice touch is that ChatSecure also encrypts the conversation logs stored on the device—the data at rest.[22]

Perhaps the best open-source option is Signal from Open Whisper Systems, which works on both iOS and Android (see page 65).

Another text-messaging app to consider is Cryptocat. It is available for iPhone and most major browsers on your traditional PC. It is not, however, available for Android.[23]

And, at the time of this writing, the Tor project, which maintains the Tor browser (see page 45), has just released Tor Messenger. Like the Tor browser, the app anonymizes your IP address, which means that messages are difficult to trace (however, please note that, like with the Tor browser, exit nodes are not by default under your control; see page 46). Instant messages are encrypted using end-to-end encryption. Like Tor, the app is a little difficult for the first-time user, but eventually it should work to provide truly private text messages.[24]

There are also commercial apps that provide end-to-end encryption. The only caveat is that their software is proprietary, and without independent review their security and integrity cannot be confirmed. Silent Phone offers end-to-end encryption text messaging. It does, however, log some data, but only to improve its services. The encryption keys are stored on the device. Having the keys on the device means that the government or law enforcement can't compel Silent Circle, its manufacturer, to release the encryption keys for any of its subscribers.

I've discussed encrypting data in motion and data at rest as well as using end-to-end encryption, PFS, and OTR to do so. What about non-app-based services, such as Web mail? What about passwords?

CHAPTER FIVE

Now You See Me, Now You Don't

In April of 2013, Khairullozhon Matanov, a twenty-two-year-old former cab driver from Quincy, Massachusetts, went to dinner with a couple of friends—a pair of brothers, in fact. Among other topics, the three men talked about events earlier in the day that occurred near the finish line of the Boston Marathon, where someone had planted rice cookers packed with nails and gunpowder and a timer. The resulting blasts claimed three lives and left more than two hundred people injured. The brothers at Matanov's table, Tamerlan and Dzhokhar Tsarnaev, would later be identified as the prime suspects.

Although Matanov said later that he had no prior knowledge of the bombing, he allegedly left an early post-bombing meeting with law enforcement officers and promptly deleted the browser history from his personal computer. That simple act—erasing his laptop's browser history—resulted in charges against him.[1]

Deleting browser history was also one of the charges against David Kernell, the college student who hacked Sarah Palin's e-mail account. What's chilling is that when Kernell cleared his browser, ran a disk defragmenter, and deleted the Palin photos he had downloaded, he wasn't yet under investigation. The message here is that in the United States you are not allowed to erase anything you do on your computer. Prosecutors want to see your entire browser history.

The charges leveled against Matanov and Kernell stem from a nearly fifteen-year-old law—the Public Company Accounting Reform and Investor Protection Act (as it's known in the Senate), or the Corporate and Auditing Accountability and Responsibility Act (as it's known in the House), more commonly called the Sarbanes-Oxley Act of 2002. The law was a direct result of corporate mismanagement at Enron, a natural gas company later found to be lying and cheating investors and the US government. Investigators in the Enron case discovered that a lot of data had been deleted at the outset of the investigation, preventing prosecutors from seeing exactly what had gone on within the company. As a result, Senator Paul Sarbanes (D-MD) and Representative Michael G. Oxley (R-OH) sponsored legislation that imposed a series of requirements aimed at preserving data. One was that browser histories must be retained.

According to a grand jury indictment, Matanov deleted his Google Chrome browser history selectively, leaving behind activity from certain days during the week of April 15, 2013.[2] Officially he was indicted on two counts: "(1) destroying, altering, and falsifying records, documents, and tangible objects in a federal investigation, and (2) making a materially false, fictitious, and fraudulent statement in a federal investigation involving international and domestic terrorism."[3] He was sentenced to thirty months in prison.

To date, the browser-history provision of Sarbanes-Oxley has rarely been invoked—either against businesses or individuals. And yes, Matanov's case is an anomaly, a high-profile national security case. In its wake, though, prosecutors, aware of its potential, have started invoking it more frequently.

If you can't stop someone from monitoring your e-mail, phone calls, and instant messages, and if you can't lawfully delete your browser history, what can you do? Perhaps you can avoid collecting such history in the first place.

Browsers such as Mozilla's Firefox, Google's Chrome, Apple's Safari, and Microsoft's Internet Explorer and Edge all offer a built-in alternative way to search anonymously on whatever device you prefer—whether you use a traditional PC or a mobile device. In each case the browser itself will open a new window and not record what you searched or where you went on the Internet during that open session. Shut down the private browser window, and all traces of the sites you visited will disappear from your PC or device. What you exchange for privacy is that unless you bookmark a site while using private browsing, you can't go back to it; there's no history—at least not on your machine.

As much as you may feel invincible using a private window on Firefox or the incognito mode on Chrome, your request for private website access, like your e-mails, still has to travel through your ISP—your Internet service provider, the company you pay for Internet or cellular service—and your provider can intercept any information that's sent without being encrypted. If you access a website that uses encryption, then the ISP can obtain the metadata—that you visited such and such site at such and such date and time.

When an Internet browser—either on a traditional PC or a mobile device—connects to a website, it first determines whether there's encryption, and if there is, what kind. The protocol for Web communications is known as http. The protocol is specified before the address, which means that a typical URL might look like this: http://www.mitnicksecurity.com. Even the "www" is superfluous in some cases.

When you connect to a site using encryption, the protocol changes slightly. Instead of "http," you see "https." So now it's https://www.mitnicksecurity.com. This https connection is more secure. For one thing, it's point-to-point, though only if you're connecting directly to the site itself. There are also a lot of Content Delivery Networks (CDNs) that cache pages for their clients to deliver them faster, no matter where you are in the world, and therefore come between you and the desired website.

Keep in mind, too, that if you are logged in to your Google, Yahoo, or Microsoft accounts, these accounts may record the Web traffic on your PC or mobile device—perhaps building your online behavioral profile so the companies can better target the ads you see. One way to avoid this is to always log out of Google, Yahoo, and Microsoft accounts when you are finished using them. You can log back in to them the next time you need to.

Moreover, there are default browsers built in to your mobile devices. These are not good browsers. They're crap, because they're mini versions of the desktop and laptop browsers and lack some of the security and privacy protections the more robust versions have. For example, iPhones ship with Safari, but you might also want to consider going to the online Apple store and downloading the mobile version of Chrome or Firefox, browsers that were designed for the mobile environment. Newer versions of Android do ship with Chrome as the default. All mobile browsers at least support private browsing.

And if you use a Kindle Fire, neither Firefox nor Chrome are download options through Amazon. Instead you have to use a few manual tricks to install Mozilla's Firefox or Chrome through Amazon's Silk browser. To install Firefox on the Kindle Fire, open the Silk browser and go to the Mozilla FTP site. Select "Go," then select the file that ends with the extension .apk.

Private browsing doesn't create temporary files, and therefore it keeps your browsing history off your laptop or mobile device. Could a third party still see your interaction with a given website? Yes, unless that interaction is first encrypted. To accomplish this, the Electronic Frontier Foundation has created a browser plug-in called HTTPS

Everywhere.[4] This is a plug-in for the Firefox and Chrome browsers on your traditional PC and for the Firefox browser on your Android device. There's no iOS version at the time of this writing. But HTTPS Everywhere can confer a distinct advantage: consider that in the first few seconds of connection, the browser and the site negotiate what kind of security to use. You want perfect forward secrecy, which I talked about in the previous chapter. Not all sites use PFS. And not all negotiations end with PFS—even if it is offered. HTTPS Everywhere can force https usage whenever possible, even if PFS is not in use.

Here's one more criterion for a safe connection: every website should have a certificate, a third-party guarantee that when you connect, say, to the Bank of America website it truly is the Bank of America site and not something fraudulent. Modern browsers work with these third parties, known as certificate authorities, to keep updated lists. Whenever you connect to a site that is not properly credentialed, your browser should issue a warning asking if you trust the site enough to continue. It's up to you to make an exception. In general, unless you know the site, don't make exceptions.

Additionally, there isn't just one type of certificate on the Internet; there are levels of certificates. The most common certificate, one you see all the time, identifies only that the domain name belongs to someone who requested the certificate, using e-mail verification. It could be anyone, but that doesn't matter—the site has a certificate that is recognized by your browser. The same is true of the second kind of certificate, an organizational certificate. This means that the site shares its certificate with other sites related to the same domain—in other words, all the subdomains on mitnicksecurity.com would share the same certificate.

The most stringent level of certificate verification, however, is what's called an extended verification certificate. On all browsers, some part of the URL turns green (ordinarily it's gray, like the rest of the URL) when an extended verification certificate has been issued. Clicking over the address—https://www.mitnicksecurity.com—should reveal additional details about the certificate and its owner, usually the city and state of the server providing the website. This physical-world confirmation indicates that the company holding the URL is legitimate and has been confirmed by a trusted third-party certificate authority.

You might expect the browser on your mobile device to track your location, but you might be surprised that the browser on your traditional PC does the same thing. It does. How?

Remember when I explained that e-mail metadata contains the IP address of all the servers that handle the e-mails on their way to you? Well, once again, the IP address coming from your browser can identify which ISP you are using and narrow down the possible geographical areas where you might be located.

The very first time you access a site that specifically requests your location data (such as a weather site), your browser should ask whether you want to share your location with the site. The advantage of sharing is that the site can customize its listing for you. For example, you might see ads on washingtonpost.com for businesses in the town where you live rather than in the DC area.

Unsure whether you answered that browser question in the past? Then try the test page at http://benwerd.com/lab/geo.php. This is one of many test sites that will tell you whether your browser is reporting your location. If it is and you want to be invisible, then disable the feature. Fortunately, you can turn off browser location tracking. In Firefox, type "about: config" in the URL address bar. Scroll down to "geo" and change the setting to "disable." Save your changes. In Chrome, go to Options>Under the Hood>Content Settings>Location. There's a "Do not allow any site to track my physical location" option that will disable geolocation in Chrome. Other browsers have similar configuration options.

You might also want to fake your location—if only just for fun. If you want to send out false coordinates—say, the White House—in Firefox, you can install a browser plug-in called Geolocator. In Google Chrome, check the plug-in's built-in setting called "emulate geolocation coordinates." While in Chrome, press Ctrl+Shift+I on Windows or Cmd+Option+I on Mac to open the Chrome Developer Tools. The Console window will open, and you can click the three vertical dots at the top right of the Console, then select more tools>sensors. A sensor tab will open. This allows you to define the exact latitude and longitude you want to share. You can use the location of a famous landmark or you can choose a site in the middle of one of the oceans. Either way, the website won't know where you really are.

You can obscure not only your physical location but also your IP address while online. Earlier I mentioned Tor, which randomizes the IP address seen by the website you are visiting. But not all sites accept Tor traffic. Until recently, Facebook did not. For those sites that don't accept Tor connections, you can use a proxy.

An open proxy is a server that sits between you and the Internet. In chapter 2 I explained that a proxy is like a foreign-language translator—you speak to the translator, and the translator speaks to the foreign-language speaker, but the message remains exactly the same. I used the term to describe the way someone in a hostile country might try to send you an e-mail pretending to be from a friendly company.

You can also use a proxy to allow you to access georestricted websites—for example, if you live in a country that limits Google search access. Or perhaps you need to hide your identity for downloading illegal or copyrighted content through BitTorrent.

Proxies are not bulletproof, however. When you use a proxy, remember that each browser must be manually configured to point to the proxy service. And even the best proxy sites admit that clever Flash or JavaScript tricks can still detect your underlying IP address—the IP address you use to connect to the proxy in the first place. You can limit the effectiveness of these tricks by blocking or restricting the use of Flash and JavaScript in your browser. But the best way to prevent JavaScript injection from monitoring you via your browser is to use the HTTPS Everywhere plug-in (see page 82).

There are many commercial proxy services. But be sure to read the privacy policy of any service you sign up for. Pay attention to the way it handles encryption of data in motion and whether it complies with law enforcement and government requests for information.

There are also some free proxies, but you must contend with a stream of useless advertising in exchange for the use of the service. My advice is to beware of free proxies. In his presentation at DEF CON 20, my friend and security expert Chema Alonso set up a proxy as an experiment: he wanted to attract bad guys to the proxy, so he advertised the IP address on xroxy.com. After a few days more than five thousand people were using his free "anonymous" proxy. Unfortunately most of them were using it to conduct scams.

The flip side, though, is that Alonso could easily use the free proxy to push malware into the bad guy's browser and monitor his or her activities. He did so using what's called a BeEF hook, a browser exploitation framework. He also used an end user license agreement (EULA) that people had to accept to *allow* him to do it. That's how he was able to read the e-mails being sent through the proxy and determine that it was handling traffic related to criminal activity. The moral here is that when something's free, you get what you pay for.

If you use a proxy with https protocol, a law enforcement or government agency would only see the proxy's IP address, not the activities on the websites you visit—that information would be encrypted. As I mentioned, normal http Internet traffic is not encrypted; therefore you must also use HTTPS Everywhere (yes, this is my answer to most browser invisibility woes).

For the sake of convenience, people often synchronize their browser settings among different devices. For example, when you sign in to the Chrome browser or a Chromebook, your bookmarks, tabs, history, and other browser preferences are all synced via your Google account. These settings load automatically every time you use Chrome, whether on traditional PCs or mobile devices. To choose what information should be synced to your account, go to the settings page on your Chrome browser. The Google Dashboard gives you full control should you ever want to remove synced information from your account. Ensure that sensitive information is not auto-synced. Mozilla's Firefox also has a sync option.

The downside is that all an attacker needs to do is lure you into signing in to your Google account on a Chrome or Firefox browser, then all your search history will load on their device. Imagine your friend using your computer and choosing to log in to the browser. Your friend's history, bookmarks, etc., will now be synced. That means that your friend's surfing history, among other information, is now viewable on your computer. Plus, if you sign in to a synchronized browser account using a public terminal and forget to sign out, all your browser's bookmarks and history will be available to the next user. If you're signed in to Google Chrome, then even your Google calendar, YouTube, and other aspects of your Google account become exposed. If you must use a public terminal, be vigilant about signing out before you leave.

Another downside of syncing is that all interconnected devices will show the same content. If you live alone, that may be fine. But if you share an iCloud account, bad things can happen. Parents who allow their children to use the family iPad, for example, might unintentionally expose them to adult content.[5]

In an Apple store in Denver, Colorado, Elliot Rodriguez, a local account executive, registered his new tablet with his existing iCloud account. Instantly all his photos, texts, and music and video downloads were available to him on the new tablet. This convenience saved him time; he didn't have to manually copy and save all that material to multiple devices. And it allowed him access to the items no matter what device he chose to use.

At some point later on Elliot thought it was a good idea to give his older-technology tablet to his eight-year-old daughter. The fact that she was connected to his devices was a short-term plus. Occasionally on his tablet Elliot would notice a new app his daughter had downloaded to her tablet. Sometimes they would even share family photos. Then Elliot took a trip to New York City, where he traveled often for business.

Without thinking, Elliot took out his iPhone and captured several moments with his New York–based mistress, some of them quite... intimate. The images from his iPhone synced automatically to his daughter's iPad back in Colorado. And of course his daughter asked her mother about the woman who was with Daddy. Needless to say, Elliot had some serious explaining to do when he got home.

And then there's the birthday-present problem. If you share devices or synced accounts, your visits to sites might tip gift recipients off to what they'll be getting for their birthdays. Or, worse, what they might have gotten. Yet another reason why sharing a family PC or tablet can present a privacy problem.

One way to avoid this is to set up different users, a relatively easy step in Windows. Keep the administrator privileges for yourself so that you can add software to the system and set up additional family or household members with their own accounts. All users will log in with their own passwords and have access to only their own content and their own browser bookmarks and histories.

Apple allows for similar divisions within its OSX operating systems. However, not many people remember to segment their iCloud space. And sometimes, seemingly through no fault of our own, technology simply betrays us.

After years of dating several women, Dylan Monroe, an LA-based

TV producer, finally found "the one" and decided to settle down. His fiancée moved in, and, as part of their new life together, he innocently connected his future wife to his iCloud account.

When you want to start a family, it makes sense to connect everyone to one account. Doing so allows you to share all your videos, texts, and music with the ones you love. Except that's in the present tense. What about your digitally stored past?

Sometimes having an automatic cloud backup service like iCloud means that we accumulate many years' worth of photos, texts, and music, some of which we tend to forget, just as we forget the contents of old boxes in the attic.

Photos are the closest thing we have to memories. And yes, spouses have been coming across shoe boxes of old letters and photographs for generations now. But a digital medium that allows you to take literally thousands of high-definition photos without too much effort creates new problems. Suddenly Dylan's old memories—some of them very private indeed—came back to haunt him in the form of photos that were now on his fiancée's iPhone and iPad.

There were items of furniture that had to be removed from the house because other women had performed intimate acts on that sofa, table, or bed. There were restaurants where his fiancée refused to go to because she had seen photos of other women there with him, at that table by the window or in that corner booth.

Dylan obliged his fiancée lovingly, even when she asked him to make the ultimate sacrifice—selling his house once the two of them were married. All because he'd connected his iPhone to hers.

The cloud creates another interesting problem. Even if you delete your browser history on your desktop, laptop, or mobile device, a copy of your search history remains in the cloud. Stored on the search engine company's servers, your history is a bit harder to delete and harder to not have stored in the first place. This is just one example of how surreptitious data collection without the proper context can be easily misinterpreted at a later date and time. It's easy to see how an innocent set of searches can go awry.

One morning in the late summer of 2013, just weeks after the Boston Marathon bombing, Michele Catalano's husband saw two black SUVs pull up in front of their house on Long Island. When he went outside to greet the officers, they asked him to confirm his identity and requested his permission to search the house. Having nothing to hide, although uncertain why they were there, he allowed them to enter. After a cursory check of the rooms, the federal agents got down to business.

"Has anyone in this household searched for information on pressure cookers?"

"Has anyone in this household searched for information on backpacks?"

Apparently the family's online searches through Google had triggered a preemptive investigation by the Department of Homeland Security. Without knowing the exact nature of the Catalano family investigation, one might imagine that in the weeks following the Boston Marathon bombing certain online searches, when combined, suggested the potential for terrorism and so were flagged. Within two hours the Catalano household was cleared of any potential wrongdoing. Michele later wrote about the experience for *Medium*—if only as a warning that what you search for today might come back to haunt you tomorrow.[6]

In her article, Catalano pointed out that the investigators must have discounted her searches for "What the hell do I do with quinoa?" and "Is A-Rod suspended yet?" She said her pressure-cooker query was about nothing more than making quinoa. And the backpack query? Her husband wanted a backpack.

At least one search engine company, Google, has created several privacy tools that allow you to specify what information you feel comfortable keeping.[7] For example, you can turn off personalized ad tracking so that if you look up Patagonia (the region in South America) you don't start seeing ads for South American travel. You can also turn off your search history altogether. Or you could not log in to Gmail, YouTube, or any of your Google accounts while you search online.

Even if you are not logged in to your Microsoft, Yahoo, or Google accounts, your IP address is still tied to each search engine request. One way to avoid this one-to-one match is to use the Google-proxy startpage.com or the search engine DuckDuckGo instead.

DuckDuckGo is already a default option within Firefox and Safari. Unlike Google, Yahoo, and Microsoft, DuckDuckGo has no provision for user accounts, and the company says your IP address is not logged by default. The company also maintains its own Tor exit relay, meaning that you can search DuckDuckGo while using Tor without much of a performance lag.[8]

Because DuckDuckGo doesn't track your use, your search results won't be filtered by your past searches. Most people don't realize it, but the results you see within Google, Yahoo, and Bing are filtered by everything you searched for on those sites in the past. For example, if the search engine sees that you're searching for sites related to health issues, it will start to filter the search results and push the results related to health issues to the very top. Why? Because very few of us bother to advance to the second page of a search result. There's an Internet joke that says that if you want to know the best place to bury a dead body, try page 2 of the search results.

Some people might like the convenience of not having to scroll through seemingly unrelated results, but at the same time it is patronizing for a search engine to decide what you may or may not be interested in. By most measures, that is censorship. DuckDuckGo does return relevant search results, but filtered by topic, not by your past history.

In the next chapter I'll talk about specific ways websites make it hard for you to be invisible to them and what you can do to surf the Web anonymously.

CHAPTER SIX

Every Mouse Click You Make, I'll Be Watching You

Be very careful what you search for on the Internet. It's not just search engines that track your online habits; every website you visit does as well. And you'd think that some of them would know better than to expose private matters to others. For example, a 2015 report found that "70 percent of health sites' URLs contain information exposing specific conditions, treatments, and diseases."[1]

In other words, if I'm on WebMD and searching for "athlete's foot," the unencrypted words *athlete's foot* will appear within the URL visible in my browser's address bar. This means that anyone—my browser, my ISP, my cellular carrier—can see that I am looking for information about athlete's foot. Having HTTPS Everywhere enabled on your browser would encrypt the contents of the site you are visiting, assuming the site supports https, but it doesn't encrypt the URL. As even the Electronic Frontier Foundation notes, https was never designed to conceal the identity of the sites you visit.

Additionally, the study found that 91 percent of health-related sites make requests to third parties. These calls are embedded in the pages themselves, and they make requests for tiny images (which may or may not be visible on the browser page), which informs these other third-party sites that you are visiting a particular page. Do a search for "athlete's foot," and as many as twenty different entities—ranging from pharmaceuticals companies to Facebook, Pinterest, Twitter, and Google—are contacted as soon as the search results load in your browser. Now all those parties know you have been searching for information about athlete's foot.[2]

These third parties use this information to target you with online advertising. Also, if you logged in to the health-care site, they might be able to obtain your e-mail address. Fortunately I can help you prevent these entities from learning more about you.

On the health-care sites analyzed in the 2015 study, the top ten third parties were Google, comScore, Facebook, AppNexus, AddThis, Twitter, Quantcast, Amazon, Adobe, and Yahoo. Some—comScore, AppNexus, and Quantcast—measure Web traffic, as does Google. Of the third parties listed above, Google, Facebook, Twitter, Amazon, Adobe, and Yahoo are spying on your activity for commercial reasons, so they can, for example, load ads for athlete's foot remedies in future searches.

Also mentioned in the study were the third parties Experian and Axiom, which are simply data warehouses—they collect as much data about a person as they possibly can. And then they sell it. Remember the security questions and the creative answers I suggested that you use? Often companies like Experian and Axiom collect, provide, and use those security questions to build online profiles. These profiles are valuable to marketers that want to target their products to certain demographics.

How does that work?

Whether you type the URL in manually or use a search engine, every site on the Internet has both a hostname and a numerical IP address (some sites exist only as numerical addresses). But you almost never see the numerical address. Your browser hides it and uses a domain name service (DNS) to translate a site's hostname name—say, Google—in to a specific address, in Google's case https://74.125.224.72/.

DNS is like a global phone book, cross-referencing the hostname with the numerical address of the server of the site you just requested. Type "Google.com" into your browser, and the DNS contacts their server at https://74.125.224.72. Then you see the familiar white screen with the day's Google Doodle above a blank search field. That, in theory, is how all Web browsers work. In practice there is more to it.

After the site has been identified through its numerical address, it will send information back to your Web browser so that it can start "building" the Web page you see. When the page is returned to your browser, you see the elements you would expect—the information you want retrieved, any related images, and ways to navigate to other parts of the site. But often there are elements that are returned to your browser that call out to other websites for additional images or scripts. Some, if not all, of these scripts are for tracking purposes, and in most cases you simply do not need them.

Almost every digital technology produces metadata, and, as you've no doubt already guessed, browsers are no different. Your browser can reveal information about your computer's configuration if queried by the site you are visiting. For example, what version of what browser and operating system you're using, what add-ons you have for that browser, and what other programs you're running on your computer (such as Adobe products) while you search. It can even reveal details of your computer's hardware, such as the resolution of the screen and the capacity of the onboard memory.

You might think after reading this far that you have taken great strides in becoming invisible online. And you have. But there's more work to be done.

Take a moment and surf over to Panopticlick.com. This is a site built by the Electronic Frontier Foundation that will determine just how common or unique your browser configuration is compared to others, based on what's running on your PC or mobile device's operating system and the plug-ins you may have installed. In other words, do you have any plug-ins that can be used to limit or otherwise protect the information that Panopticlick can glean from your browser alone?

If the numbers on the left-hand side, the results from Panopticlick, are high—say, a six-digit number—then you are somewhat unique, because your browser settings are found in fewer than one in one hundred thousand computers. Congratulations. However, if your numbers are low—say, less than three digits—then your browser settings are fairly common. You're just one in a few hundred. And that means if I'm going to target you—with ads or malware—I don't have to work very hard, because you have a common browser configuration.[3]

You might think that having a common configuration can help you become invisible—you're part of the crowd; you blend in. But from a technical perspective, this opens you up to malicious activities. A criminal hacker doesn't want to expend a lot of effort. If a house has a door open and the house next to it has a door closed, which do you think a thief would rob? If a criminal hacker knows that you have common settings, then perhaps you also lack certain protections that could enhance your security.

I understand I just jumped from discussing marketers trying to track what you view online to criminal hackers who may or may not use your personal information to steal your identity. These are very different. Marketers collect information in order to create ads that keep websites profitable. Without advertising, some sites simply could not continue. However, marketers, criminal hackers, and, for that matter, governments are all trying to get information that you may not want to give, and so, for the sake of argument, they are often lumped together in discussions about the invasion of privacy.

One way to be common yet also safe from online eavesdropping is to use a virtual machine (VM; see page 263), an operating system like Mac OSX running as a guest on top of your Windows operating system. You can install VMware on your desktop and use it to run another operating system. When you're done, you simply shut it down. The operating system and everything you did within it will disappear. The files you save, however, will remain wherever you saved them.

Something else to watch out for is that marketers and criminal hackers alike learn something about visitors to a website through what's known as a one-pixel image file or web bug. Like a blank browser pop-up window, this is a 1×1-pixel image placed somewhere on a Web page that, although invisible, nonetheless calls back to the third-party site that placed it there. The backend server records the IP address that tried to render that image. A one-pixel image placed on a health-care site could tell a pharmaceuticals company that I was interested in athlete's foot remedies.

The 2015 study I mentioned at the beginning of this chapter found that almost half of third-party requests simply open pop-up windows containing no content whatsoever. These "blank" windows generate silent http requests to third-party hosts that are used only for tracking purposes. You can avoid these by instructing your browser not to allow pop-up windows (and this will also eliminate those annoying ads as well).

Nearly a third of the remaining third-party requests, according to the study, consisted of small lines of code, JavaScript files, which usually just execute animations on a Web page. A website can identify the computer accessing the site, mostly by reading the IP address that is requesting the JavaScript file.

Even without a one-pixel image or a blank pop-up window, your

Web surfing can still be tracked by the sites you visit. For example, Amazon might know that the last site you visited was a health-care site, so it will make recommendations for health-care products for you on its own site. The way Amazon might do this is to actually see the last site you visited in your browser request.

Amazon accomplishes this by using third-party referrers—text in the request for a Web page that tells the new page where the request originated. For example, if I'm reading an article on *Wired* and it contains a link, when I click that link the new site will know that I was previously on a page within Wired.com. You can see how this third-party tracking can affect your privacy.

To avoid this, you can always go to Google.com first, so the site you want to visit doesn't know where you were previously. I don't believe third-party referrers are such a big deal, except when you're trying to mask your identity. This is one more example of a trade-off between convenience (simply going to the next website) and invisibility (always starting from Google.com).

Mozilla's Firefox offers one of the best defenses against third-party tracking through a plug-in called NoScript.[4] This add-on effectively blocks just about everything considered harmful to your computer and browser, namely, Flash and JavaScript. Adding security plug-ins will change the look and feel of your browsing session, although you can cherry-pick and enable specific features or permanently trust some sites.

One result of enabling NoScript is that the page you visit will have no ads and certainly no third-party referrers. As a result of the blocking, the Web page looks slightly duller than the version without NoScript enabled. However, should you want to see that Flash-encoded video in the upper left-hand corner of the page, you can specifically allow that one element to render while continuing to block everything else. Or, if you feel you can trust the site, you can temporarily or permanently allow all elements on that page to load—something you might want to do on a banking site, for example.

For its part, Chrome has ScriptBlock,[5] which allows you to defensively block the use of scripts on a Web page. This is useful for kids who may surf to a site that allows pop-up adult entertainment ads.

Blocking potentially harmful (and certainly privacy-compromising) elements on these pages will keep your computer from being overrun with ad-generating malware. For example, you may have noticed that ads appear on your Google home page. In fact, you should have no flashing ads on your Google home page. If you see them, your computer and browser may have been compromised (perhaps some time ago), and as a result you're seeing third-party ads that may contain Trojan horses—keyloggers, which record every keystroke you make, and other malware—if you click on them. Even if the ads don't contain malware, the advertisers' revenue comes from the number of clicks they receive. The more people they dupe into clicking, the more money they make.

As good as they are, NoScript and ScriptBlock don't block everything. For complete protection against browser threats, you might want to install Adblock Plus. The only problem is that Adblock records everything: this is another company that tracks your surfing history, despite your use of private browsing. However, in this case the good—blocking potentially dangerous ads—outweighs the bad: they know where you've been online.

Another useful plug-in is Ghostery, available for both Chrome and Firefox. Ghostery identifies all the Web traffic trackers (such as DoubleClick and Google AdSense) that sites use to follow your activity. Like NoScript, Ghostery gives you granular control over which trackers you want to allow on each page. The site says, "Blocking trackers will prevent them from running in your browser, which can help control how your behavioral data is tracked. Keep in mind that some trackers are potentially useful, such as social network feed widgets or browser-based games. Blocking may have an unintended effect on the sites you visit." Meaning that some sites will no longer work with Ghostery installed. Fortunately, you can disable it on a site-by-site basis.[6]

In addition to using plug-ins to block sites from identifying you, you might want to confuse potential hackers further by using a variety of e-mail addresses tailored for individual purposes. For example, in chapter 2 I discussed ways of creating anonymous e-mail accounts in order to communicate without detection. Similarly, for simple day-to-day browsing, it's also a good idea to create multiple e-mail accounts—not to hide but to make yourself less interesting to third parties on the Internet. Having multiple online personality profiles dilutes the privacy impact of having only one identifiable address. It makes it harder for anyone to build an online profile of you.

Let's say you want to purchase something online. You might want to create an e-mail address that you use exclusively for shopping. You might also want to have anything you purchase with this e-mail address sent to your mail drop instead of your home address.[7] In addition, you might want to use a gift card for your purchase, perhaps one you reload from time to time.

This way the company selling you products will only have your nonprimary e-mail address, your nonprimary real-world address, and your more-or-less throwaway gift card. If there's ever a data breach at that company, at least the attackers won't have your real e-mail address, real-world address, or credit card number. This kind of disconnection from an online purchasing event is good privacy practice.

You might also want to create another nonprimary e-mail address for social networks. This address might become your "public" e-mail address, which strangers and mere acquaintances can use to get in touch with you. The advantage to this is that, once again, people won't learn much about you. At least not directly. You can further protect yourself by giving each nonprimary address a unique name, either a variation on your real name or another name entirely.

Be careful if you go with the former option. You might not want to list a middle name—or, if you always go by your middle name, you might not want to list your first name. Even something innocent like JohnQDoe@xyz.com just tipped us off that you have a middle name and that it begins with *Q*. This is an example of giving out personal information when it isn't necessary. Remember that you are trying to blend into the background, not call attention to yourself.

If you use a word or phrase unrelated to your name, make it as unrevealing as possible. If your e-mail address is snowboarder@xyz .com, we may not know your name, but we do know one of your hobbies. Better to choose something generic, like silverfox@xyz.com.

You'll of course also want to have a personal e-mail address. You should only share this one with close friends and family. And the safest practices often come with nice bonuses: you'll find that not using your personal e-mail address for online purchasing will prevent you from receiving a ton of spam.

Cell phones are not immune from corporate tracking. In the summer of 2015, an eagle-eyed researcher caught AT&T and Verizon appending additional code to every Web page request made through a mobile browser. This is not the IMSI—international mobile subscriber identity—I talked about in chapter 3 (see page 52); rather, it's a unique identification code sent with each Web page request. The code, known as a unique identifier header, or UIDH, is a temporary serial number that advertisers can use to identify you on the Web. The researcher discovered what was going on because he configured his mobile phone to log all web traffic (which not many people do). Then he noticed the additional data tacked on to Verizon customers and, later, AT&T customers.[8]

The problem with this additional code is that customers were not told about it. For instance, those who had downloaded the Firefox mobile app and used plug-ins to increase their privacy were, if they used AT&T or Verizon, nonetheless being tracked by the UIDH codes.

Thanks to these UIDH codes, Verizon and AT&T could take the traffic associated with your Web requests and either use it to build a profile of your mobile online presence for future advertising or simply sell the raw data to others.

AT&T has suspended the operation—for now.[9] Verizon has made it yet another option for the end user to configure.[10] Note: by *not* opting out, you give Verizon permission to continue.

Even if you turn off JavaScript, a website may still pass a text file with data called an http cookie back to your browser. This cookie could be stored for a long time. The term *cookie* is short for *magic cookie,* a piece of text that is sent from a website and stored in the user's browser to keep track of things, such as items in a shopping cart, or even to authenticate a user. Cookies were first used on the Web by Netscape and were originally intended to help with creating virtual shopping carts and e-commerce functions. Cookies are typically stored in the browser on a traditional PC and have expiration dates, although these dates could be decades in the future.

Are cookies dangerous? No—at least not by themselves. However, cookies would provide third parties with information about your account and your specific preferences, such as your favorite cities on a weather site or your airline preferences on a travel site. The next time your browser connects to that site, if a cookie already exists, the site will remember you and perhaps say "Hello, Friend." And if it is an e-commerce site, it may also remember your last few purchases.

Cookies do not actually store this information on your traditional PC or mobile device. Like cell phones that use IMSIs as proxies, the cookie contains a proxy for the data that lives on the back end at the site. When your browser loads a Web page with a cookie attached, additional data is pulled from the site that is specific to you.

Not only do cookies store your personal site preferences, they also provide valuable tracking data for the site they came from. For example, if you are a prospective customer of a company and you have previously entered your e-mail address or other information to access a white paper, chances are there is a cookie in your browser for that company's site that matches, on the back end, information about you in a customer record management (CRM) system—say, Salesforce or HubSpot. Now every time you access that company's site, you will be identified through the cookie in your browser, and that visit will be recorded within the CRM.

Cookies are segmented, meaning that website A can't necessarily see the contents of a cookie for website B. There have been exceptions, but generally the information is separate and reasonably secure. From a privacy perspective, however, cookies do not make you very invisible.

You can only access cookies in the same domain, a set of resources assigned to a specific group of people. Ad agencies get around this by loading a cookie that can track your activity on several sites that are part of their larger networks. In general, though, cookies cannot access another site's cookies. Modern browsers provide a way for the user to control cookies. For example, if you surf the Web using incognito or private browsing features, you will not retain a historical record within the browser of your visit to a given site, nor will you acquire a new cookie for that session. If you had a cookie from an earlier visit, however, it will still apply in private mode. If you are using the normal browsing feature, on the other hand, you may from time to time want to manually remove some or all of the cookies you acquired over the years.

I should note that removing all cookies may not be advisable.

Selectively removing the cookies that are associated with one-off visits to sites you don't care about will help remove traces of you from the Internet. Sites you revisit won't be able to see you, for example. But for some sites, such as a weather site, it might be tedious to keep typing in your zip code every time you visit when a simple cookie might suffice.

Removing cookies can be accomplished by using an add-on or by going into the settings or preferences section of your browser, where there is usually an option to delete one or more (even all) of the cookies. You may want to determine the fate of your cookies on a case-by-case basis.

Some advertisers use cookies to track how long you spend on the sites where they've placed their ads. Some even record your visits to previous sites, what's known as the referrer site. You should delete these cookies immediately. You will recognize some of them because their names won't contain the names of the sites you visited. For example, instead of "CNN," a referrer cookie will identify itself as "Ad321." You may also want to consider using a cookie cleaner software tool, such as the one at piriform.com/ccleaner, to help manage your cookies easily.

There are, however, some cookies that are impervious to whatever decisions you make on the browser side. These are called super cookies because they exist on your computer, outside of your browser. Super cookies access a site's preferences and tracking data no matter what browser you use (Chrome today, Firefox tomorrow). And you should delete super cookies from your browser, otherwise your traditional PC will attempt to re-create http cookies from memory the next time your browser accesses the site.

There are two specific super cookies that live outside your browser that you can delete—Flash, from Adobe, and Silverlight, from Microsoft. Neither of these super cookies expires. And it is generally safe to delete them.[11]

Then there's the toughest cookie of them all. Samy Kamkar, once famous for creating the rapidly spreading Myspace worm called Samy, has created something he calls Evercookie, which is simply a very, very persistent cookie.[12] Kamkar achieved this persistence by storing the cookie data in as many browser storage systems as possible throughout the Windows operating system. As long as one of the storage sites remains intact, Evercookie will attempt to restore the cookie everywhere else.[13] Thus simply deleting an Evercookie from the browser's cookie storage cache is not enough. Like the kids' game whack-a-mole, Evercookies will keep popping up. You will need to delete them completely from your machine in order to win.

If you consider how many cookies you might already have on your browser, and if you multiply that by the number of potential storage areas on your machine, you can see that you'll be in for a long afternoon and evening.

It's not just websites and mobile carriers that want to track your activities online. Facebook has become ubiquitous—a platform beyond just social media. You can sign in to Facebook and then use that same Facebook log-in to sign in to various other apps.

How popular is this practice? At least one marketing report finds that 88 percent of US consumers have logged in to a website or mobile application using an existing digital identity from a social network such as Facebook, Twitter, and Google Plus.[14]

There are pros and cons to this convenience—known as OAuth, an authentication protocol that allows a site to trust you even if you don't enter a password. On the one hand, it's a shortcut: you can quickly access new sites using your existing social media password. On the other hand, this allows the social media site to glean information about you for its marketing profiles. Instead of just knowing about your visit to a single site, it knows about all the sites, all the brands you use its log-in information for. When we use OAuth, we're giving up a lot of privacy for the sake of convenience.

Facebook is perhaps the most "sticky" of all social media platforms. Logging out of Facebook may deauthorize your browser from accessing Facebook and its Web applications. Furthermore, Facebook adds trackers for monitoring user activity that function even after you're logged out, requesting information such as your geographic location, which sites you visit, what you click on within individual sites, and your Facebook username. Privacy groups have expressed concern about Facebook's intent to start tracking information from some of the websites and apps its users are visiting in order to display more personalized ads.

The point is that Facebook, like Google, wants data about you. It may not come right out and ask, but it will find ways to get it. If you link your Facebook account to other services, the platform will have information about you *and* that other service or app. Maybe you use Facebook to access your bank account—if you do, it knows what financial institution you use. Using just one authentication means that if someone gets into your Facebook account, that person will have access to every other website linked to that account—even your bank account. In the security business, having what we call a single point of failure is never a good idea. Although it takes a few seconds more, it's worth signing in to Facebook only when you need to and signing in to each app you use separately.

In addition, Facebook has deliberately chosen not to honor the "do not track" signal sent by Internet Explorer on the grounds that there's "no industry consensus" behind it.[15] The Facebook trackers come in the classic forms: cookies, JavaScript, one-pixel images, and iframes. This allows targeted advertisers to scan and access specific browser cookies and trackers to deliver products, services, and ads, both on and off Facebook.

Fortunately there are browser extensions that block Facebook services on third-party sites, e.g., Facebook Disconnect for Chrome[16] and Facebook Privacy List for Adblock Plus (which works with both

Firefox and Chrome).[17] Ultimately the goal of all of these plug-in tools is to give you control over what you share with Facebook and any other social networks as opposed to forcing you to take a backseat and allowing the service you're using to govern these things for you.

Given what Facebook knows about its 1.65 billion subscribers, the company has been fairly benevolent—so far.[18] It has a ton of data, but it, like Google, has chosen not to act on all of it. But that doesn't mean it won't.

More overt than cookies—and equally parasitic—are toolbars. The additional toolbar you see at the top of your traditional PC browser might be labeled YAHOO or MCAFEE or ASK. Or it may carry the name of any number of other companies. Chances are you don't remember how the toolbar got there. Nor do you ever use it. Nor do you know how to remove it.

Toolbars like this draw your attention away from the toolbar that came with your browser. The native toolbar allows you to choose which search engine to use as the default. The parasitic one will take you to its own search site, and the results may be filled with sponsored content. This happened to Gary More, a West Hollywood resident, who found himself with the Ask.com toolbar and no clear way to remove it. "It's like a bad houseguest," said More. "It will not leave."[19]

If you have a second or third toolbar, it may be because you've downloaded new software or had to update existing software. For example, if you have Java installed on your computer, Oracle, the maker of Java, will automatically include a toolbar unless you specifically tell it not to. When you were clicking through the download or update screens, you probably didn't notice the tiny check box that by default indicated your consent to the installation of a toolbar. There's nothing illegal about this; you did give consent, even if it means that you didn't opt out of having it install automatically. But that toolbar allows another company to track your Web habits and perhaps change your default search engine to its own service as well.

The best way to remove a toolbar is to uninstall it the way you would uninstall any program on your traditional PC. But some of the most persistent and parasitic toolbars may require you to download a removal tool, and often the process of uninstalling can leave behind enough information to allow advertising agents related to the toolbar to reinstall it.

When installing new software or updating existing software, pay attention to all the check boxes. You can avoid a lot of hassle if you don't agree to the installation of these toolbars in the first place.

What if you do use private browsing, have NoScript, HTTPS Everywhere, and you periodically delete your browser's cookies and extraneous toolbars? You should be safe, right? Nope. You can *still* be tracked online.

Websites are coded using something called Hypertext Markup Language, or HTML. There are many new features available in the current version, HTML5. Some of the features have hastened the demise of the super cookies Silverlight and Flash—which is a good thing. HTML5 has, however, enabled new tracking technologies, perhaps by accident.

One of these is canvas fingerprinting, an online tracking tool that is cool in a very creepy way. Canvas fingerprinting uses the HTML5 canvas element to draw a simple image. That's it. The drawing of the image takes place within the browser and is not visible to you. It takes only a fraction of a second. But the result is visible to the requesting website.

The idea is that your hardware and software, when combined as resources for the browser, will render the image uniquely. The image—it could be a series of variously colored shapes—is then converted into a unique number, roughly the way passwords are.

This number is then matched to previous instances of that number seen on other websites around the Internet. And from that—the number of places where that unique number is seen—a profile of websites you visit can be built up. This number, or canvas fingerprint, can be used to identify your browser whenever it returns to any particular website that requested it, even if you have removed all cookies or blocked future cookies from installing, because it uses an element built into HTML5 itself.[20]

Canvas fingerprinting is a drive-by process; it does not require you to click or do anything but simply view a Web page. Fortunately there are plug-ins for your browser that can block it. For Firefox there's CanvasBlocker.[21] For Google Chrome there's CanvasFingerprintBlock.[22] Even the Tor project has added its own anticanvas technology to its browser.[23]

If you use these plug-ins and follow all my other recommendations, you might think that you're finally free of online tracking. And you'd be wrong.

Firms such as Drawbridge and Tapad, and Oracle's Crosswise, take online tracking a step further. They claim to have technologies that can track your interests across multiple devices, including sites you visit only on your cell phones and tablets.

Some of this tracking is the result of machine learning and fuzzy logic. For example, if a mobile device and a traditional PC both contact a site using the same IP address, it's very possible that they are owned by a single person. For example, say you search for a particular item of clothing on your cell phone, then when you get home and are on your traditional PC, you find that same item of clothing in the "recently viewed" section of the retailer's website. Better yet, let's say you buy the item of clothing using your traditional PC. The more matches created between distinct devices, the more likely it is that a single individual is using both of them. Drawbridge alone claims it linked 1.2 billion users across 3.6 billion devices in 2015.[24]

Google, of course, does the same thing, as do Apple and Microsoft. Android phones require the use of a Google account. Apple devices use an Apple ID. Whether a user has a smartphone or a laptop, the Web traffic generated by each is associated with a specific user. And the latest Microsoft operating systems require a Microsoft account in order to download apps or to store photos and documents using the company's cloud service.

The big difference is that Google, Apple, and Microsoft allow you to disable some or all of this data collection activity and retroactively delete collected data. Drawbridge, Crosswise, and Tapad make the process of disabling and deletion less clear. Or it may simply not be available.

Although using a proxy service or Tor is a convenient way to obscure your true location when accessing the Internet, this masking can create interesting problems or even backfire on you, because sometimes online tracking can be justified—especially when a credit card company is trying to fight fraud. For example, just days before Edward Snowden went public, he wanted to create a website to support online rights. He had trouble, however, paying the host company for the registration with his credit card.

At the time, he was still using his real name, real e-mail address, and personal credit cards—this was just before he became a whistle-blower. He was also using Tor, which sometimes triggers fraud warnings from credit card companies when they want to verify your identity and can't reconcile some of the information you provided with what they have on file. If, say, your credit card account says you live in New York, why does your Tor exit node say you are in Germany? A geolocation discrepancy like this often flags an attempt to purchase as possible abuse and invites additional scrutiny.

Credit card companies certainly track us online. They know all our purchases. They know where we have subscriptions. They know when we leave the country. And they know whenever we use a new machine to make a purchase online.

According to Micah Lee of the EFF, at one point Snowden was in his Hong Kong hotel room discussing government secrets with Laura Poitras and Glenn Greenwald, a reporter from the *Guardian,* and at the same time he was on hold with the customer support department at DreamHost, an Internet provider based in Los Angeles. Apparently Snowden explained to DreamHost that he was overseas and didn't trust the local Internet service, hence his use of Tor. Ultimately DreamHost accepted his credit card over Tor.[25]

One way to avoid this hassle with Tor is to configure the torrec config file to use exit nodes located in your home country. That should keep the credit card companies happy. On the other hand, constantly using the same exit nodes might ultimately reveal who you are. There is some serious speculation that government agencies might control some exit nodes, so using different ones makes sense.

Another way to pay without leaving a trace is to use Bitcoin, a virtual currency. Like most currencies, it fluctuates in value based on the confidence people have in it.

Bitcoin is an algorithm that allows people to create—or, in Bitcoin terminology, mine—their own currency. But if it were easy, everyone would do it. So it's not. The process is computationally intensive, and it takes a long while just to create one Bitcoin. Thus there is a finite amount of Bitcoin in existence on any given day, and that, in addition to consumer confidence, influences its value.

Each Bitcoin has a cryptographic signature that identifies it as original and unique. Transactions made with that cryptographic signature can be traced back to the coin, but the method by which you obtain the coin can be obscured—for example, by setting up a rock-solid anonymous e-mail address and using that e-mail address to set up an anonymous Bitcoin wallet using the Tor network.

You buy Bitcoin in person, or anonymously online using prepaid gift cards, or find a Bitcoin ATM without camera surveillance. Depending on what surveillance factors could potentially reveal your true identity, every risk needs to be taken into account when choosing which purchasing method to use. You can then put these Bitcoins into what's known as a tumbler. A tumbler takes some Bitcoins from me, some from you, and some from other people chosen at random and mixes them together. You keep the value of the coins minus the tumbling fee—it's just that the cryptographic signature of each coin may be different after it's mixed with others. That anonymizes the system somewhat.

Once you have them, how do you store Bitcoins? Because there are no Bitcoin banks, and because Bitcoin is not physical currency, you will need to use a Bitcoin wallet set up anonymously using the detailed instructions described later in this book.

Now that you've bought and stored it, how do you use Bitcoin? Exchanges allow you to invest in Bitcoin and change it into other currencies, such as US dollars, or purchase goods on sites such as Amazon. Say you have one Bitcoin, valued at $618. If you only need around $80 for a purchase, then you will retain a certain percentage of the original value, depending on the exchange rate, after the transaction.

Transactions are verified in a public ledger known as a blockchain and identified by IP address. But as we have seen, IP addresses can be changed or faked. And although merchants have started accepting Bitcoin, the service fees, typically paid by the merchant, have been transferred to the purchaser. Furthermore, unlike credit cards, Bitcoin permits no refunds or reimbursements.

You can accumulate as much Bitcoin as you would hard currency. But despite its overall success (the Winklevoss brothers, famous for challenging Mark Zuckerberg over the founding of Facebook, are major investors in Bitcoin), the system has had some monumental failures as well. In 2004, Mt. Gox, a Tokyo-based Bitcoin exchange, declared bankruptcy after announcing that its Bitcoin had been stolen. There have been other reports of theft among Bitcoin exchanges, which, unlike most US bank accounts, are not insured.

Still, although there have been various attempts at virtual currency in the past, Bitcoin has become the Internet's standard anonymous currency. A work in progress, yes, but an option for anyone looking for privacy.

You might feel invisible right now—obscuring your IP address with Tor; encrypting your e-mail and text messages with PGP and Signal. I haven't, however, talked much about hardware—which can be used to both find you and hide you on the Internet.

CHAPTER SEVEN

Pay Up or Else!

The nightmare began online and ended with federal agents storming a house in suburban Blaine, Minnesota. The agents had only an IP address associated with child pornography downloads and even a death threat against Vice President Joe Biden. By contacting the Internet service provider associated with that IP address, the agents acquired the user's physical address. That sort of tracking was very successful back in the days when everyone still had a wired connection to their modems or routers. At that time, each IP address could be physically traced to a given machine.

But today most people use wireless connections within their homes. Wireless allows everyone inside to move around the house with mobile devices and remain connected to the Internet. And if you're not careful, it also allows neighbors to access that same signal. In this case the federal agents stormed the wrong house in Minnesota. They really wanted the house next door to it.

In 2010, Barry Vincent Ardolf pleaded guilty to charges of hacking, identity theft, possession of child pornography, and making threats against Vice President Biden. Court records show that the trouble between Ardolf and his neighbor began when the neighbor, who was in fact a lawyer and was not named, filed a police report saying that Ardolf allegedly "inappropriately touched and kissed" the lawyer's toddler on the mouth.[1]

Ardolf then used the IP address of his neighbor's wireless home router to open Yahoo and Myspace accounts in his victim's name. It was from these fake accounts that Ardolf launched a campaign to embarrass and cause legal troubles for the lawyer.

Many ISPs now provide their home routers with wireless capabilities built in.[2] Some ISPs, such as Comcast, are creating a second open Wi-Fi service over which you have limited control. For example, you may be able to change a few settings, such as the ability to turn it off. You should be aware of it. Someone in a van parked in front of your house might be using your free wireless. Although you don't have to pay extra for that, you might still notice a slight degradation in Wi-Fi speed if there is heavy use of the second signal. You can disable Comcast's Xfinity Home Hotspot if you don't think you will ever need to give visitors to your home free Internet access.[3]

While built-in wireless is great for getting you up and running with a new service, often these broadband routers are not configured properly and can create problems when they are not secured. For one thing, unsecured wireless access could provide a digital point of entry into your home, as it did for Ardolf. While intruders might not be after your digital files, they might be looking to cause problems nonetheless.

Ardolf was no computer genius. He confessed in court that he didn't know the difference between WEP (wired equivalent privacy) encryption, which was what the neighbor's router used, and WPA (Wi-Fi protected access) encryption, which is much more secure. He was just angry. This is just one more reason why you should take a moment to consider the security of your own household wireless network. You never know when an angry neighbor might try to use your home network against you.

If someone does do something bad on your home network, there is some protection for the router owner. According to the EFF, federal judges have rejected BitTorrent lawsuits brought by copyright holders because the defendants successfully claimed that someone else downloaded the movies using their wireless networks.[4] The EFF states that an IP address is not a person, meaning that wireless subscribers may not be responsible for the actions of others using their wireless networks.[5]

Although computer forensics will clear an innocent person whose Wi-Fi was used in the commission of a felony—as it did in the case of the Minnesota lawyer—why go through all that?

Even if you use a telephone-based dial-up modem or a cable-based ASM (any-source multicast) router (available from Cisco and Belkin, among others), these devices have had their share of software and configuration problems.

First and foremost, download the latest firmware (software installed in a hardware device). You can do that by accessing the router's configuration screen (see below) or by visiting the manufacturer's website and searching for updates for your particular make and model. Do this as often as possible. One easy way to update your router's firmware is to buy a new one every year. This can get expensive, but it will ensure that you have the latest and greatest firmware. Second, update your router's configuration settings. You don't want the default settings.

But first: what's in a name? More than you think. Common to both the ISP-provided router and a router you bought at Best Buy is the naming. All wireless routers broadcast by default what's called a service set identifier (SSID).[6] The SSID is commonly the name and model of your router, e.g., "Linksys WRT54GL." If you look at the available wireless connections in your area, you'll see what I mean.

Broadcasting the default SSID out to the world may mask the fact that the Wi-Fi signal is actually coming from a specific household, but it also allows someone on the street to know the exact make and model of the router you own. Why is that bad? That person might also know the vulnerabilities of that make and model and be able to exploit them.

So how do you change the name of the router and update its firmware?

Accessing the router is easy; you do so from your Internet browser. If you don't have the instructions for your router, there's an online list of URLs that tells you what to type into your browser window so you can connect directly to the router on your home network.[7] After typing in the local URL (you're just talking to the router, remember, not to the Internet at large), you should see a log-in screen. So what's the username and password for the log-in?

Turns out there's a list of default log-ins published on the Internet as well.[8] In the Linksys example above, the username is blank and the password is "admin." Needless to say, once you're inside the router's configuration screen, you should immediately change its default password, following the advice I gave you earlier about creating unique and strong passwords (see page 13) or using a password manager.

Remember to store this password in your password manager or write it down, as you probably won't need to access your router very often. Should you forget the password (really, how often are you going to be in the configuration screen for your router?), don't worry. There is a physical reset button that will restore the default settings. However, in conducting a physical, or hard, reset, you will also have to reenter all the configuration settings I'm about to explain below. So write down the router settings or take screenshots and print them out whenever you establish router settings that are different from the default. These screenshots will be valuable when you need to reconfigure your router.

I suggest you change "Linksys WRT54GL" to something innocuous, such as "HP Inkjet," so it won't be obvious to strangers which house the Wi-Fi signal might be coming from. I often use a generic name, such as the name of my apartment complex or even the name of my neighbor.

There is also an option to hide your SSID entirely. That means others will not be able to easily see it listed as a wireless network connection.

While you're inside your basic router configuration settings, there are several types of wireless security to consider. These are generally not enabled by default. And not all wireless encryption is created equal, nor is it supported by all devices.

The most basic form of wireless encryption, wired equivalent privacy (WEP), is useless. If you see it as an option, don't even consider it. WEP has been cracked for years, and is therefore no longer recommended. Only old routers and devices still offer it as a legacy option. Instead, choose one of the newer, stronger encryption standards, such as Wi-Fi protected access, or WPA. WPA2 is even more secure.

Turning on encryption at the router means that the devices connecting to it will also need to match encryption settings. Most new devices automatically sense the type of encryption being used, but older models still require you to indicate manually which encryption level you are using. Always use the highest level possible. You're only as secure as your weakest link, so make sure to max out the oldest device in terms of its available encryption.

Enabling WPA2 means that when you connect your laptop or mobile device, you will also need to set it to WPA2, although some new operating systems will recognize the type of encryption automatically. Modern operating systems on your phone or laptop will identify the Wi-Fi available in your area. Your SSID broadcast (now "HP Inkjet") should appear on the list at or close to the top. Padlock icons within the list of available Wi-Fi connections (usually overlaid upon the strength of each connection) indicate which Wi-Fi connections require passwords (yours should now have a padlock).

From the list of available connections, click on your own SSID. You should be prompted to enter a password—be sure to make it at least fifteen characters. Or use a password manager to create a complex password. In order to connect to your password-protected Wi-Fi, you will have to type in that password at least once on each device in order to connect, so a password manager might not work in all cases, particularly when you have to remember the complex password and type it in later yourself. Each device—including your "smart" refrigerator and digital TV—will all use the one router password you have chosen when you set the encryption on your router. You will need to do this once for every device that accesses your home or office Wi-Fi, but you won't have to do it again unless you change your home network password or acquire a new device.

You can also go one step further and limit Wi-Fi connections only to the devices you specify. This is known as whitelisting. With this process you grant access to (whitelist) some devices and forbid (blacklist) everything else. This will require you to enter your device's media access control address, or MAC address. It will also mean that when you next upgrade your cell phone, you'll have to add it to the MAC address in your router before it will connect.[9] This address is unique to every device; indeed, the first three sets of characters (octets) are the manufacturer's code, and the final three are unique to the product. The router will reject any device whose hardware MAC has not been previously stored. That said, a hacker tool called aircrack-ng can reveal the authorized MAC address of a currently connected user and then an attacker can spoof the MAC address to connect to the wireless router. Just like hidden wireless SSIDs, it's trivial to bypass MAC address filtering.

Finding the MAC address on your device is relatively easy. In Windows, go to the Start button, type "CMD," click "Command Prompt," and at the inverted caret, type "IPCONFIG." The machine will return a long list of data, but the MAC address should be there, and it will consist of twelve hexadecimal characters with every two characters separated by a colon. For Apple products it is even easier. Go to the Apple icon, select "System Preferences," and go to "Network." Then click the network device on the left panel and go to Advanced>Hardware, and you will see the MAC address. For some older Apple products, the procedure is: Apple icon>System Preferences>Networks>Built-in Ethernet. You can find the MAC address for your iPhone by selecting Settings>General>About and looking under "Wi-Fi Address." For an Android phone, go to Settings>About Phone>Status, and look under "Wi-Fi MAC address." These directions may change based on the device and model you are using.

With these twelve-digit MAC addresses in hand, you will now need to tell the router to allow only these devices and block everything else. There are a few downsides. If a guest comes over and wants to connect to your home network, you will have to decide whether to give one of your devices and its password to that person or simply turn off MAC address filtering by reentering the router configuration screen. Also, there are times when you might want to change the MAC address of a device (see page 140); if you don't change it back, you might not be able to connect to your MAC-restricted Wi-Fi network at home or work. Fortunately, rebooting the device restores the original MAC address in most cases.

To make connecting any new device to a home router easy, the Wi-Fi Alliance, a group of vendors eager to spread the use of Wi-Fi technologies, created Wi-Fi protected setup (WPS). WPS was advertised as a way for anyone—I mean anyone—to securely set up a mobile device at home or in the office. In reality, though, it's not very secure.

WPS is typically a button that you push on the router. Other methods include use of a PIN and near field communication (NFC). Simply put, you activate the WPS feature, and it communicates with any new devices you have in your home or office, automatically synchronizing them to work with your Wi-Fi network.

Sounds great. However, if the router is out in "public"—say, in your living room—then anyone can touch the WPS button and join your home network.

Even without physical access, an online attacker can use brute force to guess your WPS PIN. It could take several hours, but it's still a viable attack method, one you should protect yourself against by immediately turning off WPS on the router.

Another WPS attack method is known as Pixie Dust. This is an offline attack and affects only a few chip makers, including Ralink, Realtek, and Broadcom. Pixie Dust works by helping hackers gain access to the passwords on wireless routers. Basically the tool is very straightforward and can gain access to a device in seconds or hours depending on the complexity of the chosen or generated WPS PIN.[10] For example, one such program, Reaver, can crack a WPS-enabled router within several hours.

In general, it's a good idea to turn off WPS. You can simply connect each new mobile device to your network by typing in whatever password you've assigned for access.

So you have prevented, through the use of encryption and strong passwords, the use of your home wireless router network by others. Does that mean that no one can get inside your home network or even digitally see inside your home? Not entirely.

When high school sophomore Blake Robbins was called into the principal's office of his suburban Philadelphia school, he had no idea he was about to be reprimanded for "improper behavior"—at home. The Lower Merion School District, outside Philadelphia, had given all its high school students, including Robbins, new MacBooks to use for their course work. What the school district didn't tell the students was that software designed to recover the devices in the event they were lost could also be used to monitor all 2,300 students' behavior while they were in view of the laptops' webcams.

Robbins's alleged offense? Pill popping. The Robbins family, through their lawyer, maintained all along that the boy was simply eating Mike and Ike candy while doing his homework.

Why was this even an issue?

The school district maintains it activated the theft-tracking software only after one of its laptops was stolen. Theft-tracking software works like this: when someone using the software reports that his or her laptop has been stolen, the school can log on to a website and see images from the stolen laptop's webcam as well as hear sounds from the microphone. A school administrator could then monitor the laptop and take pictures as needed. This way the device can be located and returned and the guilty party can be identified. However, in this case it was alleged that school officials were turning on this feature to spy on the students while they were at home.

The webcam on Robbins's school-issued Mac laptop recorded hundreds of photos, including some of the boy asleep in his bed. For other students it was worse. According to court testimony, the school had even more pictures of some students, a few of whom were "partially undressed." This might have continued unnoticed by the students had Robbins not been reprimanded for something he allegedly did at home.

Robbins, along with a former student, Jalil Hasan—who had nearly five hundred images taken of him and four hundred images of his computer screen captured, revealing his online activity and the sites he visited—sued the school district. Robbins received $175,000 and Hasan $10,000.[11] The district also paid almost half a million dollars to cover the boys' legal expenses. In total the school district had to pay out, through its insurer, around $1.4 million.

It's easy for malicious software to activate the webcam and microphone on a traditional PC without the user knowing it. And this is true on a mobile device as well. In this case it was a deliberate action. But all too often it is not. One quick fix is to put tape over the webcam on your laptop until you intend to use it again.

In the fall of 2014, Sophie Curtis, a reporter for the London-based *Telegraph,* received a LinkedIn connection request in an e-mail that appeared to come from someone who worked at her newspaper. It was the kind of e-mail that Sophie received all the time, and as a professional courtesy she didn't think twice about accepting it from a colleague. A couple of weeks later she received an e-mail that appeared to be from an anonymous whistle-blower organization that was about to release sensitive documents. As a reporter who had covered groups such as Anonymous and WikiLeaks, she had received e-mails like this before, and she was curious about the request. The file attachment looked like a standard file, so she clicked to open it.

Immediately she realized something was wrong. Windows Defender, the security program that comes with every copy of Windows, started issuing warnings on her desktop. And the warnings kept piling up on the screen.

Curtis, like a lot of people today, had been tricked into clicking on an attachment that she thought was an ordinary file. While pretending to have information she wanted to see, the file downloaded and unpacked a series of other files that allowed the remote attacker to take complete control over her computer. The malicious software even took a picture of her with her own webcam. In it her face bears a look of sheer frustration as she tries to understand how someone could've taken over her computer.

Actually Curtis knew full well who had taken over her computer. As an experiment, a few months earlier she had hired a penetration tester, or pen tester. Someone like me. Individuals and companies hire professional hackers to try to break into a company's computer network to see where they need fortification. In Curtis's case, the process was spread out over several months.

At the start of jobs like this, I always try to get as much information about the client as I can. I spend time learning about his or her life and online habits. I track the client's public posts to Twitter, Facebook, and, yes, even LinkedIn. Which is exactly what Sophie Curtis's pen tester did. Amid all her e-mails was one carefully constructed message—the first one sent by her pen tester. The pen tester knew that she worked as a reporter and knew that she was open to e-mail solicitations from previously unknown individuals. In that first case Curtis later wrote that there was not enough context for her to be interested in interviewing a particular person for a future story. But she was impressed by the amount of research the hacker and his colleagues at the security company did.

Curtis said: "They were able to use Twitter to find out my work e-mail address, as well as some of my recent locations and the name of a regular social night I attend with other journalists. From objects in the background of one of the photos I had posted on Twitter they were able to discover what mobile phone I used to use, and the fact that my fiancé used to smoke roll-ups (it was an old photo), as well as the fact he likes cycling."[12] Any one of these details could have been the basis for another e-mail.

There's also a new Artificial Intelligence–based tool announced at the DEF CON 2016 conference that will analyze a target's tweets. It will then construct a spear-phishing e-mail based on their personal interests.[13] So be careful when clicking links within a tweet.

Indeed, often it is the little things—the odd comment posted here or there, the unique knickknack on the shelf behind you in a photo, the T-shirt from a camp you once attended—that provide crucial personal information that you would never have intended to share publicly. We may consider these one-off moments harmless, but the more details an attacker can learn about you, the better he can trick you into opening up e-mail attachments, and take over your online world.

Curtis points out that the pen-test team ended their attack there. Had they been real criminal hackers, the fun and games might have continued for some time, perhaps with the bad guys gaining access to her social media accounts, her office network at the *Telegraph,* even her financial accounts. And most likely they would have done it in such a way that Curtis might not have known her computer had been compromised; most attacks do not immediately trigger Windows Defender or antivirus software. Some attackers get in and persist for months or years before the user has any clue that he or she has been hacked. And it's not just your laptop: an e-mail-triggered attack could also be launched from a jailbroken iPhone or an Android mobile device.

While Google and other e-mail providers scan your messages to prevent the transmission of malware and the spread of online pornography—and to collect advertising data—they do not necessarily scan for fraud. Like privacy, the standard for which, as I've said, is different for everyone, fraud is hard to quantify. And we don't always recognize it, even when it's staring us in the face.

Within the body of Curtis's fake LinkedIn e-mail was a one-by-one-inch pixel, a tiny dot of an image, invisible to the eye, like those I said could be found on websites and used to track you online. When that tiny dot calls out, it tells a tracking server in a remote location, which could be anywhere in the world, what time you opened the e-mail, how long it remained on the screen, and on what device you opened it. It can also tell whether you saved, forwarded, or deleted the message. In addition, if the scenario used by the pen-test team had been real, the attacker might have included a link through which Curtis could have visited a fake LinkedIn page. This page would resemble a real one in every respect except that it would be hosted on a different server, perhaps in another country.

For an advertiser, this Web bug can be used to gather information about (and therefore profile) the recipient. For attackers, it can be used to obtain the technical details they need to design their next attack, which would include a way to get inside your computer. For example, if you are running an old version of a browser, there may be bugs that can be exploited.

So the second e-mail Curtis received from the pen testers included an attachment, a compressed document set to exploit a vulnerability in the software that was used to open the file (e.g., Adobe Acrobat). When we speak of malware, most people think of the computer viruses of the early 2000s, when a single infected e-mail could spread additional infected e-mails to everyone on a contact list. These types of mass-infection attacks are less common today, in part because of changes to e-mail software itself. Instead the most dangerous malware today is much more subtle and often targeted and tailored to an individual. As it was in the case of Sophie Curtis. The pen testers used a special form of phishing called spear phishing, designed to target a specific person.

Phishing is the criminally fraudulent process of trying to obtain sensitive information such as usernames, passwords, and credit card or bank information. It has been used against CFOs who are duped into wiring large sums of money because the "CEO" has authorized the transfer. Usually, the phishing e-mail or text message includes an action item such as clicking a link or opening up an attachment. In Curtis's case the intent was to plant malware on her computer for the purpose of illustrating how easy it is for someone to do this.

One of the most famous phishing schemes was Operation Aurora, in which a phishing e-mail was sent to Chinese employees of Google.

The idea was to infect their machines in China in order to gain access to the internal network at Google's world headquarters, in Mountain View, California. This the attackers did, getting dangerously close to the source code for Google's search engine. Google wasn't alone. Companies such as Adobe reported similar intrusions. As a result Google briefly pulled its operations from China.[14]

Whenever we get a LinkedIn or Facebook request, our guard is down. Perhaps because we trust those sites, we also trust their e-mail messages. And yet, as we have seen, anyone can craft a message that looks legitimate. In person, we can usually sense when someone is wearing a fake mustache or hair implants or speaking in a false voice; we have centuries' worth of evolutionary instincts to help us detect deception without thinking about it. Those instincts don't apply online, at least not for most of us. Sophie Curtis was a reporter; it was her job to be curious and skeptical, to follow leads and check facts. She could have looked through the *Telegraph*'s employee list to see who the person on LinkedIn was and learned that the e-mail was probably fake. But she didn't. And the reality is that most of us are equally unguarded.

An attacker who is phishing will have some but not all of your personal information—the little bit he has serves as his bait. For example, a phisher might send you an e-mail including the last four digits of your credit card number to establish trust, then go on to ask for even more information. Sometimes the four digits are incorrect, and the phisher will ask that you make any necessary corrections in your response. Don't do it. In short, don't interact with a phisher. In general do not respond to any requests for personal information, even if they seem trustworthy. Instead, contact the requester in a separate e-mail (if you have the address) or text (if you have the cell-phone number).

The more concerning phishing attack is one that's used to trick a target into doing an action item that directly exploits his or her computer, giving the attacker full control. That's what I do in social engineering engagements. Credential harvesting is also a popular line of attack, where a person's username and password are captured, but the real danger of spear phishing is gaining access to the target's computer system and network.

What if you did interact with a phisher and as a result lost all the data—all the personal photographs and private documents—on your infected PC or mobile device? That's what happened to author Alina Simone's mother. Writing in the *New York Times,* Simone described what it was like for her mother—who was not technologically inclined—to be up against a sophisticated enemy who was using something called ransomware.[15]

In 2014 a wave of extortionist malware hit the Internet, targeting individuals and corporations alike. Cryptowall is one example: it encrypts your entire hard drive, locking you out of every file until you pay the attacker to give you the key to unlock your files. Unless you have a full backup, the contents of your traditional PC or Android device will be inaccessible until you pay the ransom.

Don't want to pay? The extortion letter that appears on the display screen states that the key to unlock the files will be destroyed within a certain amount of time. Often there is a countdown clock included. If you don't pay, the deadline is sometimes extended, although the price increases with each delay.

In general you should avoid clicking on e-mail attachments (unless you open them in Google Quick View or Google Docs). Still, there are other ways in which Cryptowall spreads—banner ads on websites, for example. Just viewing a page with an infected banner ad can infect your traditional PC—this is called a drive-by because you didn't actively click on the ad. Here's where having ad-removal plug-ins such as Adblock Plus in your browser is really effective.

In the first six months of 2015, the FBI's Internet Crime Complaint

Center (IC3) recorded nearly one thousand cases of Cryptowall 3.0, with losses estimated to be around $18 million. This figure includes ransom that was paid, the cost to IT departments and repair shops, and lost productivity. In some cases the encrypted files contain personally identifiable information such as Social Security numbers, which may qualify the attack as a data breach and thus incur more costs.

Although the key to unlock the files can always be purchased for a flat fee of $500 to $1000, those who are infected typically try other means—such as breaking the encryption themselves—to remove the ransomware. That's what Simone's mother tried. When she finally called her daughter, they were almost out of time.

Almost everyone who tries to break the ransomware encryption fails. The encryption is really strong and requires more powerful computers and more time to break it than most people have at their disposal. So the victims usually pay. According to Simone, the Dickson County, Tennessee, sheriff's office paid in November 2014 a Cryptowall ransom to unlock 72,000 autopsy reports, witness statements, crime scene photographs, and other documents.

The hackers often demand payment in Bitcoin, meaning that many average people will have a hard time paying.[16] Bitcoin, as I mentioned, is a decentralized, peer-to-peer virtual currency, and most people do not have Bitcoin wallets available for withdrawal.

Throughout the *Times* piece, Simone reminds readers that they should never pay the ransom—yet she did just that in the end. In fact the FBI now advises people whose computers are infected with ransomware to simply pay up. Joseph Bonavolonta, the assistant special agent in charge of the FBI's cyber and counterintelligence program in Boston, said, "To be honest, we often advise people just to pay the ransom." He said not even the FBI is able to crack the ultra-secure encryption used by the ransomware authors, and he added that because so many people have paid the attackers, the $500 cost has remained fairly consistent over the years.[17] The FBI later came out to say it's up to the individual companies to decide whether to pay or contact other security professionals.

Simone's mother, who had never purchased an app in her life, called her daughter at the eleventh hour only because she needed to figure out how to pay with the virtual currency. Simone said she found a Bitcoin ATM in Manhattan from which, after a software glitch and a service call to the ATM owner, she ultimately made the payment. At that day's exchange rate, each Bitcoin was a bit more than $500.

Whether these extortionists receive their payment in Bitcoin or in cash, they remain anonymous, although technically there are ways of tracing both forms of payment. Transactions conducted online using Bitcoin can be connected to the purchaser—but not easily. The question is, who is going to put forth the time and effort to pursue these criminals?

In the next chapter I will describe what can happen when you connect to the Internet via public Wi-Fi. From a privacy perspective you want the anonymity of a public Wi-Fi but at the same time you will need to take precautions.

CHAPTER EIGHT

Believe Everything, Trust Nothing

When the telephone was still a novelty, it was physically wired into the home and perhaps placed in a nook built into the wall. Getting a second line was considered a status symbol. Similarly, public phone booths were built for privacy. Even banks of pay phones in hotel lobbies were equipped with sound baffles between them to give the illusion of privacy.

With mobile phones, that sense of privacy has fallen away entirely. It is common to walk down the street and hear people loudly sharing some personal drama or — worse — reciting their credit card number within earshot of all who pass by. In the midst of this culture of openness and sharing, we need to think carefully about the information we're volunteering to the world.

Sometimes the world is listening. I'm just saying.

Suppose you like to work at the café around the corner from your home, as I sometimes do. It has free Wi-Fi. That should be okay, right? Hate to break it to you, but no. Public Wi-Fi wasn't created with online banking or e-commerce in mind. It is merely convenient, and it's also incredibly insecure. Not all that insecurity is technical. Some of it begins—and, I hope, ends—with you.[1]

How can you tell if you are on public Wi-Fi? For one thing, you won't be asked to input a password to connect to the wireless access point. To demonstrate how visible you are on public Wi-Fi, researchers from the antivirus company F-Secure built their own access point, or hotspot. They conducted their experiment in two different locations in downtown London—a café and a public space. The results were eye-opening.

In the first experiment, the researchers set up in a café in a busy part of London. When patrons considered the choices of available networks, the F-Secure hotspot came up as both strong and free. The researchers also included a banner that appeared on the user's browser stating the terms and conditions. Perhaps you've seen a banner like this at your local coffee shop stipulating what you can and cannot do while using their service. In this experiment, however, terms for use of this free Wi-Fi required the surrender of the user's firstborn child or beloved pet. Six people consented to those terms and conditions.[2] To be fair, most people don't take the time to read the fine print—they just want whatever is on the other end. Still, you should at least skim the terms and conditions. In this case, F-Secure said later that neither it nor its lawyers wanted anything to do with children or pets.

The real issue is what can be seen by third parties while you're on public Wi-Fi. When you're at home, your wireless connection should be encrypted with WPA2 (see page 116). That means if anyone is snooping, he or she can't see what you're doing online. But when you're using open, public Wi-Fi at a coffee shop or airport, that destination traffic is laid bare.

Again you might ask, what's the problem with all this? Well, first of all, you don't know who's on the other end of the connection. In this case the F-Secure research team ethically destroyed the data they collected, but criminals probably would not. They'd sell your e-mail address to companies that send you spam, either to get you to buy something or to infect your PC with malware. And they might even use the details in your unencrypted e-mails to craft spear-phishing attacks.

In the second experiment, the team set the hotspot on a balcony in close proximity to the Houses of Parliament, the headquarters of the Labour and Conservative parties, and the National Crime Agency. Within thirty minutes a total of 250 people connected to the experimental free hotspot. Most of these were automatic connections made by whatever device was being used. In other words, the users didn't consciously choose the network: the device did that for them.

A couple of issues here. Let's first look at how and why your mobile devices automatically join a Wi-Fi network.

Your traditional PC and all your mobile devices remember your last few Wi-Fi connections, both public and private. This is good because it saves you the trouble of continually reidentifying a frequently used Wi-Fi access point—such as your home or office. This is also bad because if you walk into a brand-new café, a place you've never been before, you might suddenly find that you have wireless connectivity there. Why is that bad? Because you might be connected to something other than the café's wireless network.

Chances are your mobile device detected an access point that matches a profile already on your most recent connection list. You may sense something amiss about the convenience of automatically connecting to Wi-Fi in a place you've never been before, but you may also be in the middle of a first-person shooter game and don't want to think much beyond that.

How does automatic Wi-Fi connection work? As I explained in the last chapter, maybe you have Comcast Internet service at home, and if you do you might also have a free, nonencrypted public SSID called Xfinity as part of your service plan. Your Wi-Fi-enabled device may have connected to it once in the past.[3] But how do you know that the guy with a laptop at the corner table isn't broadcasting a spoofed wireless access point called Xfinity?

Let's say you *are* connected to that shady guy in the corner and not to the café's wireless network. First, you will still be able to surf the Net. So you can keep on playing your game. However, every packet of unencrypted data you send and receive over the Internet will be visible to this shady character through his spoofed laptop wireless access point.

If he's taken the trouble to set up a fake wireless access point, then he's probably capturing those packets with a free application such as Wireshark. I use this app in my work as a pen tester. It allows me to see the network activity that's going on around me. I can see the IP addresses of sites people are connecting to and how long they are visiting those sites. If the connection is not encrypted, it is legal to intercept the traffic because it is generally available to the public. For example, as an IT admin, I would want to know the activity on my network.

Maybe the shady guy in the corner is just sniffing, seeing where you go and not influencing the traffic. Or maybe he is actively influencing your Internet traffic. This would serve multiple purposes.

Maybe he's redirecting your connection to a proxy that implants a javascript keylogger in your browser so when you visit Amazon your keystrokes will be captured as you interact with the site. Maybe he gets paid to harvest your credentials—your username and password. Remember that your credit card may be associated with Amazon and other retailers.

When delivering my keynote, I give a demonstration that shows how I can intercept a victim's username and password when accessing sites once he or she is connected to my spoofed access point. Because I'm sitting in the middle of the interaction between the victim and the website, I can inject JavaScript and cause fake Adobe updates to pop up on his or her screen, which, if installed will infect the victim's computer with malware. The purpose is usually to trick you into installing the fake update to gain control of your computer.

When the guy at the corner table is influencing the Internet traffic, that's called a man-in-the-middle attack. The attacker is proxying your packets through to the real site, but intercepting or injecting data along the way.

Knowing that you could unintentionally connect to a shady Wi-Fi access point, how can you prevent it? On a laptop the device will go through the process of searching for a preferred wireless network and then connect to it. But some laptops and mobile devices automatically choose what network to join. This was designed to make the process of taking your mobile device from one location to another as painless as possible. But as I mentioned, there are downsides to this convenience.

According to Apple, its various products will automatically connect to networks in this order of preference:

1. the private network the device most recently joined,
2. another private network, and
3. a hotspot network.

Laptops, fortunately, provide the means to delete obsolete Wi-Fi connections—for example, that hotel Wi-Fi you connected to last summer on a business trip. In a Windows laptop, you can uncheck the "Connect Automatically" field next to the network name before you connect. Or head to Control Panel>Network and Sharing Center and click on the network name. Click on "Wireless Properties," then uncheck "Connect automatically when this network is in range." On a Mac, head to System Preferences, go to Network, highlight Wi-Fi on the left-hand panel, and click "Advanced." Then uncheck "Remember networks this computer has joined." You can also individually remove networks by selecting the name and pressing the minus button underneath it.

Android and iOS devices also have instructions for deleting previously used Wi-Fi connections. On an iPhone or iPod, go into your settings, select "Wi-Fi," click the "i" icon next to the network name, and choose "Forget This Network." On an Android phone, you can go into your settings, choose "Wi-Fi," long-press the network name, and select "Forget Network."

Seriously, if you really have something sensitive to do away from your house, then I recommend using the cellular connection on your mobile device instead of using the wireless network at the airport or coffee shop. You can also tether to your personal mobile device using USB, Bluetooth, or Wi-Fi. If you use Wi-Fi, then make sure you configure WPA2 security as mentioned earlier. The other option is to purchase a portable hotspot to use when traveling. Note, too, this won't make you invisible, but is a better alternative than using public Wi-Fi. But if you need to protect your privacy from the mobile operator—say, to download a sensitive spreadsheet—then I suggest you use HTTPS Everywhere or a Secure File Transfer Protocol (SFTP). SFTP is supported using the Transmit app on Mac and the Tunnelier app on Windows.

A virtual private network (VPN) is a secure "tunnel" that extends a private network (from your home, office, or a VPN service provider) to your device on a public network. You can search Google for VPN providers and purchase service for approximately $60 a year. The network you'll find at the local coffee shop or the airport or in other public places is not to be trusted—it's public. But by using a VPN you can tunnel through the public network back to a private and secure network. Everything you do within the VPN is protected by encryption, as all your Internet traffic is now secured over the public network. That's why it's important to use a VPN provider you can trust—it can see your Internet traffic. When you use a VPN at the coffee shop, the sketchy guy in the corner can only see that you have connected to a VPN server and nothing else—your activities and the sites you visit are all completely hidden behind tough-to-crack encryption.

However, you will still touch the Internet with an IP address that is traceable directly to you, in this case the IP address from your home or office. So you're still not invisible, even using a VPN. Don't forget—your VPN provider knows your originating IP address. Later we'll discuss how to make this connection invisible (see page 253).

Many companies provide VPNs for their employees, allowing them to connect from a public network (i.e., the Internet) to a private internal corporate network. But what about the rest of us?

There are many commercial VPNs available. But how do you know whether to trust them? The underlying VPN technology, IPsec (Internet protocol security), automatically includes PFS (perfect forward secrecy; see page 66), but not all services—even corporate ones—actually bother to configure it. OpenVPN, an open-source project, includes PFS, so you might infer that when a product says it uses OpenVPN it also uses PFS, but this is not always the case. The product might not have OpenVPN configured properly. Make sure the service specifically includes PFS.

One disadvantage is that VPNs are more expensive than proxies.[4] And, since commercial VPNs are shared, they can also be slow, or in some cases you simply can't get an available VPN for your personal use and you will have wait until one becomes available. Another annoyance is that in some cases Google will pop up a CAPTCHA request (which asks you to type in the characters you see on the screen) before you can use its search engine because it wants to make sure you are a human and not a bot. Finally, if your particular VPN vendor keeps logs, read the privacy policy to make sure that the service doesn't retain your traffic or connection logs—even encrypted—and that it doesn't make the data easy to share with law enforcement. You can figure this out in the terms of service and privacy policy. If they can report activities to law enforcement, then they do log VPN connections.

Airline passengers who use an in-air Internet service such as GoGo run the same risk as they do going online while sitting in a

Starbucks or airport lounge, and VPNs aren't always great solutions. Because they want to prevent Skype or other voice-call applications, GoGo and other in-air services throttle UDP packets—which will make most VPN services very slow as UDP is the protocol most use by default. However, choosing a VPN service that uses the TCP protocol instead of UDP, such as TorGuard or ExpressVPN, can greatly improve performance. Both of these VPN services allow the user to set either TCP or UDP as their preferred protocol.

Another consideration with a VPN is its privacy policy. Whether you use a commercial VPN or a corporate-provided VPN, your traffic travels over its network, which is why it's important to use https so the VPN provider can't see the contents of your communications.[5]

If you work in an office, chances are your company provides a VPN so that you can work remotely. Within an app on your traditional PC, you type in your username and password (something you know). The app also contains an identifying certificate placed there by your IT department (something you already have), or it may send you a text on your company-issued phone (also something you have). The app may employ all three techniques in what's known as multifactor authentication.

Now you can sit in a Starbucks or an airport lounge and conduct business as though you were using a private Internet service. However, you should not conduct personal business, such as remote banking, unless the actual session is encrypted using the HTTPS Everywhere extension.

The only way to trust a VPN provider is to be anonymous from the start. If you really want to be completely anonymous, never use an Internet connection that could be linked to you (i.e., one originating from your home, office, friends' homes, a hotel room reserved in your name, or anything else connected to you). I was caught when the FBI traced a cell-phone signal to my hideout in Raleigh, North Carolina, back in the 1990s. So never access personal information using a burner device in the same location if you're attempting to avoid governmental authorities. Anything you do on the burner device has to be completely separate in order to remain invisible. Meaning that no metadata from the device can be linked to your real identity.

You can also install a VPN on your mobile device. Apple provides instructions for doing so,[6] and you can find instructions for Android devices as well.[7]

If you have been following my advice in the book so far, you'll probably fare much better than the average Joe. Most of your Internet usage will probably be safe from eavesdropping or manipulation by an attacker.

So will your social media. Facebook uses https for all its sessions.

Checking your e-mail? Google has also switched over to https only. Most Web mail services have followed, as have most major instant messaging services. Indeed, most major sites—Amazon, eBay, Dropbox—all now use https.

To be invisible, it's always best to layer your privacy. Your risk of having your traffic viewed by others in a public network declines with each additional layer of security you employ. For example, from a public Wi-Fi network, access your paid VPN service, then access Tor with the HTTPS Everywhere extension installed by default in the Firefox browser.

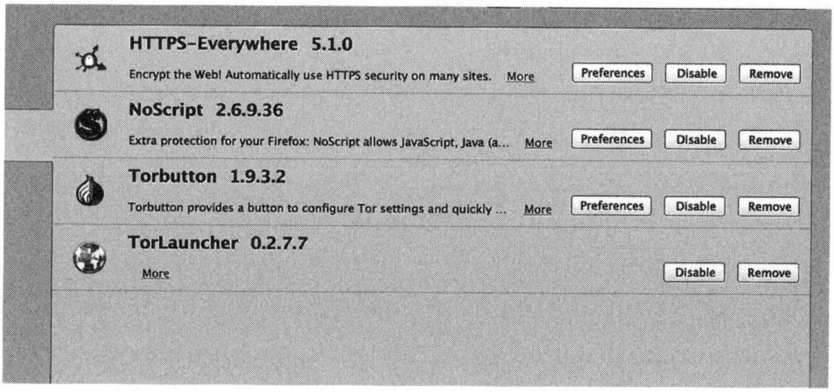

Then whatever you do online will be encrypted and hard to trace.

Say you just want to check the weather and not do anything financial or personal, and you are using your own personal laptop outside your home network—that should be secure, right? Once again, not really. There are a few precautions you still need to take.

First, turn off Wi-Fi. Seriously. Many people leave Wi-Fi on their laptops turned on even when they don't need it. According to documents released by Edward Snowden, the Communications Security Establishment Canada (CSEC) can identify travelers passing through Canadian airports just by capturing their MAC addresses. These are readable by any computer that is searching for any probe request sent from wireless devices. Even if you don't connect, the MAC address can be captured. So if you don't need it, turn off your Wi-Fi.[8] As we've seen, convenience often works against privacy and safety.

So far we've skirted around an important issue—your MAC address. This is unique to whatever device you are using. And it is not permanent; you can change it.

Let me give you an example.

In the second chapter, I told you about encrypting your e-mail using PGP (Pretty Good Privacy; see page 34). But what if you don't want to go through the hassle, or what if the recipient doesn't have a public PGP key for you to use? There is another clandestine way to exchange messages via e-mail: use the drafts folder on a shared e-mail account.

This is how former CIA director General David Petraeus exchanged information with his mistress, Paula Broadwell—his biographer. The scandal unfolded after Petraeus ended the relationship and noticed that someone had been sending threatening e-mails to a friend of his. When the FBI investigated, they found not only that the threats had come from Broadwell but that she had also been leaving romantic messages for Petraeus.[9]

What's interesting is that the messages between Broadwell and

Petraeus were not transmitted but rather left in the drafts folder of the "anonymous" e-mail account. In this scenario the e-mail does not pass through other servers in an attempt to reach the recipient. There are fewer opportunities for interceptions. And if someone does get access to the account later on, there will be no evidence if you delete the e-mails and empty the trash beforehand.

Broadwell also logged in to her "anonymous" e-mail account using a dedicated computer. She did not contact the e-mail site from her home IP address. That would have been too obvious. Instead she went to various hotels to conduct her communications.

Although Broadwell had taken considerable pains to hide, she still was not invisible. According to the *New York Times,* "because the sender's account had been registered anonymously, investigators had to use forensic techniques—including a check of what other e-mail accounts had been accessed from the same computer address—to identify who was writing the e-mails."[10]

E-mail providers such as Google, Yahoo, and Microsoft retain log-in records for more than a year, and these reveal the particular IP addresses a consumer has logged in from. For example, if you used a public Wi-Fi at Starbucks, the IP address would reveal the store's physical location. The United States currently permits law enforcement agencies to obtain these log-in records from the e-mail providers with a mere subpoena—no judge required.

That means the investigators had the physical location of each IP address that contacted that particular e-mail account and could then match Broadwell's device's MAC address on the router's connection log at those locations.[11]

With the full authority of the FBI behind them (this was a big deal, because Petraeus was the CIA director at the time), agents were able to search all the router log files for each hotel and see when Broadwell's MAC address showed up in hotel log files. Moreover, they were able to show that on the dates in question Broadwell was a registered guest. The investigators did note that while she logged in to these e-mail accounts, she never actually sent an e-mail.

When you connect to a wireless network, the MAC address on your computer is automatically recorded by the wireless networking equipment. Your MAC address is similar to a serial number assigned to your network card. To be invisible, prior to connecting to any wireless network you need to change your MAC address to one not associated with you.

To stay invisible, the MAC address should be changed each time you connect to the wireless network so your Internet sessions cannot easily be correlated to you. It's also important not to access any of your personal online accounts during this process, as it can compromise your anonymity.

Instructions for changing your MAC address vary with each operating system—i.e., Windows, Mac OS, Linux, even Android and iOS.[12] Each time you connect to a public (or private) network, you might want to remember to change your MAC address. After a reboot, the original MAC address returns.

Let's say you don't own a laptop and have no choice but to use a public computer terminal, be it in a café, a library, or even a business center in a high-end hotel. What can you do to protect yourself?

When I go camping I observe the "leave no trace" rule—that is, the campsite should look just as it did when I first arrived. The same is true with public PC terminals. After you leave, no one should know you were there.

This is especially true at trade shows. I was at the annual Consumer Electronics Show one year and saw a bank of public PCs set out so that attendees could check their e-mail while walking the convention floor. I even saw this at the annual security-conscious RSA conference, in San Francisco. Having a row of generic terminals out in public is a bad idea for a number of reasons.

One, these are leased computers, reused from event to event. They may be cleaned, the OS reinstalled, but then again they might not be.

Two, they tend to run admin rights, which means that the conference attendee can install any software he or she wants to. This includes malware such as keyloggers, which can store your username and password information. In the security business, we speak of the principle of "least privilege," which means that a machine grants a user only the minimum privileges he or she needs to get the job done. Logging in to a public terminal with system admin privileges, which is the default position on some public terminals, violates the principle of least privilege and only increases the risk that you are using a device previously infected with malware. The only solution is to somehow be certain that you are using a guest account, with limited privileges, which most people won't know how to do.

In general I recommend never trusting a public PC terminal. Assume the person who last used it installed malware—either consciously or unconsciously. If you log in to Gmail on a public terminal, and there's a keylogger on that public terminal, some remote third party now has your username and password. If you log in to your bank—forget it. Remember, you should enable 2FA on every site you access so an attacker armed with your username and password cannot impersonate you. Two-factor authentication will greatly mitigate the chances of your account being hacked if someone does gain knowledge of your username and password.

The number of people who use public kiosks at computer-based conferences such as CES and RSA amazes me. Bottom line, if you're at a trade show, use your cellular-enabled phone or tablet, your personal hotspot (see page 134), or wait until you get back to your room.

If you have to use the Internet away from your home or office, use your smartphone. If you absolutely have to use a public terminal, then do not by any means sign in to any personal account, even Web mail. If you're looking for a restaurant, for example, access only those websites that do *not* require authentication, such as Yelp. If you use a public terminal on a semiregular basis, then set up an e-mail account to use only on public terminals, and only forward e-mail from your legitimate accounts to this "throwaway" address when you are on the road. Stop forwarding once you return home. This minimizes the information that is findable under that e-mail address.

Next, make sure the sites you access from the public terminal have https in the URL. If you don't see https (or if you do see it but suspect that someone has put it there to give you a false sense of security), then perhaps you should reconsider accessing sensitive information from this public terminal.

Let's say you get a legitimate https URL. If you're on a log-in page, look for a box that says "Keep me logged in." Uncheck that. The reason is clear: this is not your personal PC. It is shared by others. By keeping yourself logged in, you are creating a cookie on that machine. You don't want the next person at the terminal to see your e-mail or be able to send e-mail from your address, do you?

As noted, don't log in to financial or medical sites from a public terminal. If you do log in to a site (whether Gmail or otherwise), make sure you log off when you are done and perhaps consider changing your password from your own computer or mobile device afterward just to be safe. You may not always log off from your accounts at home, but you must always do this when using someone else's computer.

After you've sent your e-mail (or looked at whatever you wanted to look at) and logged off, then try to erase the browser history so the next person can't see where you've been. Also delete any cookies if you can. And make sure you didn't download personal files to the computer. If you do, then try to delete the file or files from the desktop or downloads folder when you're finished.

Unfortunately, though, just deleting the file isn't enough. Next you will need to empty the trash. That still doesn't fully remove the deleted stuff from the computer—I can retrieve the file after you leave if I want to. Thankfully, most people don't have the ability to do that, and usually deleting and emptying the trash will suffice.

All these steps are necessary to be invisible on a public terminal.

CHAPTER NINE

You Have No Privacy? Get Over It!

At some point during the time that former antivirus software creator John McAfee spent as a fugitive from authorities in Belize, he started a blog. Take it from me: if you're trying to get off the grid and totally disappear, you don't want to start a blog. For one thing, you're bound to make a mistake.

McAfee is a smart man. He made his fortune in the early days of Silicon Valley by pioneering antivirus research. Then he sold his company, sold all his assets in the United States, and for around four years, from 2008 to 2012, he lived in Belize, on a private estate off the coast. Toward the end of that period, the government of Belize had him under near-constant surveillance, raiding his property and accusing him of assembling a private army in addition to engaging in drug trafficking.

McAfee denied doing either. He claimed he was fighting the drug lords on the island. He said, for example, that he had offered a flat-screen TV to a small-time marijuana dealer on the condition that the man stop dealing. And he was known to pull over cars that he suspected were carrying drug dealers.[1]

McAfee in fact did have a drug lab, but not necessarily for recreational drugs. He claimed he was creating a new generation of "helpful" drugs. Hence his growing suspicion that cars full of white men outside his property were spies from pharmaceuticals companies such as GlaxoSmithKline. He further claimed that the raids by the local police were instigated by these same pharmaceuticals companies.

Guarding his property were several men with guns and eleven dogs. A neighbor two houses to the south, Greg Faull, complained regularly to the authorities about the dogs barking late at night. Then one night in November of 2012, some of McAfee's dogs were poisoned. And later that same week, Faull was shot, found facedown in a pool of blood in his house.

The Belize authorities naturally considered McAfee a person of interest in their investigation. As McAfee relates in his blog, when he heard from his housekeeper that the police wanted to talk to him, he went into hiding. He became a fugitive.

But it wasn't the blog that ultimately led law enforcement to McAfee. It was a photo. And it wasn't even his own.

A security researcher named Mark Loveless (better known in security circles as Simple Nomad) noticed a picture of McAfee published on Twitter by *Vice* magazine in early December of 2012. The photo showed *Vice*'s editor standing next to McAfee in a tropical location—maybe in Belize, maybe somewhere else.

Loveless knew that digital photos capture a lot of information about when, where, and how they are taken, and he wanted to see what digital information this photo might contain. Digital photos store what is known as exchangeable image file, or EXIF, data. This is photo metadata, and it contains mundane details such as the amount of color saturation in the image so that the photo can be accurately reproduced on a screen or by a printer. It can also, if the camera is equipped to do so, include the exact longitude and latitude of the place where the photo was taken.

Apparently the photo of McAfee with the *Vice* magazine editor was taken with an iPhone 4S camera. Some cell phones ship with geolocation automatically enabled. Loveless got lucky: the image posted in the online file included the exact geolocation of John McAfee, who was, it turned out, in neighboring Guatemala.

In a subsequent blog McAfee said he faked the data, but that seems unlikely. Later he said he intended to reveal his location. More likely he got lazy.

Long story short, the Guatemalan police detained McAfee and wouldn't let him leave the country. He then suffered a health condition, was hospitalized, and was eventually allowed to return to the United States.

The murder of Greg Faull remains unsolved. McAfee now lives in Tennessee, and in 2015 he decided to run for president to advocate for more cyberfriendly policies in the US government. He doesn't blog nearly as often nowadays.

Let's say you are an ambitious young jihadist, and you are proud to be posted to a recently established military headquarters of Daesh, or ISIL. What's the first thing you do? You pull out your cell phone and take a selfie. Worse, in addition to the photo of you and your new digs, you post a few words about the sophisticated equipment available at this particular facility.

Half a world away, reconnaissance airmen at Florida's Hurlburt Field are combing social media and see the photo. "We got an in," one of them says. Sure enough, a few hours later three JDAMs (joint direct attack munitions) take out that shiny new military building.[2] All because of a selfie.[3]

We don't always consider what *else* lies inside the frame of a selfie we've just taken. In film and theater this is called the mise-en-scène, roughly translated from the French as "what's in the scene." Your picture might show a crowded city skyline, including the Freedom Tower, outside your apartment window. Even a picture of you in a rural setting—maybe a prairie extending out to the flat horizon—gives me valuable information about where you live. These visuals provide tiny location clues that might tip off someone who is eager to find you.

In the young jihadist's case, what was in the scene was a military headquarters.

Embedded in the metadata of the selfie were the precise longitude and latitude, or geolocation, of the place where the photo was taken. General Hawk Carlisle, the head of the US Air Combat Command, estimated it was a mere twenty-four hours from the time that selfie was first posted on social media to the complete destruction of that headquarters.

Certainly the metadata inside your image files can be used to locate you. EXIF data in a digital image contains, among other things, the date and time when the picture was snapped, the make and model number of the camera, and, if you have geolocation activated on the device taking the photo, the longitude and latitude of the place where you took the image. It is this information, within the file, that the US military used to find the Daesh headquarters in the desert, just as Mark Loveless used EXIF data to identify John McAfee's location. Anyone can use this tool—it's native in the file inspector on Apple OSX and in downloadable tools such as FOCA for Windows and Metagoofil for Linux—to gain access to the metadata stored in photos and documents.

Sometimes it's not a photo but an app that gives up your spot. In the summer of 2015, drug lord Joaquin "El Chapo" Guzman escaped from a Mexican prison and immediately went off the grid. Or did he?

Two months after his escape—from Mexico's maximum-security Altiplano prison—El Chapo's twenty-nine-year-old son, Jesus Alfredo Guzman Salazar, posted an image to Twitter. Although the two men seated at a dinner table with Salazar are obscured by emoticons, the build of the man on the left bears a strong resemblance to El Chapo.

Further, Salazar captioned the image: "August here, you already know with whom." The tweet also contained the Twitter location data—Costa Rica—suggesting that El Chapo's son failed to switch off the autotagging function on Twitter's smartphone app.[4]

Even if you don't have an escaped convict in your family, you need to be aware that the digital and visual information hidden (sometimes in plain sight) in your photos can reveal a lot to someone who does not know you and it can come back to haunt you.

Online photos can do more than just reveal your location. They can, in conjunction with certain software programs, reveal personal information about you.

In 2011 Alessandro Acquisti, a researcher from Carnegie Mellon University, posed a simple hypothesis: "I wanted to see if it was possible to go from a face on the street to a Social Security number," he said. And he found that it was indeed possible.[5] By taking a simple webcam photograph of a student volunteer, Acquisti and his team had enough information to obtain personal information about that individual.

Think about that. You could take a photo of a person out on the street and, using facial recognition software, attempt to identify that person. Without that person's confirmation of his or her identity, you may get a few false positives. But chances are a majority of the "hits" would reveal one name more than another.

"There's a blending of online and offline data, and your face is the conduit—the veritable link between these two worlds," Acquisti told *Threatpost*. "I think the lesson is a rather gloomy one. We have to face the reality that our very notion of privacy is being eroded. You're no longer private in the street or in a crowd. The mashup of all these technologies challenges our biological expectation of privacy."

For his study, Acquisti and others stopped students on the Carnegie Mellon campus and asked them to fill out an online survey. The webcam on the laptop took a picture of each student as he or she was taking the survey, and the picture was immediately cross-referenced online using facial recognition software. At the conclusion of each survey, several of the retrieved photos had already appeared on the screen. Acquisti said that 42 percent of the photos were positively identified and linked to the students' Facebook profiles.

If you use Facebook, you are perhaps already aware of its limited facial recognition technology. Upload a photo to the site, and Facebook will attempt to phototag the people within your network, people with whom you are already friends. You do have some control over this. By going into your Facebook settings you can require the site to notify you every time that happens and choose whether to be identified in the photo. You can also choose to post the photo to your wall or timeline only after you've been notified, if at all.

To make tagged photos invisible in Facebook, open your account and go to "Privacy Settings." There are various options, including limiting the images to your personal timeline. Other than that, Facebook has not yet provided an option to stop people from tagging you without permission.

Companies such as Google and Apple also have facial-recognition technology built into some of their applications, such as Google Photo and iPhoto. It may be worth looking at the configuration settings for those apps and services so that you can limit what facial recognition technology can do in each. Google has so far held back from including facial recognition technology in its image search feature (indicated by that little camera icon you see in the Google search window). You can upload an existing picture, and Google will find the picture, but it will not attempt to find other photos showing the same person or people within the image. Google has, in various public statements, said that letting people identify strangers by face "crosses the creepy line."[6]

Even so, some repressive governments have done just that. They have taken photos of protesters at large antigovernment rallies and then put the images on the Web. This is not using image recognition software so much as it is crowdsourcing the identification process. Also, some US states have used their motor vehicle departments' photo databases to identify suspects in criminal cases. But those are fancy state-based operations. What could a lone academic do?

Acquisti and his fellow researchers wanted to see how much image-derived information about a person could be cross-referenced online. To find out they used a facial recognition technology called Pittsburgh Pattern Recognition, or PittPatt, now owned by Google. The algorithms used in PittPatt have been licensed to various security companies and government institutions. Shortly after the acquisition, Google went on record about its intentions: "As we've said for over a year, we won't add face recognition to Google unless we can figure out a strong privacy model for it. We haven't figured it out."[7] Let's hope the company sticks to its word.

At the time of his research, Acquisti was able to use PittPatt paired with data-mined Facebook images from what he and his team considered to be searchable profiles, i.e., those on which the Carnegie Mellon volunteers had already posted photos of themselves along with certain pieces of personal information. They then applied this set of known faces to the "anonymous" faces on a popular online dating site. There the researchers found that they could identify 15 percent of these supposedly "anonymous" digital heartbreakers.

The creepiest experiment, however, involved linking a person's face to his or her Social Security number. To do that, Acquisti and his team looked for Facebook profiles that included the person's date and city of birth. Previously, in 2009, the same group of researchers had shown that this information by itself was enough to enable them to obtain a person's Social Security number (Social Security numbers are issued sequentially per a state's own formula, and since 1989 SSNs have been issued on or very near the date of birth, making it even easier to guess a person's last four digits).[8]

After some initial calculations, the researchers then sent a follow-up survey to each of their CMU student volunteers asking whether the first five digits of his or her Social Security number as predicted by their algorithm was correct. And a majority of them were.[9]

I'll bet there are some photos that you now don't want online. Chances are you won't be able to take them all back, even if you could delete them from your social media site. That's in part because once you post something to a social network, it's owned by that network and out of your hands. And you agreed to this in the terms of service.

If you use the popular Google Photos app, even deleting a photo there doesn't necessarily mean it's gone. Customers have found that images are still there even after they delete the app from their mobile devices. Why? Because once the image hits the cloud, it is app-independent, meaning that other apps may have access to it and may continue to display the image you deleted.[10]

This has real-world consequences. Say you posted some stupid caption on a photo of someone who now works at the very company that you are applying to work for. Or you posted a photo of yourself with someone you don't want your current spouse to know about. Although it may be your personal social network *account,* it is the social network's *data*.

You've probably never taken the trouble to read the terms of use for any website where you post your personal data, daily experiences, thoughts, opinions, stories, gripes, complaints, and so on, or where you shop, play, learn, and interact, perhaps on a daily or even hourly basis. Most social networking sites require users to agree to terms and conditions before they use their services. Controversially, these terms often contain clauses permitting the sites to store data obtained from users and even share it with third parties.

Facebook has attracted attention over the years for its data storage policies, including the fact that the site makes it difficult to delete an account. And Facebook isn't alone. Many websites have nearly identical language in their terms of use that would very likely scare you away if you had read the terms before signing on. Here's one example, from Facebook, as of January 30, 2015:

> *You own all of the content and information you post on Facebook, and you can control how it is shared through your privacy and application settings. In addition:*
>
> *1. For content that is covered by intellectual property rights, like photos and videos (IP content), you specifically give us the following permission, subject to your privacy and application settings: you grant us a non-exclusive, transferable, sub-licensable, royalty-free, worldwide license to use any IP content that you post on or in connection with Facebook (IP License). This IP License ends when you delete your IP content or your account unless your content has been shared with others, and they have not deleted it.*[11]

In other words, the social media company has the right to use anything you post to the site in any way it wants. It can even sell your picture, your opinions, your writing, or anything else you post, making money from your contribution without paying you a penny. It can use your posted comments, criticisms, opinions, libel, slander (if you're into that sort of thing), and the most personal details you've posted about your children, your boss, or your lover. And it doesn't have to do it anonymously: if you have used your real name, the site can use it, too.

All this means, among other things, that images you post to Facebook can end up on other sites. To find out whether there are any embarrassing photos of you out there in the world, you can perform what's called a reverse image search in Google. To do this, click on the tiny camera within the Google search window and upload any photo from your hard drive. In a few minutes you will see any copies of that image findable online. In theory, if it's your photo, you should know all the sites that come up in the results. However, if you find that someone has posted your photo on a site you don't like, you have limited options.

Reverse image searches are limited by what's already posted. In other words, if there is a similar image online but not the exact same image, Google won't find it. It will find cropped versions of the image you searched for, but in that case the central data, or enough of it, remains the same.

Once, for my birthday, someone tried to create a stamp with my image on it. The company, Stamps.com, has a strict policy against using images of convicted persons. My image was rejected. Perhaps they did an online image search.

I was in a database somewhere as Kevin Mitnick, convicted of a crime.

The following year my friend tried an earlier photo under a different name, one taken before I was well known. She reasoned that perhaps this photo had not been uploaded online. And guess what? It worked. The second photo, showing a much younger me, was approved. This shows the limitations of image searches.

That said, if you do find photos of yourself that you'd rather not see online, you have a few options.

First, contact the site. Most sites have an "abuse@nameofthesite.com" e-mail address. You might also contact the site's webmaster at "admin@nameofthesite.com." Explain that you own the image and don't give permission for it to be posted. Most webmasters will take down the image without much fuss. However, if you need to you can file a Digital Millennium Copyright Act, or DMCA, request by e-mailing "DMCA@nameofthesite.com."

Be careful. Misrepresenting a DMCA request might get you into trouble, so seek legal advice if it gets to this level. If you still can't get the image removed, then consider going upstream and contacting the website's ISP (whether it's Comcast, GoDaddy, or another company). Most will take a legitimate DMCA request seriously.

Besides photos, what else is in your social media profile? You wouldn't share everything there is to know about you with the person sitting next to you on the subway. In the same way, it's not a good idea to share too much personal information on impersonal websites. You never know who is looking at your profile. And once it's out there, you can't take it back. Think carefully about what you put in your profile—you don't have to fill in all the blanks, such as the university you attended (or even when you attended). In fact, fill in the least amount of information you possibly can.

You may also want to create a dedicated social media profile. Don't lie, just be deliberately vague with the facts. For example, if you grew up in Atlanta, say you grew up in the "southeastern United States" or simply "I'm from the South."

You may also want to create a "security" birthday—a day that is not your real birthday—to mask personal information even further. Be sure to keep track of your security birthdays, since they are sometimes used to verify your identity when you phone technical support or need to reenter a site after you've been locked out.

After creating or tweaking your online profiles, take a few minutes to look at the privacy options on each site. For example, within Facebook you should enable privacy controls, including tag review. Disable "Suggest photos of me to friends." Disable "Friends can check me into places."

Kids with Facebook accounts are perhaps the most worrisome. They tend to fill in every blank box they can, even their relationship status. Or they innocently reveal the names of the schools they attend and the teachers they have as well as the numbers of the buses they ride each morning. While they don't necessarily tell the world specifically where they live, they might just as well. Parents need to friend their kids, monitor what they post, and, ideally, discuss in advance what is acceptable and what is not.

Being invisible doesn't mean you can't share updates about your personal life securely, but it involves both common sense and visiting and revisiting the privacy settings of the social media sites you use—because privacy policies do change, and sometimes not for the better. Do not display your birthday, even your security birthday, or at the very least hide it from the Facebook "friends" you do not personally know.

Consider a post that says Mrs. Sanchez is a great teacher. Another post might be about a crafts fair at Alamo Elementary. From Google we can find that Mrs. Sanchez teaches the fifth grade at Alamo Elementary—and from this we can assume the student account holder is around ten years old.

Despite warnings from Consumer Reports and other organizations to those who do post personal information, people continue to tell all online. Remember that it is perfectly legal for third parties to come along and to take that information once it is out in public.[12]

Remember also that no one is compelling you to post personal information. You can post as much or as little as you want. In some cases you are required to fill in some information. Beyond that, you decide how much sharing is right for you. You need to determine your own personal privacy level and understand that whatever information you provide cannot be taken back.

To help you get on top of all the choices you have, Facebook launched a new privacy checkup tool in May of 2015.[13] Despite tools like these, almost thirteen million Facebook users back in 2012 told *Consumer Reports* magazine that they had never set, or didn't know about, Facebook's privacy tools. And 28 percent shared all, or almost all, their wall posts with an audience wider than just their friends. More tellingly, 25 percent of those interviewed by *Consumer Reports* said they falsified information in their profiles to protect their identity, and this figure was up from 10 percent in 2010.[14] At least we're learning.

While you do have the right to post information about yourself that isn't strictly accurate, be aware that in California it is illegal to post online as someone else. You cannot impersonate another living individual. And Facebook has a policy that will not allow you to create an account under a false name.

This actually happened to me. My account was suspended by Facebook because Facebook accused me of impersonating Kevin Mitnick. At the time there were twelve Kevin Mitnicks on Facebook. The situation was fixed when CNET ran a story about the "real" Kevin Mitnick getting locked out of Facebook.[15]

There are, however, many reasons why individuals might need to post under a different name. If it is important to you, then find a social media service that allows you to post anonymously or under a different name. Such sites, however, will not match the breadth and reach of Facebook.

Be careful whom you friend. If you have met the person face-to-face, fine. Or if the person is a friend of someone you know, maybe. But if you receive an unsolicited request, think carefully. While you can unfriend that person at any point, he or she will nonetheless have a chance to see your entire profile—and a few seconds is all it takes for someone with malicious intent to interfere with your life. The best recommendation is to limit all the personal information you share on Facebook, because there have been very personal attacks, *even among friends,* over social networking websites. And data visible to your friends can still be reposted by them elsewhere without your consent or control.

I'll give you an example. A guy once wanted to hire me because he was the victim of extortion. He had met an amazing, beautiful girl on Facebook and began sending her nude photos of himself.

This continued for a time. Then one day he was told to send this woman — who might have been some guy living in Nigeria using a woman's photo — $4,000. He did, but then contacted me after he was asked to send another $4,000 or his nude photos would be sent to all his friends, including his parents, on Facebook. He was desperate to fix this situation. I told him his only real option was to tell his family or to wait and see if the extortionist went through with the threat. I told him to stop paying the money — the extortionist wasn't going to quit as long he continued to pay.

Even legitimate social networks can be hacked: someone could friend you just to get access to someone you know. A law enforcement officer could be seeking information on a person of interest who happens to be part of your social network. It happens.

According to the Electronic Frontier Foundation, social networks have been used for passive surveillance by federal investigators for years. In 2011 the EFF released a thirty-eight-page training course for IRS employees (obtained through the Freedom of Information Act) that the foundation said was used for conducting investigations via social networks.[16] Although federal agents can't legally pretend to be someone else, they can legally ask to be your friend. In doing so they can see all your posts (depending on your privacy settings) as well as those of others in your network. The EFF continues to study the privacy issues associated with this new form of law enforcement surveillance.

Sometimes corporations follow you, or at least monitor you, if you post or tweet something that they find objectionable — something as innocent as a comment about a test you took in school, for example. For one student, a tweet like that caused a lot of trouble.

When Elizabeth C. Jewett, the superintendent of the Watchung Hills Regional High School, in Warren, New Jersey, received a communication from the testing company that provided her school with a statewide exam, her reaction was surprise rather than concern. She was surprised that Pearson Education was watching a student's Twitter account in the first place. Minors are given a certain amount of privacy and leeway when it comes to what they post on social media. But students—whether they're in middle school, high school, or college—need to realize that what they are doing online is public and being watched. In this case one of Jewett's students had allegedly tweeted material from a standardized test.

In fact the student had actually posted a question about a question—not a picture of the exam page, just a few words—on a one-day statewide test given in New Jersey, the Partnership for Assessment of Readiness for College and Careers, or PARCC, test. The tweet was posted around 3:00 p.m.—well after students in the district had taken the test. After the superintendent spoke with a parent of the student who posted the tweet, the student removed it. There was no evidence of cheating. The tweet—not revealed to the public—was a subjective comment rather than a solicitation of an answer.

But the revelation about Pearson unnerved people. "The DOE [Department of Education] informed us that Pearson is monitoring all social media during PARCC testing," Jewett wrote to her colleagues in an e-mail that a local columnist made public without her permission. In that e-mail Jewett confirmed that at least three more cases had been identified by Pearson and passed along to the state DOE.

While Pearson is not alone in monitoring social media in order to detect theft of intellectual property, its behavior does raise questions. How, for example, did the company know the identity of the student involved from his Twitter handle? In a statement provided to the *New York Times,* Pearson said: "A breach includes any time someone shares information about a test outside of the classroom—from casual conversations to posts on social media. Again, our goal is to ensure a fair test for all students. Every student deserves his or her chance to take the test on a level playing field."[17]

The *Times* said it confirmed through officials in Massachusetts, which is also administering the PARCC test, that Pearson does cross-reference tweets about standardized tests with lists of students who have registered to take the tests. On this Pearson declined to comment for the *Times*.

For years the state of California also monitored social media during its annual Standardized Testing and Reporting (STAR) tests. In 2013, the last year the tests were given statewide, the California Department of Education identified 242 schools whose students posted on social media during administration of the tests, only sixteen of which included postings of test questions or answers.[18]

"The incident highlighted the degree to which students are under surveillance, both within and outside of traditional school environments," said Elana Zeide, a privacy research fellow at New York University's Information Law Institute. "Social media is generally seen as a separate domain from school. Twitter seems more like 'off campus' speech—so that Pearson's monitoring is more like spying on students' conversations in carpools than school hallways."[19]

However, she goes on to say, "The conversation also needs to shift from focusing on individual interests and harms to take the broader consequences of information practices into account. Schools and vendors need to stop dismissing parents as Luddites simply because they can't articulate a specific and immediate harm to their child. Parents, in turn, need to understand that schools can't defer to all their privacy preferences because there are also collective interests at stake that affect the entire educational system."

Twitter, with its iconic 140-character limit, has become pervasive, collecting a lot of seemingly tiny details about our daily lives. Its privacy policy acknowledges that it collects—and retains—personal information through its various websites, applications, SMS services, APIs (application programming interfaces), and other third parties. When people use Twitter's service, they consent to the collection, transfer, storage, manipulation, disclosure, and other uses of this information. In order to create a Twitter account, one must provide a name, username, password, and e-mail address. Your e-mail address cannot be used for more than one Twitter account.

Another privacy issue on Twitter concerns leaked tweets—private tweets that have been made public. This occurs when friends of someone with a private account retweet, or copy and paste, that person's private tweet to a public account. Once public, it cannot be taken back.

Personal information can still be dangerous to share over Twitter, especially if your tweets are public (the default). Avoid sharing addresses, phone numbers, credit card numbers, and Social Security numbers over Twitter.[20] If you must share sensitive information, use the direct message feature to contact a specific individual. But be aware that even private or direct-message tweets can become public.

For today's youth, so-called Generation Z, Facebook and Twitter are already old. Generation Z's actions on their mobile devices center around WhatsApp (ironically, now part of Facebook), Snapchat (not Facebook), and Instagram and Instagram Stories (also Facebook). All these apps are visual in that they allow you to post photos and videos or primarily feature photos or videos taken by others.

Instagram, a photo- and video-sharing app, is Facebook for a younger audience. It allows follows, likes, and chats between members. Instagram has terms of service and appears to be responsive to take-down requests by members and copyright holders.

Snapchat, perhaps because it is not owned by Facebook, is perhaps the creepiest of the bunch. Snapchat advertises that it allows you to send a self-destructing photo to someone. The life of the image is short, about two seconds, just long enough for the recipient to see the image. Unfortunately, two seconds is long enough for someone to grab a quick screenshot that lasts.

In the winter of 2013, two underage high school girls in New Jersey snapped photos of themselves, naked, and sent them to a boy at their school over Snapchat, naturally assuming that the images would be automatically deleted two seconds after they sent them. At least that's what the company said would happen.

However, the boy knew how to take a screenshot of the Snapchat message and later uploaded the images to his Instagram app. Instagram does not delete photos after two seconds. Needless to say the images of the naked underage girls went viral, and the school superintendent had to send a note home to the parents asking that the images be deleted from all students' phones or they would risk being arrested on child pornography charges. As for the three students, as minors they couldn't be charged with a crime, but each was subjected to disciplinary action within the school district.[21]

And it's not just girls sending nude photos to boys. In the United Kingdom, a fourteen-year-old boy sent a naked picture of himself to a girl at his school via Snapchat, again thinking the image would disappear after a few seconds. The girl, however, took a screenshot and...you know the rest of the story. According to the BBC, the boy—and the girl—will be listed in a UK database for sex crimes even though they are too young to be prosecuted.[22]

Like WhatsApp, with its inconsistent image-blurring capabilities, Snapchat, despite the app's promises, does not really delete images. In fact Snapchat agreed in 2014 to a Federal Trade Commission settlement over charges that the company had deceived users about the disappearing nature of its messages, which the federal agency alleged could be saved or retrieved at a later time.[23] Snapchat's privacy policy also says that it does not ask for, track, or access any location-specific information from your device at any time, but the FTC found those claims to be false as well.[24]

It is a requirement of all online services that individuals be thirteen years of age or older to subscribe. That is why these services ask for your birth date. A user could, however, just say, under penalty of perjury, "I swear that I am over the age of thirteen"—or twenty-one or whatever. Parents who find that their ten-year-olds have signed up for Snapchat or Facebook can report them and have those accounts removed. On the other hand, parents who want their kids to have an account often alter the child's birth date. That data becomes part of the child's profile. Suddenly your ten-year-old is fourteen, which means that he or she might be getting online ads targeted at older children. Also note that every e-mail address and photo your child shares over the service is recorded.

The Snapchat app also transmits Wi-Fi-based and cellular-based location information from Android users' mobile devices to its analytics tracking service provider. If you're an iOS user and enter your phone number to find friends, Snapchat collects the names and phone numbers of all the contacts in your mobile device's address book without your notice or consent, although iOS will prompt for permission the first time it is requested. My recommendation is to try another app if you want true privacy.

In North Carolina, a high school student and his girlfriend were charged with possessing naked photos of minors even though the photos were of themselves and had been taken and shared consensually. The girlfriend faced two charges of sexual exploitation of a minor: one for taking the photo and another for possessing it. Sexting aside, that means it is illegal for North Carolina teens to take or possess nude photos of *themselves*. In the police warrant, the girlfriend is listed as both victim and criminal.

The boyfriend faced five charges, two for each photo he took of himself plus one for possessing a photo of his girlfriend. If convicted he could face up to ten years in prison and have to register as a sex offender for the rest of his life. All for taking naked photos of himself and keeping one that his girlfriend sent him.[25]

When I was in high school, I simply met someone and asked her out. Today you have to put some information online so people can check you out first. But be careful.

If you are using a dating site and access it from someone else's computer, or should you happen to use a public computer to access it, always log out. Seriously. You don't want someone to hit the Back button on the browser and see your dating information. Or change it. Also, remember to uncheck the box that says "Remember me" on the log-in screen. You don't want this—or any other—computer to automatically log someone else in to your dating account.

Say you go on a first date, maybe a second date. People don't always reveal their true selves on a first or second date. Once your date has friended you on Facebook or followed you on Twitter or on any other social network, he or she can see all your friends, your pictures, your interests... things can get weird fast.

We've covered online services: what about mobile apps?

Dating apps can report your location, and part of that is by design. Say you see someone you like in your area: you can then use the app to find out if that person is nearby. The mobile dating app Grindr gives very precise location information for its subscribers... perhaps too precise.

Researchers Colby Moore and Patrick Wardle from the cybersecurity firm Synack were able to spoof requests to Grindr in order to follow some of the people in its service as they moved about a single city. They also found that if they had three accounts search for one individual, they could triangulate the results to get a much more precise measurement of where that person was at any given moment.[26]

Maybe dating apps aren't your thing, but even logging in to the Yelp service to search for a good restaurant gives third-party businesses information about your sex, age, and location. A default setting within the app allows it to send information back to the restaurant, telling it, for example, that a woman, age thirty-one, from New York City was looking at its review. You can, however, go into your settings and choose "Basics," which reveals only your city (unfortunately you cannot disable the feature entirely).[27] Perhaps the best way to avoid this is to not log in and simply use Yelp as a guest.

Regarding geolocation, it is a good idea in general to check if *any* mobile apps you use broadcast your location. In most cases you can turn this feature off, either in each individual app or entirely.[28]

And before agreeing to download any Android app, always read the permissions first. You can view these permissions in Google Play by going to the app, then scrolling down to the section above Google Play content that says "Permissions." If the permissions make you feel uncomfortable, or if you think they give the app developer too much control, then do not download the app. Apple does not provide similar information about the apps in its store, and instead permissions are prompted as they are needed when using the app. In fact, I prefer to use iOS devices because the operating system always prompts before disclosing private information—like my location data. Also iOS is much more secure than Android if you don't jailbreak your iPhone or iPad. Of course, well-funded adversaries could purchase exploits for any operating system in the marketplace, but iOS exploits are quite expensive—costing over a million dollars.[29]

CHAPTER TEN

You Can Run but Not Hide

If you carry your cell phone with you throughout the day, as most of us do, then you are not invisible. You are being surveilled—even if you don't have geolocation tracking enabled on your phone. For example, if you have iOS 8.2 or earlier, Apple will turn off GPS in airplane mode, but if you have a newer version, as most of us do, GPS remains on—even if you are in airplane mode—unless you take additional steps.[1] To find out how much his mobile carrier knew about his daily activity, a prominent German politician, Malte Spitz, filed suit against the carrier, and a German court ordered the company to turn over its records. The sheer volume of those records was astounding. Just within a six-month period, they had recorded his location 85,000 times while also tracking every call he had made and received, the phone number of the other party, and how long each call lasted. In other words, this was the metadata produced by Spitz's phone. And it was not just for voice communication but for text messages as well.[2]

Spitz teamed up with other organizations, asking them to format the data and make it public. One organization produced daily summaries like the one below. The location of that morning's Green Party meeting was ascertained from the latitude and longitude given in the phone company records.

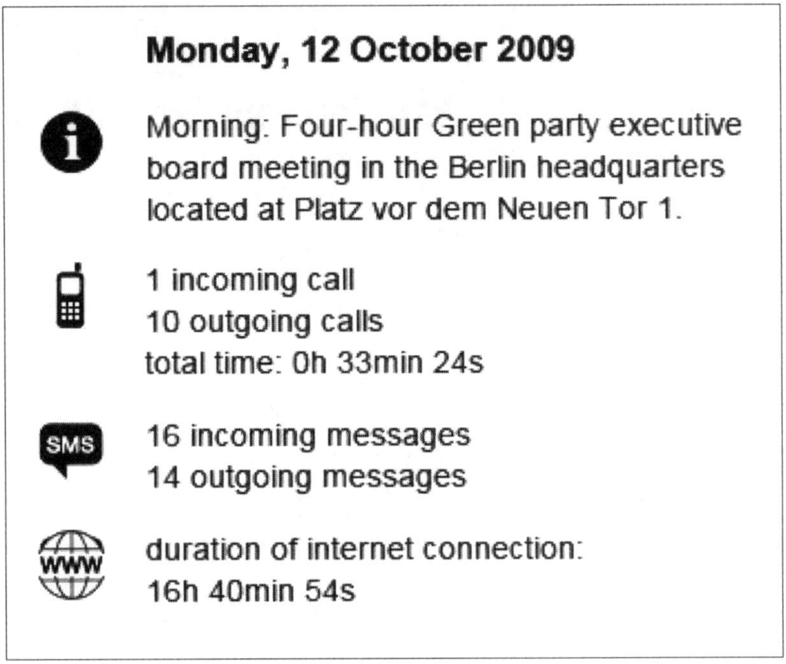

Malte Spitz activity for October 12, 2009

From this same data, another organization created an animated map. It shows Spitz's minute-by-minute movements all around Germany and displays a flashing symbol every time he made or received a call. This is an amazing level of detail captured in just few ordinary days.[3]

The data on Spitz isn't a special case, of course, nor is this situation confined to Germany. It's simply a striking example of the data that *your* cell-phone carrier keeps. And it can be used in a court of law.

In 2015, a case before the United States Court of Appeals for the

Fourth Circuit involved the use of similar cell-phone records in the United States. The case concerned two robbers who robbed a bank, a 7-Eleven, several fast-food restaurants, and a jewelry store in Baltimore. By having Sprint hand over information about the location of the prime suspects' phones for the previous 221 days, police were able to tie the suspects to a series of crimes, both by the crimes' proximity to each other and by the suspects' proximity to the crime scenes themselves.[4]

A second case, heard by the United States District Court for the Northern District of California, didn't detail specifics of the crime, but it also centered on "historical cell site information" available from Verizon and AT&T for the targets' phones. In the words of the American Civil Liberties Union, which filed an amicus brief in the case, this data "generates a near-continuous record of an individual's locations and movements." When a federal judge mentioned cell-phone privacy during the California case, the federal prosecutor suggested that "cellphone users who are concerned about their privacy could either not carry phones or turn them off," according to the official record.

This would seem to violate our Fourth Amendment right to be protected against unreasonable searches. Most people would never equate simply carrying a cell phone with forfeiting their right not to be tracked by the government—but that's what carrying a phone amounts to these days. Both cases note that Verizon, AT&T, and Sprint don't tell customers in privacy policies how pervasive location tracking is. Apparently AT&T, in a letter to Congress in 2011, said it stores cellular data for five years "in case of billing disputes."[5]

And location data is not stored only with the carrier; it's also stored with the vendor. For example, your Google account will retain all your Android geolocation data. And if you use an iPhone, Apple will also have a record of your data. To prevent someone from looking at this data on the device itself and to prevent it from being backed up to the cloud, periodically you should delete location data from your smartphone. On

Android devices, go to Google Settings>Location>Delete location history. On an iOS device you need to drill down a bit; Apple doesn't make it easy. Go to Settings>Privacy>Location Services, then scroll down to "System Services," then scroll down to "Frequent Locations," then "Clear Recent History."

In the case of Google, unless you've turned the feature off, the geolocation data available online can be used to reconstruct your movements. For example, much of your day might be spent at a single location, but there might be a burst of travel as you meet with clients or grab a bite to eat. More disturbing is that if anyone ever gains access to your Google or Apple account, that person can perhaps also pinpoint where you live or who your friends are based on where you spend the majority of your time. At the very least someone can figure out what your daily routine might be.

So it's clear that the simple act of going for a walk today is fraught with opportunities for others to track your behavior. Knowing this, say you consciously leave your cell phone at home. That should solve the problem of being tracked, right? Well, that depends.

Do you wear a fitness-tracking device such as Fitbit, Jawbone's UP bracelet, or the Nike+ FuelBand? If not, maybe you wear a smartwatch from Apple, Sony, or Samsung. If you wear one or both of these—a fitness band and/or a smartwatch—you can still be tracked. These devices and their accompanying apps are designed to record your activity, often with GPS information, so whether it is broadcast live or uploaded later, you can still be tracked.

The word *sousveillance,* coined by privacy advocate Steve Mann, is a play off the word *surveillance.* The French word for "above" is *sur;* the French word for "below" is *sous.* So sousveillance means that instead of being watched from above—by other people or by security cameras, for example, we're being watched from "below" by the small devices that we carry around and maybe even wear on our bodies.

Fitness trackers and smartwatches record biometrics such as your heart rate, the number of steps you take, even your body temperature. Apple's app store supports lots of independently created applications to track health and wellness on its phones and watches. Same with the Google Play store. And—surprise!—these apps are set to radio home the data to the company, ostensibly just to collect it for future review by the owner but also to share it, sometimes without your active consent.

For example, during the 2015 Amgen Tour of California, participants in the bicycle race were able to identify who had passed them and later, while online, direct-message them. That could get a little creepy when a stranger starts talking to you about a particular move you made during a race, a move you might not even remember making.

A similar thing happened to me. On the freeway, driving from Los Angeles to Las Vegas, I had been cut off by a guy driving a BMW. Busy on his cell phone, he suddenly switched lanes, swerving within inches of me, scaring the crap out of me. He almost wiped out the both of us.

I grabbed my cell phone, called the DMV, and impersonated law enforcement. I got the DMV to run his plate, then they gave me his name, address, and Social Security number. Then I called AirTouch Cellular, impersonating an AirTouch employee, and had them do a search on his Social Security number for any cellular accounts. That's how I was able to get his cell number.

Hardly more than five minutes after the other driver had cut me off, I called the number and got him on the phone. I was still shaking, pissed and angry. I shouted, "Hey, you idiot, I'm the guy you cut off five minutes ago, when you almost killed us both. I'm from the DMV, and if you pull one more stunt like that, we're going to cancel your driver's license!"

He must be wondering to this day how some guy on the freeway was able to get his cell-phone number. I'd like to think the call scared him into becoming a more considerate driver. But you never know.

What goes around comes around, however. At one point my AT&T mobile account was hacked by some script kiddies (a term for unsophisticated wannabe hackers) using social engineering. The hackers called an AT&T store in the Midwest and posed as an employee at another AT&T store. They persuaded the clerk to reset the e-mail address on my AT&T account so they could reset my online password and gain access to my account details, including all my billing records!

In the case of the Amgen Tour of California, riders used the Strava app's Flyby feature to share, by default, personal data with other Strava users. In an interview in *Forbes,* Gareth Nettleton, director of international marketing at Strava, said "Strava is fundamentally an open platform where athletes connect with a global community. However, the privacy of our athletes is very important to us, and we've taken measures to enable athletes to manage their privacy in simple ways."[6]

Strava does offer an enhanced privacy setting that allows you to control who can see your heart rate. You can also create device privacy zones so others can't see where you live or where you work. At the Amgen Tour of California, customers could opt out of the Flyby feature so that their activities were marked as "private" at the time of upload.

Other fitness-tracking devices and services offer similar privacy protections. You might think that since you don't bike seriously and probably won't cut someone off while running on the footpath around your office complex, you don't need those protections. What could be the harm? But there are other activities you do perform, some in private, that could still be shared over the app and online and therefore create privacy issues.

By itself, recording actions such as sleeping or walking up several flights of stairs, especially when done for a specific medical purpose, such as lowering your health insurance premiums, might not compromise your privacy. However, when this data is combined with other data, a holistic picture of you starts to emerge. And it may reveal more information than you're comfortable with.

One wearer of a health-tracking device discovered upon reviewing his online data that it showed a significant increase in his heart rate whenever he was having sex.[7] In fact, Fitbit as a company briefly reported sex as part of its online list of routinely logged activities. Although anonymous, the data was nonetheless searchable by Google until it was publicly disclosed and quickly removed by the company.[8]

Some of you might think, "So what?" True: not very interesting by itself. But when heart rate data is combined with, say, geolocation data, things could get dicey. *Fusion* reporter Kashmir Hill took the Fitbit data to its logical extreme, wondering, "What if insurance companies combined your activity data with GPS location data to determine not just when you were likely having sex, but *where* you were having sex? Could a health insurance company identify a customer who was getting lucky in multiple locations per week, and give that person a higher medical risk profile, based on his or her alleged promiscuity?"[9]

On the flip side of that, Fitbit data has been successfully used in court cases to prove or disprove previously unverifiable claims. In one extreme case, Fitbit data was used to show that a woman had lied about a rape.[10]

To the police, the woman—while visiting Lancaster, Pennsylvania—said she'd awakened around midnight with a stranger on top of her. She further claimed that she'd lost her Fitbit in the struggle for her release. When the police found the Fitbit and the woman gave them her consent to access it, the device told a different story. Apparently the woman had been awake and walking around all night. According to a local TV station, the woman was "charged with false reports to law enforcement, false alarms to public safety, and tampering with evidence for allegedly overturning furniture and placing a knife at the scene to make it appear she had been raped by an intruder."[11]

On the other hand, activity trackers can also be used to support disability claims. A Canadian law firm used activity-tracker data to show the severe consequences of a client's work injury. The client had provided the data company Vivametrica, which collects data from wearable devices and compares it to data about the activity and health of the general population, with Fitbit data showing a marked decrease in his activity. "Till now we've always had to rely on clinical interpretation," Simon Muller, of McLeod Law, LLC, in Calgary, told *Forbes*. "Now we're looking at longer periods of time through the course of a day, and we have hard data."[12]

Even if you don't have a fitness tracker, smartwatches, such as the Galaxy Gear, by Samsung, can compromise your privacy in similar ways. If you receive quick-glance notifications, such as texts, e-mails, and phone calls, on your wrist, others might be able to see those messages, too.

There's been tremendous growth recently in the use of GoPro, a tiny camera that you strap to your helmet or to the dashboard of your car so that it can record a video of your movements. But what happens if you forget the password to your GoPro mobile app? An Israeli researcher borrowed his friend's GoPro and the mobile app associated with it, but he did not have the password. Like e-mail, the GoPro app allows you to reset the password. However, the procedure—which has since been changed—was flawed. GoPro sent a link to your e-mail as part of the password reset process, but this link actually led to a ZIP file that was to be downloaded and inserted onto the device's SD card. When the researcher opened the ZIP file he found a text file named "settings" that contained the user's wireless credentials—including the SSID and password the GoPro would use to access the Internet. The researcher discovered that if he changed the number in the link—8605145—to another number, say 8604144, he could access other people's GoPro configuration data, which included their wireless passwords.

You could argue that Eastman Kodak jump-started the discussion of privacy in America—or at least made it interesting—in the late 1800s. Until that point, photography was a serious, time-consuming, inconvenient art requiring specialized equipment (cameras, lights, darkrooms) and long stretches of immobility (while subjects posed in a studio). Then Kodak came along and introduced a portable, relatively affordable camera. The first of its line sold for $25—around $100 today. Kodak subsequently introduced the Brownie camera, which sold for a mere $1. Both these cameras were designed to be taken outside the home and office. They were the mobile computers and mobile phones of their day.

Suddenly people had to deal with the fact that someone on the beach or in a public park might have a camera, and that person might actually include you within the frame of a photo. You had to look nice. You had to act responsibly. "It was not only changing your attitude toward photography, but toward the thing itself that you were photographing," says Brian Wallis, former chief curator at the International Center of Photography. "So you had to stage a dinner, and stage a birthday party."[13]

I believe we actually do behave differently when we are being watched. Most of us are on our best behavior when we know there's a camera on us, though of course there will always be those who couldn't care less.

The advent of photography also influenced how people felt about their privacy. All of a sudden there could be a visual record of someone behaving badly. Indeed, today we have dash cams and body cameras on our law enforcement officers so there will be a record of our behavior when we're confronted with the law. And today, with facial recognition technology, you can take a picture of someone and have it matched to his or her Facebook profile. Today we have selfies.

But in 1888, that kind of constant exposure was still a shocking and disconcerting novelty. The *Hartford Courant* sounded an alarm: "The sedate citizen can't indulge in any hilariousness without incurring the risk of being caught in the act and having his photograph passed around among his Sunday-school children. And the young fellow who wishes to spoon with his best girl while sailing down the river must keep himself constantly sheltered by his umbrella."[14]

Some people didn't like the change. In the 1880s, in the United States, a group of women smashed a camera on board a train because they didn't want its owner to take their picture. In the UK, a group of British boys ganged together to roam the beaches, threatening anyone who tried to take pictures of women coming out of the ocean after a swim.

Writing in the 1890s, Samuel Warren and Louis Brandeis—the latter of whom subsequently served on the Supreme Court—wrote in an article that "instantaneous photographs and newspaper enterprise have invaded the sacred precincts of private and domestic life." They proposed that US law should formally recognize privacy and, in part to stem the tide of surreptitious photography, impose liability for any intrusions.[15] Such laws were passed in several states.

Today several generations have grown up with the threat of instantaneous photographs—Polaroid, anyone? But now we have to also contend with the *ubiquity* of photography. Everywhere you go you are bound to be captured on video—whether or not you give your permission. And those images might be accessible to anyone, anywhere in the world.

We live with a contradiction when it comes to privacy. On the one hand we value it intensely, regard it as a right, and see it as bound up in our freedom and independence: shouldn't anything we do on our own property, behind closed doors, remain private? On the other hand, humans are curious creatures. And we now have the means to fulfill that curiosity in previously unimaginable ways.

Ever wonder what's over that fence across the street, in your neighbor's backyard? Technology may be able to answer that question for almost anyone. Drone companies such as 3D Robotics and CyPhy make it easy today for the average Joe to own his own drone (for example, I have the DJI Phantom 4 drone). Drones are remote-controlled aircraft and significantly more sophisticated than the kind you used to be able to buy at Radio Shack. Almost all come with tiny video cameras. They give you the chance to see the world in a new way. Some drones can also be controlled from your cell phone.

Personal drones are Peeping Toms on steroids. Almost nothing is out of bounds now that you can hover a few hundred feet above the ground.

Currently the insurance industry uses drones for business reasons. Think about that. If you are an insurance adjuster and need to get a sense of the condition of a property you are about to insure, you can fly a drone around it, both to visually inspect areas you didn't have access to before and to create a permanent record of what you find. You can fly high and look down to get the type of view that previously you could only have gotten from a helicopter.

The personal drone is now an option for spying on our neighbors; we can just fly high over someone's roof and look down. Perhaps the neighbor has a pool. Perhaps the neighbor likes to bathe in the nude. Things have gotten complicated: we have the expectation of privacy within our own homes and on our own property, but now that's being challenged. Google, for example, masks out faces and license plates and other personal information on Google Street View and Google Earth. But a neighbor with a private drone gives you none of those assurances—though you can try asking him nicely not to fly over your backyard. A video-equipped drone gives you Google Earth and Google Street View combined.

There are some regulations. The Federal Aviation Administration, for instance, has guidelines stating that a drone cannot leave the operator's line of sight, that it cannot fly within a certain distance of airports, and that it cannot fly at heights exceeding certain levels.[16] There's an app called B4UFLY that will help you determine where to fly your drone.[17] And, in response to commercial drone use, several states have passed laws restricting or severely limiting their use. In Texas, ordinary citizens can't fly drones, although there are exceptions—including one for real estate agents. The most liberal attitude toward drones is perhaps found in Colorado, where civilians can legally shoot drones out of the sky.

At a minimum the US government should require drone enthusiasts to register their toys. In Los Angeles, where I live, someone crashed a drone into power lines in West Hollywood, near the intersection of Larrabee Street and Sunset Boulevard. Had the drone been registered, authorities might know who inconvenienced seven hundred people for hours on end while dozens of power company employees worked into the night to restore power to the area.

Retail stores increasingly want to get to know their customers. One method that actually works is a kind of cell-phone IMSI catcher (see page 225). When you walk into a store, the IMSI catcher grabs information from your cell phone and somehow figures out your number. From there the system is able to query tons of databases and build a profile on you. Brick-and-mortar retailers are also using facial recognition technology. Think of it as a supersize Walmart greeter.

"Hello, Kevin," could be the standard greeting I get from a clerk in the not-too-distant future, even though I might never have been in that store before. The personalization of your retail experience is another, albeit very subtle, form of surveillance. We can no longer shop anonymously.

In June of 2015, barely two weeks after leaning on Congress to pass the USA Freedom Act—a modified version of the Patriot Act with some privacy protection added—nine consumer privacy groups, some of which had lobbied heavily in favor of the Freedom Act, grew frustrated with several large retailers and walked out of negotiations to restrict the use of facial recognition.[18]

At issue was whether consumers should by default have to give permission before they can be scanned. That sounds reasonable, yet not one of the major retail organizations involved in the negotiations would cede this point. According to them, if you walk into their stores, you should be fair game for scanning and identification.[19]

Some people may want that kind of personal attention when they walk into a store, but many of us will find it just plain unsettling. The stores see it another way. They don't want to give consumers the right to opt out because they're trying to catch known shoplifters, who would simply opt out if that were an option. If automatic facial recognition is used, known shoplifters would be identified the moment they enter a store.

What do the customers say? At least in the United Kingdom, seven out of ten survey respondents find the use of facial recognition technology within a store "too creepy."[20] And some US states, including Illinois, have taken it upon themselves to regulate the collection and storage of biometric data.[21] These regulations have led to lawsuits. For example, a Chicago man is suing Facebook because he did not give the online service express permission to use facial recognition technology to identify him in other people's photos.[22]

Facial recognition can be used to identify a person based solely on his or her image. But what if you already know who the person is and you just want to make sure he's where he should be? This is another potential use of facial recognition.

Moshe Greenshpan is the CEO of the Israel- and Las Vegas–based facial-recognition company Face-Six. Their software Churchix is used for—among other things—taking attendance at churches. The idea is to help churches identify the congregants who attend irregularly so as to encourage them to come more often and to identify the congregants who *do* regularly attend so as to encourage them to donate more money to the church.

Face-Six says there are at least thirty churches around the world using its technology. All the church needs to do is upload high-quality photos of its congregants. The system will then be on the lookout for them at services and social functions.

When asked if the churches tell their congregants they are being tracked, Greenshpan told *Fusion,* "I don't think churches tell people. We encourage them to do so but I don't think they do."[23]

Jonathan Zittrain, director of Harvard Law School's Berkman Center for Internet and Society, has facetiously suggested that humans need a "nofollow" tag like the ones used on certain websites.[24] This would keep people who want to opt out from showing up in facial recognition databases. Toward that end, the National Institute of Informatics, in Japan, has created a commercial "privacy visor." The eyeglasses, which sell for around $240, produce light visible only to cameras. The photosensitive light is emitted around the eyes to thwart facial recognition systems. According to early testers, the glasses are successful 90 percent of the time. The only caveat appears to be that they are not suitable for driving or cycling. They may not be all that fashionable, either, but they're perfect for exercising your right to privacy in a public place.[25]

Knowing that your privacy can be compromised when you're out in the open, you might feel safer in the privacy of your car, your home, or even your office. Unfortunately that is no longer the case. In the next few chapters I'll explain why.

CHAPTER ELEVEN

Hey, KITT, Don't Share My Location

Researchers Charlie Miller and Chris Valasek were no strangers to hacking cars. Previously the two had hacked a Toyota Prius—but they had done so while physically connected to the car and sitting in the backseat. Then, in the summer of 2015, Miller and Valasek succeeded in taking over the main controls of a Jeep Cherokee while it was traveling at seventy miles per hour down a freeway in St. Louis. They could remotely control a car without being anywhere near it.[1]

The Jeep in question did have a driver—*Wired* reporter Andy Greenberg. The researchers had told Greenberg beforehand: no matter what happens, don't panic. That turned out to be a tall order, even for a guy who was expecting to have his car hacked.

"Immediately my accelerator stopped working," Greenberg wrote of the experience. "As I frantically pressed the pedal and watched the RPMs climb, the Jeep lost half its speed, then slowed to a crawl. This occurred just as I reached a long overpass, with no shoulder to offer an escape. The experiment had ceased to be fun."

Afterward, the researchers faced some criticism for being "reckless" and "dangerous." Greenberg's Jeep was on a public road, not on a test track, so Missouri law enforcement is, at the time of this writing, still considering pressing charges against Miller and Valasek—and possibly Greenberg.

Hacking connected cars remotely has been talked about for years, but it took Miller and Valasek's experiment to get the automobile industry to pay attention. Whether it was "stunt hacking" or legitimate research, it got car manufacturers to start thinking seriously about cybersafety—and about whether Congress should prohibit the hacking of automobiles.[2]

Other researchers have shown they can reverse engineer the protocol controlling your vehicle by intercepting and analyzing the GSM or CDMA traffic from your car's onboard computer to the automaker's systems. The researchers were able to spoof the automotive control systems by sending SMS messages to lock and unlock car doors. Some have even hijacked remote start capabilities using the same methods as well. But Miller and Valasek were the first to be able to take complete control of a car remotely.[3] And they claim that, by using the same methods, they could take over cars in other states as well.

Perhaps the most important result of the Miller-Valasek experiment was a recall by Chrysler of more than 1.4 million of its cars because of a programming issue—the first recall of its kind. As an interim measure, Chrysler also suspended the affected cars' connection to the Sprint network, which the cars had used for telematics, the data that cars collect and share with the manufacturer in real time. Miller and Valasek told an audience at DEF CON 23 that they had realized they could do that—take over cars in other states—but they knew it wasn't ethical. Instead they conducted their controlled experiment with Greenberg in Miller's hometown.

In this chapter I'll discuss the various ways the cars we drive, the trains we ride, and the mobile apps we use to power our daily commute to work are vulnerable to cyberattacks, not to mention the numerous privacy compromises that our connected cars introduce into our lives.

When Johana Bhuiyan, a reporter for BuzzFeed, arrived at the New York offices of Uber, the car-calling service, in one of Uber's own cars, Josh Mohrer, the general manager, was waiting. "There you are," he said, holding up his iPhone. "I was tracking you." It was not an auspicious start to their interview, which touched upon, among other things, consumer privacy.[4]

Until Bhuiyan's story appeared, in November of 2014, few outside of Uber were even aware of God View, a tool with which Uber tracks the location of its thousands of contract drivers as well as their customers, all in real time.

As I mentioned earlier, apps routinely ask users for various permissions, including the right to access their geolocation data. The Uber app goes even further: it asks for your approximate (Wi-Fi) and precise (GPS) location, the right to access your contacts, and does not allow your mobile device to sleep (so it can keep tabs on where you are).

Bhuiyan allegedly told Mohrer up front that she did not give the company permission to track her anytime and anywhere. But she did, although maybe not explicitly. The permission was in the user agreement she consented to upon downloading the service to her mobile device. After their meeting, Mohrer e-mailed Bhuiyan logs of some of her recent Uber trips.

Uber compiles a personal dossier for every customer, recording every single trip he or she makes. That's a bad idea if the database isn't secure. Known in the security business as a honeypot, the Uber database can attract all sorts of snoops, from the US government to Chinese hackers.[5]

In 2015, Uber changed some of its privacy policies—in some instances to the detriment of the consumer.[6] Uber now collects geolocation data from all US-based users—even if the app runs only in the background and even if satellite and cellular communications are turned off. Uber said it will use Wi-Fi and IP addresses to track the users "offline." That means the Uber app acts as a silent spy on your mobile device. The company did not, however, say why it needs this ability.[7]

Nor has Uber fully explained why it needs God View. On the other hand, according to the company's privacy policy: "Uber has a strict policy prohibiting all employees at every level from accessing a rider or driver's data. The only exception to this policy is for a limited set of legitimate business purposes." Legitimate business might include monitoring accounts suspected of fraud and resolving driver issues (for example, missed connections). It probably doesn't include tracking a reporter's travels.

You might think Uber would give its customers the right to delete tracking information. No. And if after reading this you've deleted the app from your phone, well, guess what? The data still exists within Uber.[8]

Under the revised privacy policy, Uber also collects your address book information. If you have an iPhone, you can go into your settings and change your preference for contact sharing. If you own an Android, that's not an option.

Uber representatives have claimed that the company is not currently collecting this kind of customer data. By including data collection in the privacy policy, however, which existing users have already agreed to and which new users must agree to, the company ensures that it can roll out these features at any time. And the user won't have any redress.

Uber's God View is perhaps enough to make you nostalgic for regular old taxicabs. In the past, you would jump into a taxi, state your destination, and pay cash for the ride once you arrived. In other words, your trip would be almost completely anonymous.

With the advent of nearly universal acceptance of credit cards in the early twenty-first century, a lot of ordinary transactions have become traceable, and so there probably is a record of your taxi ride somewhere—maybe it doesn't reside with a specific driver or company, but it certainly resides with your credit card company. Back in the 1990s I used to work as a private investigator, and I could figure out my target's movements by obtaining their credit card transactions. One need only look at a statement to know that last week you rode a taxi in New York City and paid $54 for that trip.

Around 2010 taxis began to use GPS data. Now the taxi company knows your pickup and drop-off location, the amount of your fare, and perhaps the credit card number associated with your trip. This data is kept private by New York, San Francisco, and other cities that support the open data movement in government, providing researchers with rich—and anonymized—data sets. As long as names are not included, what harm could there be in making such anonymized data public?

In 2013, Anthony Tockar, then a Northwestern University graduate student interning for a company called Neustar, looked at the anonymized metadata publicly released by the New York City Taxi and Limousine Commission. This data set contained a record of every trip taken by the cars in its fleet during the previous year and included the cab number, the pickup and drop-off times, the locations, the fare and tip amounts, and anonymized (hashed) versions of the taxis' license and medallion numbers.[9] By itself, this data set isn't very interesting. The hash value in this case is unfortunately relatively easy to undo.[10]

When you combine the public data set with other data sets, however, you start to get a complete picture of what's going on. In this case, Tockar was able to determine where specific celebrities such as Bradley Cooper and Jessica Alba had taken their taxis within New York City during the previous year. How did he make this leap?

He already had geolocation data, so he knew where and when the taxis picked up and dropped off their fares, but he had to go further to determine who was inside the cab.[11] So he combined the New

York City Taxi and Limousine Commission metadata with online photos from ordinary tabloid websites available online. A paparazzi database.

Think about that. Paparazzi frequently photograph celebrities just as they enter and exit New York City's taxis. In these cases the cab's unique medallion number is often visible within the image. It's printed on the side of every cab. So a cab number photographed alongside Bradley Cooper, for instance, could be matched to the publicly available data regarding pickup and drop-off locations and fare and tip amounts.

Fortunately, not all of us have paparazzi on our trail. That doesn't mean there aren't other ways to trace our travels, though. Maybe you don't take taxis. Are there other ways to determine your location? There are. Even if you take public transportation.

If you ride a bus, train, or ferry to work, you're no longer invisible among the masses. Transit systems are experimenting with using mobile apps and near field communication (NFC) to tag riders as they get on and get off public transportation. NFC is a short-distance radio signal that often requires physical contact. Payment systems such as Apple Pay, Android Pay, and Samsung Pay all use NFC to make fumbling for quarters a thing of the past.

Let's say you have an NFC-enabled phone with an app from your local transit authority installed. The app will want a connection to your bank account or credit card so that you can always board any bus or train or ferry without worrying about a negative balance on your account. That connection to your credit card number, if it is not obscured by a token, or placeholder, number, could reveal to the transit authority who you are. Replacing your credit card number with a token is a new option that Apple, Android, and Samsung offer. That way the merchant—in this case the transit authority—only has a token and not your real credit card number. Using a token will cut down on data breaches affecting credit cards in the near future because the criminal would then need two databases: the token, and the real credit card number behind the token.

But say you don't use an NFC-enabled phone. Instead you have a transit card, like the CharlieCard in Boston, the SmarTrip card in Washington, DC, and the Clipper card in San Francisco. These cards use tokens to alert the receiving device—whether a turnstile or a fare-collection box—that there is enough of a balance for you to ride the bus, train, or ferry. However, transit systems don't use tokens on the back end. The card itself has only an account number—not your credit card information—on its magnetic strip. But if the transit authority were to be breached on the back end, then your credit card or bank information could also be exposed. Also, some transit systems want you to register for their cards online so that they can send you e-mail, meaning your e-mail addresses could also be exposed in a future hack. Either way, the ability to anonymously ride a bus has largely gone out the window unless you pay for the card using cash, not credit.[12]

This development is enormously helpful for law enforcement. Because these commuter-card companies are privately owned third parties, not governments, they can set whatever rules they want about sharing data. They can share it not only with law enforcement but also with lawyers pursuing civil cases—in case your ex wants to harass you.

So someone looking at the transit authority logs might know exactly who went through a subway station at such-and-such a time—but that person might not know which train his target boarded, especially if the station is a hub for several lines. What if your mobile device could resolve the question of which train you then rode and therefore infer your destination?

Researchers at Nanjing University, in China, decided to answer that question by focusing their work on something inside our phones called an accelerometer. Every mobile device has one. It's a tiny chip responsible for determining the orientation of your device—whether you are holding it in landscape or portrait view. These chips are so sensitive that the researchers decided to use accelerometer data alone in their calculations. And sure enough, they were able to accurately predict which subway train a user is riding. This is because most subway lines include turns that affect the accelerometer. Also important is the length of time between station stops—you need only to look at a map to see why. The accuracy of their predictions improved with each station a rider passed. The researchers claim their method has a 92 percent accuracy rate.

Let's say you own an old-model car and drive yourself to work. You might think you're invisible—just one of a million cars on the road today. And you might be right. But new technology—even if it is not part of the car itself—is eroding your anonymity. Chances are, with effort, someone could still identify you whizzing by on the freeway pretty quickly.

In the city of San Francisco, the Municipal Transportation Agency has started to use the FasTrak toll system, which allows you to cross any of the eight Bay Area bridges with ease, to track the movements of FasTrak-enabled cars throughout the city. Using technology similar to what toll bridges use to read the FasTrak (or E-ZPass) device in your car, the city has started searching for those devices as users circle around looking for parking. But officials are not always interested in *your* movements: rather, they're interested in the parking spaces—most of which are equipped with electronic parking meters. Spaces that are highly sought after can charge a higher rate. The city can wirelessly adjust the price at specific meters—including meters near a popular event.

In addition, in 2014 officials decided not to use human toll takers at the Golden Gate Bridge, so everyone, even tourists, is required to pay electronically or receive a bill in the mail. How do the authorities know where to send your bill? They photograph your license plate when you cross the toll plaza. These license-plate photographs are also used to nab red-light runners at problematic intersections. And increasingly, police are using a similar strategy as they drive by parking lots and residential driveways.

Police departments passively track your car's movements every day with automated license plate recognition (ALPR) technology. They can photograph your car's license plate and store that data, sometimes for years, depending on the police department's policy. ALPR cameras scan and read every plate they pass, whether the car is registered to a criminal or not.

Ostensibly ALPR technology is used primarily to locate stolen cars, wanted criminals, and assist with AMBER Alerts. The technology involves three cameras mounted to the top of a patrol car that are hooked up to a computer screen inside the vehicle. The system is further linked to a Department of Justice database that keeps track of the license plates of stolen cars and vehicles associated with crimes. As an officer drives, the ALPR technology can scan up to sixty plates per second. If a scanned plate matches a plate in the DOJ database, the officer receives an alert both visually and audibly.

The *Wall Street Journal* first reported on license plate recognition technology in 2012.[13] At issue for those who oppose or question ALPR technology is not the system itself but rather how long the data is kept and why some law enforcement agencies will not release it, even to the owner of the car being tracked. It's a disturbing tool that the police can use to figure out where you've been.

"Automatic license plate readers are a sophisticated way of tracking drivers' locations, and when their data is aggregated over time they can paint detailed pictures of people's lives," notes Bennett Stein of the ACLU's Project on Speech, Privacy, and Technology.[14]

One California man who filed a public records request was

disturbed by the number of photos (more than one hundred) that had been taken of his license plate. Most were at bridge crossings and other very public locations. One, however, showed him and his daughters exiting their family car while it was parked in their own driveway. Mind you, this person *wasn't* under suspicion for committing a crime. Documents obtained by the ACLU show that even the office of the FBI's general counsel has questioned the use of ALPR in the absence of a coherent government policy.[15]

Unfortunately, you don't have to file a public records request to see some of the ALPR data. According to the EFF, the images from more than a hundred ALPR cameras are available to anyone online. All you need is a browser. Before it went public with its findings, the EFF worked with law enforcement to correct the leakage of data. The EFF said this misconfiguration was found in more than just those one hundred instances and urged law enforcement around the country to take down or limit what's posted on the Internet. But as of this writing, it is still possible, if you type the right query into a search window, to gain access to license plate images in many communities. One researcher found more than 64,000 plate images and their corresponding locational data points during a one-week period.[16]

Perhaps you don't own a car and only rent one occasionally. Still, you are definitely not invisible, given all the personal and credit card information you must supply at the time of rental. What's more, most rental cars today have GPS built in. I know. I found out the hard way.

When you are given a loaner car from a dealership because your car is being serviced, you typically agree not to take it across state lines. The dealership wants to keep the car in the state where it was borrowed. This rule mostly concerns their insurance, not yours.

This happened to me. I brought my car into a Lexus dealer in Las Vegas for servicing, and they let me use a loaner car. Since it was past closing time at the dealership, I just signed the paperwork without reading it, mostly because I was being rushed by the service associate. Later, I drove the car to Northern California, to the Bay Area, for a consulting gig. When the service guy called me to discuss his recommendations, he asked, "Where are you?" I said, "San Ramon, California." He said, "Yeah, that's where we see the car." He then read me the riot act about taking the car out of state. Apparently the loaner agreement I had quickly signed stipulated that I was not to take the car out of Nevada.

When you rent or borrow a car today, there's a temptation to pair your wireless device to the entertainment system, to re-create the audio experience you have at home. Of course there are some immediate privacy concerns. This isn't your car. So what happens to your infotainment data once you return the car to the rental agency?

Before you pair your device with a car that isn't yours, take a look at the entertainment system. Perhaps by tapping the mobile phone setting you will see previous users' devices and/or names listed on the Bluetooth screen. Think about whether you want to join that list.

In other words, your data doesn't just disappear when you leave the car. You have to remove it yourself.

You might be thinking, "What harm is there in sharing my favorite tunes with others?" The problem is that your music isn't the only thing that gets shared. When most mobile devices connect to an automobile infotainment system, they automatically link your contacts to the car's system. The assumption is that you might want to make a hands-free call while driving, so having your contacts stored in the car makes it that much easier. Trouble is, it's not your car.

"When I get a rental car," says David Miller, chief security officer for Covisint, "the last thing I do is pair my phone. It downloads all my contacts because that's what it wants to do. In most rental cars you can go in and—if somebody's paired with it—see their contacts."

The same is true when you finally sell your car. Modern cars give you access to your digital world while on the road. Want to check Twitter? Want to post to Facebook? Cars today bear an increasing resemblance to your traditional PC and your cell phone: they contain personal data that you should remove before the machine or device is sold.

Working in the security business will get you in the habit of thinking ahead, even about mundane transactions. "I spend all this time connecting my vehicle to my whole life," says Miller, "and then in five years I sell it—how do I disconnect it from my whole life? I don't want the guy who buys [my car] to be able to see my Facebook friends, so you have to de-provision. Security guys are much more interested in the security vulnerabilities around de-provisioning than provisioning."[17]

And, just as you do with your mobile device, you will need to password protect your car. Except at the time of this writing, there is no mechanism available that will allow you to password lock your infotainment system. Nor is it easy to delete all the accounts you've put into your car over the years—how you do it varies by manufacturer, make, and model. Perhaps that will change—someone could invent a one-stop button that removes an entire user profile from your car. Until then, at least go online and change all your social media passwords after you sell your car.

Perhaps the best example of a computer on wheels is a Tesla, a state-of-the-art all-electronic vehicle. In June of 2015, Tesla reached a significant milestone: collectively, Tesla cars worldwide had been driven more than one billion miles.[18]

I drive a Tesla. They're great cars, but given their sophisticated dashboards and constant cellular communication, they raise questions about the data they collect.

When you take possession of a Tesla you are offered a consent form. You have the ability to control whether Tesla will record any information about your car over a wireless communication system. You can enable or disable sharing your personal data with Tesla via a touch screen on the dashboard. Many people accept the argument that their data will help Tesla make a better car in the future.

According to Tesla's privacy policy, the company may collect the vehicle identification number, speed information, odometer readings, battery usage information, battery charging history, information about electrical system functions, software version information, infotainment system data, and safety-related data (including information regarding the vehicle's SRS systems, brakes, security, and e-brake system), among other things, to assist in analyzing the performance of the vehicle. Tesla states that they may collect such information in person (e.g., during a service appointment) or via remote access.

That's what they say in their printed policy.

In practice, they can also determine your car's location and status at any time. To the media, Tesla has been cagey about what data it collects in real time and how it uses that data. Like Uber, Tesla sits in a God-like position that allows it to know everything about each car and its location at any moment.

If that unnerves you, you can contact Tesla and opt out of its telematics program. However, if you do, you will miss out on automatic software updates, which include security fixes and new features.

Of course the security community is interested in the Tesla, and independent security researcher Nitesh Dhanjani has identified some problems. While he agrees with me that the Tesla Model S is a great car and a fantastic product of innovation, Dhanjani found that Tesla uses a rather weak one-factor authentication system to access the car's systems remotely.[19] The Tesla website and app lack the ability to limit the number of log-in attempts on a user account, which means an attacker could potentially use brute force to crack a user's password. That means a third party could (assuming your password is cracked) log in and use the Tesla API to check the location of your vehicle. That person could also log in remotely to the Tesla app and control the vehicle's systems—its air conditioner, lights, and so on, although the vehicle must be stationary.

Most of Dhanjani's concerns have been addressed by Tesla at the time of this writing, but the situation is an example of how much more auto manufacturers need to do today to secure their cars. Just offering an app to remotely start and check the status of your car isn't good enough. It also has to be secure. The most recent update, a feature called Summon, allows you to tell the car to pull itself out of the garage or park itself in a tight spot. In the future, Summon will allow the car to pick you up from any location across the country. Kinda like the old TV show *Knight Rider.*

In refuting a negative review in the *New York Times,* Tesla admitted to the power of data they have on their side. *Times* reporter John Broder said that his Tesla Model S had broken down and left him stranded. In a blog, Tesla countered, identifying several data points they said called into question Broder's version of the story. For example, Tesla noted that Broder drove at speeds ranging from sixty-five miles per hour to eighty-one miles per hour, with an average cabin temperature setting of seventy-two degrees Fahrenheit.[20] According to *Forbes,* "data recorders in the Model S knew the temperature settings in the car, the battery level throughout the trip, the car's speed from minute to minute, and the exact route taken—down to the fact that the car reviewer drove circles in a parking lot when the car's battery was almost dead."[21]

Telematics capability is a logical extension of the black boxes mandatory in all cars produced for sale in the United States after 2015. But black boxes in cars aren't new at all. They date back to the 1970s, when air bags were first introduced. In collisions, people back then sustained life-threatening injuries from air bags, and some died from the force of the bags hitting their bodies. In some cases, had the car not been equipped with those bags, the occupants might be alive today. In order to make improvements, engineers needed the data on the deployment of the bags in the moments before and after a crash, collected by the air bags' sensing and diagnostic modules (SDMs). However, the vehicle owners were not told until very recently that the sensors in their cars recorded data about their driving.

Triggered by sudden changes in g-forces, black boxes in cars, like black boxes in airplanes, record only the last few seconds or so surrounding a g-force event, such as sudden acceleration, torque, and hard braking.

But it is easy to envision more kinds of data being collected in these black boxes and transmitted in real time via cellular connections. Imagine, in the future, that data collected over a three-to-five-day period could be stored either on the vehicle or in the cloud. Instead of trying to describe that *ping-ping* noise you hear when your car travels thirty-five miles per hour or more, you'd just give your mechanic access to the recorded data. The real question is, who else has access to all this data? Even Tesla admits that the data it collects might be used by third parties.

What if the third party was your bank? If it had an agreement with your car's manufacturer, it could track your driving ability and judge your eligibility for future auto loans accordingly. Or your health insurer could do the same. Or even your car insurer. It might be necessary for the federal government to weigh in on who owns data from your car and what rights you have to keep such data private.

There is little you can do about this today, but it's worth paying attention to in the future.

Even if you don't own a Tesla, your auto manufacturer might offer an app that allows you to open the car doors, start the engine, or even inspect certain diagnostics on your car. One researcher has shown that these signals—between the car, the cloud, and the app—can be hacked and used to track a target vehicle, effortlessly unlock it, trigger the horn and alarm, and even control its engine. The hacker can do just about everything except put the car in gear and drive it away. That still requires the driver's key. Although, I recently figured how to disable the Tesla key fob so that the Tesla is completely grounded. By using a small transmitter at 315 MHz you can make it so the key fob cannot be detected, thus disabling the car.

Speaking at DEF CON 23, Samy Kamkar, the security researcher best known for developing the Myspace-specific Samy worm back in 2005, demonstrated a device he built called OwnStar, which can impersonate a known vehicle network. With it he could open your OnStar-enabled General Motors vehicle, for example. The trick involves physically placing the device on the bumper or underside of a target car or truck. The device spoofs the automobile's wireless access point, which automatically associates the unsuspecting driver's mobile device with the new access point (assuming the driver has previously associated with the original access point). Whenever the user launches the OnStar mobile app, on either iOS or Android, the OwnStar code exploits a flaw in the app to steal the driver's OnStar credentials. "As soon as you're on my network and you open the app, I've taken over," Kamkar said.[22]

After obtaining the user's log-in credentials for RemoteLink, the software that powers OnStar, and listening for the locking or unlocking sound (*beep-beep*), an attacker can track down a car in a crowded parking lot, open it, and steal anything valuable inside. The attacker would then remove the device from the bumper. It's a very neat attack, since there's no sign of a forced intrusion. The owner and the insurance company are left to puzzle out what happened.

Researchers have found that connected-car standards designed to improve traffic flow can also be tracked. The vehicle-to-vehicle (V2V) and vehicle-to-infrastructure (V2I) communications, together known as V2X, call for cars to broadcast messages ten times a second, using a portion of the Wi-Fi spectrum at 5.9 gigahertz known as 802.11p.[23]

Unfortunately this data is sent unencrypted—it has to be. When cars are speeding down a highway, the millisecond of delay needed to decrypt the signal could result in a dangerous crash, so the designers have opted for open, unencrypted communications. Knowing this, they insist that the communications contain no personal information, not even a license plate number. However, to prevent forgeries, the messages are digitally signed. It's these digital signatures, like the IMEI (mobile phone serial number) data sent from our cell phones, that can be traced back to the registered owners of the vehicle.

Jonathan Petit, one of the researchers behind the study, told *Wired,* "The vehicle is saying 'I'm Alice, this is my location, this is my speed and my direction.' Everyone around you can listen to that.... They can say, 'There's Alice, she claimed she was at home, but she drove by the drug store, went to a fertility clinic,' this kind of thing... Someone can infer a lot of private information about the passenger."[24]

Petit has designed a system for around $1,000 that can listen for the V2X communications, and he suggests that a small town could be covered with his sensors for about $1 million. Rather than having a large police force, the town would use the sensors to identify drivers and, more important, their habits.

One proposal from the National Highway Traffic Safety Administration and European authorities is to have the 802.11p signal—the vehicle's "pseudonym"—change every five minutes. That won't, however, stop a dedicated attacker—he will just install more roadside sensors that will identify the vehicle before and after it makes the change. In short, there appear to be very few options to avoid vehicle identification.

"Pseudonym changing doesn't stop tracking. It can only mitigate this attack," says Petit. "But it's still needed to improve privacy... We want to demonstrate that in any deployment, you still have to have this protection, or someone will be able to track you."

Car connectivity to the Internet is actually good for vehicle owners: manufacturers are able to push out software bug fixes instantly should they be required. At the time of this writing, Volkswagen,[25] Land Rover,[26] and Chrysler[27] have experienced high-profile software vulnerabilities. However, only a few automakers, such as Mercedes, Tesla, and Ford, send over-the-air updates to all their cars. The rest of us still have to go into the shop to get our automobile software updated.

If you think the way Tesla and Uber are tracking every ride you take is scary, then self-driving cars will be even scarier. Like the personal surveillance devices we keep in our pockets—our cell phones—self-driving cars will need to keep track of where we want to go and perhaps even know where we are at a given moment in order to be always at the ready. The scenario proposed by Google and others is that cities will no longer need parking lots or garages—your car will drive around until it is needed. Or perhaps cities will follow the on-demand model, in which private ownership is a thing of the past and everyone shares whatever car is nearby.

Just as our cell phones are less like copper-wire phones than they are like traditional PCs, self-driving cars will also be a new form of computer. They'll be self-contained computing devices, able to make split-second autonomous decisions while driving in case they are cut off from their network communications. Using cellular connections, they will be able to access a variety of cloud services, allowing them to receive real-time traffic information, road construction updates, and weather reports from the National Weather Service.

These updates are available on some conventional vehicles right now. But it's predicted that by 2025 a majority of the cars on the road will be connected—to other cars, to roadside assistance services—and it's likely that a sizable percentage of these will be self-driving.[28] Imagine what a software bug in a self-driving car would look like.

Meanwhile, every trip you take will be recorded somewhere. You will need an app, much like the Uber app, that will be registered to you and to your mobile device. That app will record your travels and, presumably, the expenses associated with your trip if they would be charged to the credit card on file, which could be subpoenaed, if not from Uber then from your credit card company. And given that a private company will most likely have a hand in designing the software that runs these self-driving cars, you would be at the mercy of those companies and their decisions about whether to share any or all of your personal information with law enforcement agencies.

Welcome to the future.

I hope that by the time you read this there will be tougher regulations—or at least the hint of tougher regulations in the near future—regarding the manufacture of connected cars and their communications protocols. Rather than use widely accepted software and hardware security practices that are standard today, the auto industry, like the medical-device industry and others, is attempting to reinvent the wheel—as though we haven't learned much about network security over the last forty years. We have, and it would be best if these industries started following existing best practices instead of insisting that what they are doing is radically different from what's been done before. It's not. Unfortunately, failure to secure code in a car has much greater consequences than a mere software crash, with its blue screen of death. In a car, that failure could harm or kill a human being. At the time of this writing, at least one person has died while a Tesla was in beta autopilot mode—whether the result of faulty brakes or an error in judgment by the car's software remains to be resolved.[29]

Reading this, you may not want to leave your home. In the next chapter, I'll discuss ways in which the gadgets in our homes are listening and recording what we do behind closed doors. In this case it's not the government that we need to be afraid of.

CHAPTER TWELVE

The Internet of Surveillance

A few years ago nobody cared about the thermostat in your home. It was a simple manually operated thermostat that kept your home at a comfortable temperature. Then thermostats became programmable. And then a company, Nest, decided that you should be able to control your programmable thermostat with an Internet-based app. You can sense where I'm going with this, right?

In one vengeful product review of the Honeywell Wi-Fi Smart Touchscreen Thermostat, someone who calls himself the General wrote on Amazon that his ex-wife took the house, the dog, and the 401(k), but he retained the password to the Honeywell thermostat. When the ex-wife and her boyfriend were out of town, the General claimed he would jack up the temperature in the house and then lower it back down before they returned: "I can only imagine what their electricity bills might be. It makes me smile."[1]

Researchers at Black Hat USA 2014, a conference for people in the information security industry, revealed a few ways in which the firmware of a Nest thermostat could be compromised.[2] It is important to note that many of these compromises require physical access to the device, meaning that someone would have to get inside your house and install a USB port on the thermostat. Daniel Buentello, an independent security researcher, one of four presenters who talked about hacking the device, said, "This is a computer that the user can't put an antivirus on. Worse yet, there's a secret back door that a bad person could use and stay there forever. It's a literal fly on the wall."[3]

The team of researchers showed a video in which they changed the Nest thermostat interface (they made it look like the HAL 9000 fishbowl camera lens) and uploaded various other new features. Interestingly, they were not able to turn off the automatic reporting feature within the device—so the team produced their own tool to do so.[4] This tool would cut off the stream of data flowing back to Google, the parent company of Nest.

Commenting on the presentation, Zoz Cuccias of Nest later told *VentureBeat,* "All hardware devices—from laptops to smartphones—are susceptible to jailbreaking; this is not a unique problem. This is a physical jailbreak requiring physical access to the Nest Learning Thermostat. If someone managed to get in your home and had their choice, chances are they would install their own devices, or take the jewelry. This jailbreak doesn't compromise the security of our servers or the connections to them and to the best of our knowledge, no devices have been accessed and compromised remotely. Customer security is very important to us, and our highest priority is on remote vulnerabilities. One of your best defenses is to buy a Dropcam Pro so you can monitor your home when you're not there."[5]

With the advent of the Internet of Things, companies like Google are eager to colonize parts of it—to own the platforms that other products will use. In other words, these companies want devices developed by other companies to connect to their services and not someone else's. Google owns both Dropcam and Nest, but they want other Internet of Things devices, such as smart lightbulbs and baby monitors, to connect to your Google account as well. The advantage of this, at least to Google, is that they get to collect more raw data about your personal habits (and this applies to any large company—Apple, Samsung, even Honeywell).

In talking about the Internet of Things, computer security expert Bruce Schneier concluded in an interview, "This is very much like the computer field in the '90s. No one's paying any attention to security, no one's doing updates, no one knows anything—it's all really, really bad and it's going to come crashing down.... There will be vulnerabilities, they'll be exploited by bad guys, and there will be no way to patch them."[6]

To prove that point, in the summer of 2013 journalist Kashmir Hill did some investigative reporting and some DIY computer hacking. By using a Google search she found a simple phrase that allowed her to control some Insteon hub devices for the home. A hub is a central device that provides access to a mobile app or to the Internet directly. Through the app, people can control the lighting in their living rooms, lock the doors to their houses, or adjust the temperature of their homes. Through the Internet, the owner can adjust these things while, say, on a business trip.

As Hill showed, an attacker could also use the Internet to remotely contact the hub. As further proof, she reached out to Thomas Hatley, a complete stranger, in Oregon, and asked if she could use his home as a test case.

From her home in San Francisco, Hill was able to turn on and off the lights within Hatley's home, some six hundred miles up the Pacific coast. She also could have controlled his hot tubs, fans, televisions, water pumps, garage doors, and video surveillance cameras if he had had those connected.

The problem—now corrected—was that Insteon made all Hatley's information available on Google. Worse, access to this information wasn't protected by a password at the time—anyone who stumbled upon this fact could control any Insteon hub that could be found online. Hatley's router did have a password, but that could be bypassed by looking for the port used by Insteon, which is what Hill did.

"Thomas Hatley's home was one of eight that I was able to access," Hill wrote. "Sensitive information was revealed — not just what appliances and devices people had, but their time zone (along with the closest major city to their home), IP addresses and even the name of a child; apparently, the parents wanted the ability to pull the plug on his television from afar. In at least three cases, there was enough information to link the homes on the Internet to their locations in the real world. The names for most of the systems were generic, but in one of those cases, it included a street address that I was able to track down to a house in Connecticut."[7]

Around the same time, a similar problem was found by Nitesh Dhanjani, a security researcher. Dhanjani was looking in particular at the Philips Hue lighting system, which allows the owner to adjust the color and brightness of a lightbulb from a mobile device. The bulb has a range of sixteen million colors.

Dhanjani found that a simple script inserted onto a home computer on the home network was enough to cause a distributed denial-of-service attack — or DDoS attack — on the lighting system.[8] In other words, he could make any room with a Hue lightbulb go dark at will. What he scripted was a simple code so that when the user restarted the bulb, it would quickly go out again — and would keep going out as long as the code was present.

Dhanjani said that this could spell serious trouble for an office building or apartment building. The code would render all the lights inoperable, and the people affected would call the local utility only to find there was no power outage in their area.

While Internet-accessible home-automation devices can be the direct targets of DDoS attacks, they can also be compromised and joined to a botnet — an army of infected devices under one controller that can be used to launch DDoS attacks against other systems on the Internet. In October 2016, a company called Dyn, which handles DNS infrastructure services for major Internet brands like Twitter, Reddit, and Spotify, was hit hard by one of these attacks. Millions of users on the eastern part of the United States couldn't access many major sites because their browsers couldn't reach Dyn's DNS services.

The culprit was a piece of malware called Mirai, a malicious program that scours the Internet looking for insecure Internet of Things devices, such as CCTV cameras, routers, DVRs, and baby monitors, to hijack and leverage in further attacks. Mirai attempts to take over the device by simple password guessing. If the attack is successful, the device is joined to a botnet where it lies in wait for instructions. Now with a simple one-line command, the botnet operator can instruct every device—hundreds of thousands or millions of them—to send data to a target site and flood it with information, forcing it to go offline.

While you cannot stop hackers from launching DDoS attacks against others, you can become invisible to their botnets. The first item of business when deploying an Internet of Things device is to change the password to something hard to guess. If you already have a device deployed, rebooting it should remove any existing malicious code.

Computer scripts can affect other smart-home systems.

If you have a newborn in your home, you may also have a baby monitor. This device, either a microphone or a camera or a combination of both, allows parents to be out of the nursery but still keep track of their baby. Unfortunately, these devices can invite others to observe the child as well.

Analog baby monitors use retired wireless frequencies in the 43–50 MHz range. These frequencies were first used for cordless phones in the 1990s, and anyone with a cheap radio scanner could easily intercept cordless phone calls without the target ever knowing what happened.

Even today, a hacker could use a spectrum analyzer to discover the frequency that a particular analog baby monitor uses, then employ various demodulation schemes to convert the electrical signal to audio. A police scanner from an electronics store would also suffice. There have been numerous legal cases in which neighbors using the same brand of baby monitor set to the same channel eavesdropped on one other. In 2009 Wes Denkov of Chicago sued the manufacturers of the Summer Infant Day & Night baby video monitor, claiming that his neighbor could hear private conversations held in his home.[9]

As a countermeasure, you might want to use a digital baby monitor. These are still vulnerable to eavesdropping, but they have better security and more configuration options. For example, you can update the monitor's firmware (the software on the chip) immediately after purchase. Also be sure to change the default username and password.

Here again you might come up against a design choice that is out of your control. Nitesh Dhanjani found that the Belkin WeMo wireless baby monitor uses a token in an app that, once installed on your mobile device and used on your home network, remains active—from anywhere in the world. Say you agree to babysit your newborn niece and your brother invites you to download the Belkin app to your phone through his local home network (with any luck, it is protected with a WPA2 password). Now you have access to your brother's baby monitor from across the country, from across the globe.

Dhanjani notes that this design flaw is present in many interconnected Internet of Things devices. Basically, these devices assume that everything on the local network is trusted. If, as some believe, we'll all have twenty or thirty such devices in our homes before long, the security model will have to change. Since everything on the network is trusted, then a flaw in any one device—your baby monitor, your lightbulb, your thermostat—could allow a remote attacker onto your smart home network and give him an opportunity to learn even more about your personal habits.

* * *

Long before mobile apps, there were handheld remotes. Most of us are too young to remember the days before TVs had remote controls—the days when people had to physically get up off the couch and turn a dial to change the channel. Or to pump up the volume. Today, from the comfort of our sofas, we can just instruct the TV with our words. That may be very convenient, but it also means that the TV is listening—if only for the command to turn itself on.

In the early days, remote controls for TVs required direct line of sight and functioned by using light—specifically, infrared technology. A battery-operated remote would emit a sequence of flashes of light barely visible to the human eye but visible (again, within a line of sight) to a receptor on the TV. How would the TV know if you wanted to turn it on when it was off? Simple: the infrared sensor located within the TV was always on, on standby, waiting for a particular sequence of infrared light pulses from the handheld remote to wake it up.

Remote-control TVs evolved over the years to include wireless signals, which meant you didn't have to stand directly in front of the TV; you could be off to one side, sometimes even in another room. Again, the TV was on in standby mode, waiting for the proper signal to wake it up.

Fast-forward to voice-activated TVs. These TVs do away with the remote you hold in your hand—which, if you're like me, you can never find when you want it anyway. Instead you say something silly like "TV on" or "Hi, TV," and the TV—magically—turns on.

In the spring of 2015 security researchers Ken Munro and David Lodge wanted to see whether voice-activated Samsung TVs were listening in on conversations in the room even when the TV was not in use. While they found that digital TVs do in fact sit idle when they are turned off—which is reassuring—the TVs record everything spoken after you give them a simple command, such as "Hi, TV" (that is, they record everything until the TV is commanded to turn off again). How many of us will remember to keep absolutely quiet while the TV is on?

We won't, and to make matters even more disturbing, what we say (and what is recorded) after the "Hi, TV" command is not encrypted. If I can get on your home network, I can eavesdrop on whatever conversation you're having in your home while the TV is turned on. The argument in favor of keeping the TV in listening mode is that the device needs to hear any additional commands you might give it, such as "Volume up," "Change the channel," and "Mute the sound." That might be okay, except the captured voice commands go up to a satellite before they come back down again. And because the entire string of data is not encrypted, I can carry out a man-in-the-middle attack on your TV, inserting my own commands to change your channel, pump up your volume, or simply turn off the TV whenever I want.

Let's think about that for a second. That means if you're in a room with a voice-activated TV, in the middle of a conversation with someone, and you decide to turn on the TV, the stream of conversation that follows may be recorded by your digital TV. Moreover, that recorded conversation about the upcoming bake sale at the elementary school may be streamed back to a server somewhere far from your living room. In fact, Samsung streams that data not only to itself but also to another company called Nuance, a voice-recognition software company. That's two companies that have vital information about the upcoming bake sale.

And let's get real here: the average conversation you're having in your TV room probably isn't about a bake sale. Maybe you're talking about something illegal, which law enforcement might want to know about. It is entirely likely that these companies would inform law enforcement, but if law enforcement, for example, were already interested in you, then officers might get a warrant forcing these companies to provide complete transcripts. "Sorry, but it was your smart TV that narc'd on you…"

Samsung has, in its defense, stated that such eavesdropping scenarios are mentioned in the privacy agreement that all users implicitly agree to when they turn on the TV. But when was the last time you read a privacy agreement before turning on a device for the first time? Samsung says in the near future all its TV communications will be encrypted.[10] But as of 2015, most models on the market are not protected.

Fortunately, there are ways to disable this HAL 9000–like feature on your Samsung and presumably on other manufacturers' TVs as well. On the Samsung PN60F8500 and similar products, go into the Settings menu, select "Smart Features," and then under "Voice Recognition," select "Off." But if you want to stop your TV from being able to record sensitive conversations in your home, you'll have to sacrifice being able to walk into a room and voice-command your TV to turn on. You can still, with remote in hand, select the microphone button and speak your commands. Or you could get up off the couch and switch the channels yourself. I know. Life is hard.

Unencrypted data streams are not unique to Samsung. While testing LG smart TVs, a researcher found that data is being sent back to LG over the Internet every time the viewer changes the channel. The TV also has a settings option called "Collection of watching info," enabled by default. Your "watching info" includes the names of files stored on any USB drive you connect to your LG television—say, one that contains photos from your family vacation. Researchers carried out another experiment in which they created a mock video file and loaded it to a USB drive, then plugged it into their TV. When they analyzed network traffic, they found that the video file name was transmitted unencrypted within http traffic and sent to the address GB.smartshare.lgtvsdp.com.

Sensory, a company that makes embedded speech-recognition solutions for smart products, thinks it can do even more. "We think the magic in [smart TVs] is to leave it always on and always listening," says Todd Mozer, CEO of Sensory. "Right now [listening] consumes too much power to do that. Samsung's done a really intelligent thing and created a listening mode. We want to go beyond that and make it always on, always listening no matter where you are."[11]

Now that you know what your digital TV is capable of, you might be wondering: Can your cell phone eavesdrop when it's turned off? There are three camps. Yes, no, and it depends.

There are those in the privacy community who swear you have to take the battery out of your turned-off smartphone to be sure that it is not listening. There doesn't seem to be a lot of evidence to support this; it's mostly anecdotal. Then there are the people who swear that just turning off your phone is good enough; case closed. But I think in reality there are instances—say, if malware is added to a smartphone—when it doesn't turn off entirely and could still record conversations held nearby. So it depends on a variety of factors.

There are some phones that wake up when you say a magic phrase, just as voice-activated TVs do. This would imply that the phones are listening at all times, waiting for the magic phrase. This would also imply that what is said is somehow being recorded or transmitted. In some malware-infected phones that is true: the phone's camera or microphone is activated when there is not a call in progress. These cases, I think, are rare.

But back to the main question. There are some in the privacy community who swear that you can activate a phone when it is turned off. There *is* malware that can make the phone appear to be off when it is not. However, the possibility that someone could activate a turned-off phone (no battery power) strikes me as impossible. Basically any device that has battery power that allows its software to be in a running state can be exploited. It's not hard for a firmware back door to make the device appear that it's off when it isn't. A device with no power can't do anything. Or can it? Some still argue that the NSA has put chips in our phones that provide power and allow tracking even when the phone is physically powered off (even if the physical battery is pulled).

Whether or not your phone is capable of listening, the browser you use on it certainly is. Around 2013 Google started what's called hotwording, a feature that allows you to give a simple command that activates the listening mode in Chrome. Others have followed suit, including Apple's Siri, Microsoft's Cortana, and Amazon's Alexa. So your phone, your traditional PC, and that stand-alone device on your coffee table all contain back-end, in-the-cloud services that are designed to respond to voice commands such as "Siri, how far to the nearest gas station?" Which means they listen. And if that doesn't concern you, know that the searches conducted by these services are recorded and saved indefinitely.[12]

Indefinitely.

So how much do these devices hear? Actually, it's a little unclear what they do when they are not answering questions or turning your TV on and off. For example, using the traditional PC version of the Chrome browser, researchers found that someone—Google?—appeared to be listening all the time by enabling the microphone. This feature came to Chrome from its open-source equivalent, a browser known as Chromium. In 2015, researchers discovered that someone—Google?—appeared to be listening all the time. Upon further investigation, they discovered that this is because the browser turns the microphone on by default. Despite being included in open-source software, this code was not available for inspection.

There are several problems with this. First, "open source" means that people should be able to look at the code, but in this case the code was a black box, code that no one had vetted. Second, this code made its way to the popular version of the browser via an automatic update from Google, which users weren't given a chance to refuse. And as of 2015 Google has not removed it. They did offer a means for people to opt out, but that opt-out requires coding skills so complicated that average users can't do it on their own.[13]

There are other, more low-tech ways to mitigate this creepy eavesdropping feature in Chrome and other programs. For the webcam, simply put a piece of tape over it. For the microphone, one of the best defenses is to put a dummy mic plug in the microphone socket of your traditional PC. To do this, get an old, broken set of headphones or earbuds and simply cut the wire near the microphone jack. Now plug that stub of a mic jack into the socket. Your computer will think there's a microphone there when there isn't. Of course if you want to make a call using Skype or some other online service, then you will need to remove the plug first. Also—and this is very important—make sure the two wires on the mic stub do not touch so that you don't fry your microphone port.

Another connected device that lives in the home is the Amazon Echo, an Internet hub that allows users to order movies on demand and other products from Amazon just by speaking. The Echo is also always on, in standby mode, listening to every word, waiting for the "wake word." Because Amazon Echo does more than a smart TV does, it requires first-time users to speak up to twenty-five specific phrases into the device before they give it any commands. Amazon can tell you the weather outside, provide the latest sports scores, and order or reorder items from its collection if you ask it to. Given the generic nature of some of the phrases Amazon recognizes—for example, "Will it rain tomorrow?"—it stands to reason that your Echo might be listening more than your smart TV is.

Fortunately, Amazon provides ways to remove your voice data from Echo.[14] If you want to delete everything (for example, if you plan to sell your Echo to another party), then you need to go online to do that.[15]

While all these voice-activated devices require a specific phrase to wake up, it remains unclear what each device is doing during downtime—the time when no one is commanding it to do anything. When possible, turn off the voice activation feature in the configuration settings. You can always turn it back on again when you need it.

Joining the Amazon Echo in the Internet of Things, in addition to your TV and thermostat, is your refrigerator.

Refrigerator?

Samsung has announced a model of refrigerator that connects with your Google calendar to display upcoming events on a flat screen embedded in the appliance's door—kind of like that whiteboard you once had in its place. Only now the refrigerator connects to the Internet through your Google account.

Samsung did several things right in designing this smart fridge. They included an SSL/https connection so traffic between the refrigerator and the Google Calendar server is encrypted. And they submitted their futuristic refrigerator for testing at DEF CON 23—one of the most intense hacker conventions on earth.

But according to security researchers Ken Munro and David Lodge, the individuals who hacked the digital TV communications, Samsung failed to check the certificate to communicate with Google servers and obtain Gmail calender information. A certificate would validate that the communications between the refrigerator and the Google servers are secure. But without it someone with malicious intent could come along and create his own certificate, allowing him to eavesdrop on the connection between your refrigerator and Google.[16]

So what?

Well, in this case, by being on your home network, someone could not only gain access to your refrigerator and spoil your milk and eggs but also gain access to your Google account information by performing a man-in-the-middle attack on the fridge calendar client and stealing your Google log-in credentials—allowing him or her to read your Gmail and perhaps do even greater damage.

Smart refrigerators are not the norm yet. But it stands to reason that as we connect more devices to the Internet, and even to our home networks, there will be lapses in security. Which is frightening, especially when the thing being compromised is something really precious and private, like your home.

Internet of Things companies are working on apps that will turn any device into a home security system. Your TV, for instance, might someday contain a camera. In that scenario an app on a smartphone or tablet could allow you to view any room in your home or office from any remote location. Lights, too, can be turned on when there is motion inside or outside the house.

In one scenario, you might drive up to your house, and as you do so the alarm system app on your phone or in your car uses its built-in geolocation capabilities to sense your arrival. When you're fifty feet away, the app signals the home alarm system to unlock the front or garage door (the app on your phone has already connected to the house and authenticated). The alarm system further contacts the in-home lighting system, asking it to illuminate the porch, entryway, and maybe either the living room or kitchen. Additionally, you may want to enter your home while soft chamber music or the latest Top 40 tune from a service such as Spotify is playing on the stereo. And of course the temperature of the house warms or cools, according to the season and your preferences, now that you are home again.

Home alarms became popular around the turn of the twenty-first century. Home alarm systems at that time required a technician to mount wired sensors in the doors and windows of the house. These wired sensors were connected to a central hub that used a wired landline to send and receive messages from the monitoring service. You would set the alarm, and if anyone compromised the secured doors and windows, the monitoring service would contact you, usually by phone.

A battery was often provided in case the power went out. Note that a landline usually never loses power unless the wire to the house is cut.

When a lot of people got rid of their copper-wire landlines and relied solely upon their mobile communication services, the alarm monitoring companies began offering cellular-based connections. Lately they've switched to Internet-based app services.

The alarm sensors on the doors and windows themselves are now wireless. There is certainly less drilling and stringing of ugly cable, but there is also more risk. Researchers have repeatedly found that the signals from these wireless sensors are not encrypted. A would-be attacker need only listen to the communications between devices in order to compromise them. For example, if I can breach your local network, I can eavesdrop on the communications between your alarm company servers and your in-home device (assuming it's on the same local network and not encrypted), and by manipulating those communications I can start to control your smart home, spoofing commands to control the system.

Companies are now providing "do-it-yourself" home monitoring services. If any sensors are disturbed, your cell phone lights up with a text message informing you of the change. Or perhaps the app provides a webcam image from inside the house. Either way, you are in control and are monitoring the house yourself. That's great until your home Internet goes out.

Even when the Internet is working, the bad guys can still subvert or suppress these do-it-yourself wireless alarm systems. For example, an attacker can trigger false alarms (which in some cities the homeowner has to pay for). Devices that create false alarms could be set off from the street in front of your house or up to 250 yards away. Too many false alarms could render the system unreliable (and the homeowner out of pocket for a hefty fee).

Or the attacker could jam the do-it-yourself wireless sensor signals by sending radio noise to prevent communication back to the main hub or control panel. It suppresses the alarm and prevents it from sounding, effectively neutralizing the protection and allowing the criminal to walk right in.

A lot people have installed webcams in their homes—whether for security, for monitoring a cleaning person or nanny, or for keeping tabs on a homebound senior or loved one with special needs. Unfortunately, a lot of these over-the-Internet webcams are vulnerable to remote attacks.

There's a publicly available Web search engine known as Shodan that exposes nontraditional devices configured to connect to the Internet.[17] Shodan displays results not only from your Internet of Things devices at home but also from internal municipal utilities networks and industrial control systems that have been misconfigured to connect their servers to the public network. It also displays data streams from countless misconfigured commercial webcams all over the world. It has been estimated that on any given day there may be as many as one hundred thousand webcams with little or no security transmitting over the Internet.

Among these are Internet cameras without default authentication from a company called D-Link, which can be used to spy on people in their private moments (depending on what these cameras are set to capture). An attacker can use Google filters to search for "D-Link Internet cameras." The attacker can then look for the models that default to no authentication, then go to a website such as Shodan, click a link, and view the video streams at his leisure.

To help prevent this, keep your Internet-accessible webcams turned off when they're not in use. Physically disconnect them to be sure they're off. When they are in use, make sure they have proper authentication and are set to a strong customized password, not the default one.

If you think your home is a privacy nightmare, wait until you see your workplace. I'll explain in the next chapter.

CHAPTER THIRTEEN

Things Your Boss Doesn't Want You to Know

If you've read this far, you're obviously concerned about privacy, but for most of us it's not a matter of hiding from the federal government. Rather, we know that when we're at work, our employers can see exactly what we're doing online over their networks (e.g., shopping, playing games, goofing off). A lot of us just want to cover our asses!

And that's getting harder to do, thanks in part to the cell phones we carry. Whenever Jane Rodgers, finance manager of a Chicago landscaping company, wants to know whether her employees in the field are where they should be, she pulls up their exact locations on her laptop. Like many managers and company owners, she is turning to tracking software on corporate-owned, personally enabled (COPE) smartphones and service trucks with GPS devices to surveil her employees. One day a customer asked Jane whether one of her landscapers had been out to perform a service. After a few keystrokes, Jane verified that between 10:00 a.m. and 10:30 a.m. one of her employees had been to the specified place.

The telematics service Rodgers uses provides capabilities beyond geolocation. For example, on her nine company-owned phones she can also view photos, text messages, and e-mails sent by her gardeners. She also has access to their call logs and website visits. But Rodgers says she only uses the GPS feature.[1]

GPS tracking in the service industry has been available for a long time. It, along with United Parcel Service's own ORION system of algorithmic route selection, has allowed the package delivery company to cut down on gas expenses by monitoring and suggesting optimized routes for its drivers. The company was also able to crack down on lazy drivers. In these ways, UPS has increased its volume by 1.4 million additional packages per day—with one thousand fewer drivers.[2]

All this is good for the employers, who argue that by squeezing out higher margins they can in turn afford to pay better wages. But how do employees feel? There is a downside to all this surveillance. In an analysis, *Harper's* magazine featured a profile of a driver who was electronically monitored while at work. The driver, who did not give his name, said that the software timed his deliveries to the second and informed him whenever he was under or over optimal time. At the end of a typical day, the driver said he might be over by as much as four hours.

Slacking off? The driver pointed out that a single stop might include multiple packages—which the ORION software does not always account for. The driver described coworkers in his New York distribution center who were battling chronic pain in their lower backs and knees from trying to carry too much in a single trip—despite constant reminders from the company regarding proper handling of heavy loads—in order to keep up with the software. So there's one kind of human cost to this employee monitoring.

Another place where work surveillance is used regularly is the food service industry. From cameras in the ceilings of restaurants to kiosks at the tabletop, wait staff can be watched and rated by various software systems. A 2013 study by researchers from Washington University, Brigham Young University, and MIT found that theft-monitoring software used in 392 restaurants produced a 22 percent reduction in server-side financial theft after it was installed.[3] As I mentioned, actively monitoring people does change their behavior.

There are currently no federal statutes in the United States to prohibit companies from tracking their employees. Only Delaware and Connecticut require employers to tell employees when they are being tracked. In most states, employees have no idea whether they are being watched at work.

What about employees in the office? The American Management Association found that 66 percent of employers monitor the Internet use of their employees, 45 percent track employee keystrokes at the computer (noting idle time as potential "breaks"), and 43 percent monitor the contents of employee e-mail.[4] Some companies monitor employees' Outlook calendar entries, e-mail headers, and instant-messaging logs. The data is ostensibly used to help companies figure out how their employees are spending their time—from how much time salespeople are spending with customers to which divisions of the company are staying in touch by e-mail to how much time employees are spending in meetings or away from their desks.

Of course there's a positive spin: having such metrics means that the company can be more efficient in scheduling meetings or in encouraging teams to have more contact with each other. But the bottom line is that someone is collecting all this corporate data. And it could someday be turned over to law enforcement or at the very least used against you in a performance review.

You are not invisible at work. Anything passing through a corporate network belongs to the company—it is not yours. Even if you are checking your personal e-mail account, your last order with Amazon, or planning a vacation, you are probably using a company-issued phone, laptop, or VPN, so expect to have someone monitoring everything you do.

Here's an easy way to keep your manager and even your coworkers from snooping: when you leave your desk to go to a meeting or the bathroom, lock your computer screen. Seriously. Don't leave your e-mail, or details about the project you've spent weeks on, open — just sitting there for someone to mess with. Lock your computer until you return to your screen. It takes a few extra seconds, but it'll spare you a lot of grief. Set a timer in the operating system to lock the screen after a certain number of seconds. Or look into one of the Bluetooth apps that will automatically lock your screen if your mobile phone is not near the computer. That said, there is a new attack that uses a weaponized USB device. A lot of offices seal the USB ports on their laptops and desktops, but if yours doesn't a weaponized USB stick could still unlock your computer without a password.[5]

In addition to corporate secrets, there's also a fair amount of personal e-mail that passes through our computers during the workday, and sometimes we print it out for ourselves while in the office. If you are concerned about privacy, don't do *anything* personal while at work. Keep a strict firewall between your work life and your home life. Or bring a personal device such as a laptop or an iPad from home if you feel the need to do personal stuff while on break. And if your mobile device is cellular-enabled, never use the company Wi-Fi, and, further, turn off the SSID broadcast if you are using a portable hotspot (see page 134). Only use cellular data when conducting personal business at work.

Really, once you arrive at your office, your public game face needs to be on. Just as you wouldn't talk about really personal things with your casual office mates, you need to keep your personal business off the company computer systems (especially when you're searching for health-related topics or looking for a new job).

It's harder than it sounds. For one thing, we're used to the ubiquity of information and the nearly universal availability of the Internet. But if you are going to master the art of invisibility, you have to prevent yourself from doing private things in public.

Assume that everything you type into your office computer is public. That doesn't mean that your IT department is actively monitoring your particular device or will ever act on the fact that you printed out your child's science fair project on the expensive color printer on the fifth floor—although they might. The point is, there's a record that you did these things, and should there be suspicion in the future, they *can* access the records of everything you did on that machine. It's their machine, not yours. And it's their network. That means they're scanning the content that flows in and out of the company.

Consider the case of Adam, who downloaded his free credit report on his work computer. He logged in to the credit bureau's site using the company computer over the company network. Let's say you, like Adam, also download your credit report at work. You want to print it out, right? So why not send it to the company printer over in the corner? Because if you do, there will be a copy of the PDF file containing your credit history sitting on the hard drive of the printer. You don't control that printer. And after the printer is retired and removed from the office, you don't have control over how that hard drive is disposed of. Some printers are now encrypting their drives, but can you be sure that the printer in your office is encrypted? You can't.

That's not all. Every Word or Excel document that you create using Microsoft Office includes metadata that describes the document. Typically document metadata includes the author's name, the date created, the number of revisions, and the file size as well as an option to add more details. This is not enabled by default by Microsoft; you have to go through some hoops to see it.[6] Microsoft has, however, included a Document Inspector that can remove these details before you export the document elsewhere.[7]

A 2012 study sponsored by Xerox and McAfee found that 54 percent of employees say they don't always follow their company's IT security policies, and 51 percent of employees whose workplace has a printer, copier, or multifunction printer say they've copied, scanned, or printed confidential personal information at work. And it's not just work: the same goes for printers at the local copy shop and the local library. They all contain hard drives that remember everything they've printed over their lifetimes. If you need something personal printed out, perhaps you should print it out later at home, on a network and printer over which *you* have control.

Spying, even on employees, has gotten very creative. Some companies enlist nontraditional office devices that we might otherwise take for granted, never imagining they could be used to spy on us. Consider the story of a young Columbia University graduate student named Ang Cui. Wondering if he could hack into a corporate office and steal sensitive data through nontraditional means, Cui decided first to attack laser printers, a staple in most offices today.

Cui noticed that printers were way behind the times. During several pen tests, I have observed this as well. I have been able to leverage the printer to get further access into the corporate network. This is because workers rarely change the admin password on printers that are internally deployed.

The software and the firmware used in printers—especially commercial printers for the home office—contain a lot of basic security flaws. The thing is, very few people see an office printer as vulnerable. They think they're enjoying what's sometimes called "security by obscurity"—if no one notices the flaw, then you are safe.

But as I've said, printers and copy machines, depending on the model, have one important thing in common—they both may contain hard drives. And unless that hard drive is encrypted—and many are still not—it is possible to access what has been printed at a later date. All this has been known for years. What Cui wondered was if he could turn a company printer against its owners and exfiltrate whatever was printed.

To make things more interesting, Cui wanted to attack the printer's firmware code, the programming embedded inside a chip within the printer. Unlike our traditional PCs and mobile devices, digital TVs and other "smart" electronics do not have the power or the processing resources to run a full-blown operating system such as Android, Windows, and iOS. Instead these devices use what's called real-time operating systems (RTOS), which are stored on individual chips inside the device (frequently known as fireware). These chips store only the commands needed to operate the system and not much else. Occasionally even these simple commands need to be updated by the manufacturer or vendor by flashing or replacing the chips. Given that this is done so infrequently, it's obvious that many manufacturers simply did not build in the proper security measures. This, the lack of update, was the vector that Cui decided to pursue for his attack.

Cui wanted to see what would happen if he hacked the file format HP used for its firmware updates, and he discovered that HP didn't check the validity of each update. So he created printer firmware of his own—and the printer accepted it. Just like that. There was no authentication on the printer's side that the update came from HP. The printer only cared that the code was in the expected format.

Cui now was free to explore.

In one famous experiment, Cui reported that he could turn on the fuser bar, the part of the printer that heats the paper after the ink has been applied, and leave it on, which would cause the printer to catch fire. The vendor—not HP—immediately responded by arguing that there was a thermo fail-safe within the fuser bar, meaning the printer could not overheat. However, that was Cui's point—he'd managed to turn that fail-safe feature off so that the machine could actually catch fire.

As a result of these experiments, Cui and his adviser, Salvatore Stolfo, argued that printers were weak links in any organization or home. For example, the HR department of a Fortune 500 company might receive a maliciously-coded résumé file over the Internet. In the time it takes the hiring manager to print that document, the printer through which it travels could be fully compromised by installing a malicious version of the firmware.

Preventing someone from grabbing your documents off the printer, secure printing, also known as pull printing, ensures that documents are only released upon a user's authentication at the printer (usually a passcode must be entered before the document will print). This can be done by using a PIN, smart card, or biometric fingerprint. Pull printing also eliminates unclaimed documents, preventing sensitive information from lying around for everyone to see.[8]

Building on his printer attacks, Cui began to look around the typical office for other common objects that might be vulnerable and settled on Voice over Internet Protocol (VoIP) telephones. As with printers, no one had appreciated the hidden yet obvious-once-you-thought-about-it value of these devices in collecting information. And as with a printer, an update to the system can be faked and accepted by the VoIP phone.

Most VoIP phones have a hands-free option that allows you to put someone on speakerphone in your cubicle or office. Which means there's not only a speaker but also a microphone on the outside of the handset. There's also an "off the hook" switch, which tells the phone when someone has picked up the receiver and wants to make or listen to a call as well as when the receiver has been put back and the speakerphone is enabled. Cui realized that if he could compromise the "off the hook" switch, he could make the phone listen to conversations nearby via the speakerphone microphone—even when the receiver was on the hook!

One caveat: unlike a printer, which can receive malicious code via the Internet, VoIP phones need to be "updated" individually by hand. This requires the code to be propagated using a USB drive. Not a problem, Cui decided. For a price, a night janitor could install the code on each phone with a USB stick as he or she cleaned the office.

Cui has presented this research at a number of conferences, each time using different VoIP telephones. And each time the vendor was notified in advance, and each time the vendor did produce a fix. But Cui has pointed out that just because a patch exists doesn't mean it gets applied. Some of the unpatched phones might still be sitting in offices, hotels, and hospitals right now.

So how did Cui get the data off the phone? Since office computer networks are monitored for unusual activity, he needed another means of extracting the data. He decided to go "off network" and use radio waves instead.

Previously, researchers at Stanford University and in Israel found that having your mobile phone positioned next to your computer can allow a remote third party to eavesdrop on your conversations. The trick requires malware to be inserted onto your mobile device. But with maliciously coded apps available for download from rogue app stores, that's easy enough, right?

With the malware installed on your mobile phone, the gyroscope within the phone is now sensitive enough to pick up slight vibrations. The malware in this case, researchers say, can also pick up minute air vibrations, including those produced by human speech. Google's Android operating system allows movements from the sensors to be read at 200 Hz, or 200 cycles per second. Most human voices range from 80 to 250 Hz. That means the sensor can pick up a significant portion of those voices. Researchers even built a custom speech-recognition program designed to interpret the 80–250 Hz signals further.[9]

Cui found something similar within the VoIP phones and printers. He found that the fine pins sticking out of just about any microchip within any embedded device today could be made to oscillate in unique sequences and therefore exfiltrate data over radio frequency (RF). This is what he calls a funtenna, and it is a virtual playground for would-be attackers. Officially, says security researcher Michael

Ossmann, whom Cui credits for the idea, "a funtenna is an antenna that was not intended by the designer of the system to be an antenna, particularly when used as an antenna by an attacker."[10]

Aside from a funtenna, what are some other ways people can spy on what you do at work?

Researchers in Israel have found that ordinary cell phones can—with malware installed—be made to receive binary data from computers. And previously, Stanford researchers found that mobile phone sensors could intercept the sound of electronic emissions from a wireless keyboard.[11] This builds on similar research conducted by scientists at MIT and Georgia Tech.[12] Suffice it to say that everything you type or view or use in the office can be listened to in one way or another by a remote third party.

For instance, say you use a wireless keyboard. The wireless radio signal sent from the keyboard to the laptop or desktop PC can be intercepted. Security researcher Samy Kamkar developed something called KeySweeper that's designed to do just that: a disguised USB charger that wirelessly and passively looks for, decrypts, logs, and reports back (over GSM) all keystrokes from any Microsoft wireless keyboard in the vicinity.[13]

We've discussed the danger of using bogus hotspots at cafés and airports. The same can be true in offices. Someone in your office may set up a wireless hotspot, and your device might automatically connect to it. IT departments typically scan for such devices, but sometimes they don't.

A modern equivalent of bringing your own hotspot to the office is bringing your own cellular connection. Femtocells are small devices available from your mobile carrier. They're designed to boost cellular connections within a home or office where the signal might be weak. They are not without privacy risks.

First of all, because femtocells are base stations for cellular communications, your mobile device will often connect to them without informing you. Think about that.

In the United States, law enforcement uses something called a StingRay, also known as an IMSI catcher, a cell-site simulator. Additionally there are TriggerFish, Wolfpack, Gossamer, and swamp box. Though the technologies vary, these devices basically all act like a femtocell without the cellular connection. They're designed to collect the international mobile subscriber identity, or IMSI, from your cellular phone. Their use in the United States is significantly behind that of Europe—for now. IMSI catchers are used at large social protests, for example, to help law enforcement identify who was at the assembly. Presumably the organizers will be on their phones, coordinating events.

After a protracted legal battle, the American Civil Liberties Union of Northern California obtained documents from the government detailing how it goes about using StingRay. For example, law enforcement agents are told to obtain a pen register or a trap-and-trace court order. Pen registers have been used to obtain phone numbers, a record of digits dialed on a phone. Trap-and-trace technology has been used to collect information about received calls. In addition, law enforcement can, with a warrant, legally obtain the voice recording of a phone call or the text of an e-mail. According to *Wired,* the documents received by the ACLU state that the devices "may be capable of intercepting the contents of communications and, therefore, such devices must be configured to disable the interception function, unless interceptions have been authorized by a Title III order."[14] A Title III order allows for real-time interception of communication.

Let's say you're not under surveillance by law enforcement. Let's say you're in an office that is highly regulated—for example, at a public utility. Someone may install a femtocell to allow personal communications outside the utility's normal call-logging system.

The danger is that the coworker with the modified femtocell at his or her desk could perform a man-in-the-middle attack, and he or she could also listen in on your calls or intercept your texts.

In a demonstration at Black Hat USA 2013, researchers were able to capture voice calls, SMS text messages, and even Web traffic from volunteers in the audience on their Verizon femtocells. The vulnerability in Verizon-issued femtocells had already been patched, but the researchers wanted to show companies that they should avoid using them anyway.

Some versions of Android will inform you when you switch cellular networks; iPhones will not. "Your phone will associate to a femtocell without your knowledge," explained researcher Doug DePerry. "This is not like Wi-Fi; you do not have a choice."[15]

One company, Pwnie Express, produces a device called Pwn Pulse that identifies femtocells and even IMSI catchers such as StingRay.[16] It gives companies the ability to monitor cellular networks around them. Tools like these, which detect the full spectrum of potential cellular threats, were once bought largely by the government—but not anymore.

As user-friendly as it is, Skype is not the friendliest when it comes to privacy. According to Edward Snowden, whose revelations were first published in the *Guardian,* Microsoft worked with the NSA to make sure that Skype conversations could be intercepted and monitored. One document boasts that an NSA program known as Prism monitors Skype video, among other communications services. "The audio portions of these sessions have been processed correctly all along, but without the accompanying video. Now, analysts will have the complete 'picture'," the *Guardian* wrote.[17]

In March of 2013, a computer-science graduate student at the University of New Mexico found that TOM-Skype, a Chinese version of Skype created through a collaboration between Microsoft and the Chinese company TOM Group, uploads keyword lists to every Skype user's machine—because in China there are words and phrases you are not permitted to search for online (including "Tiananmen Square"). TOM-Skype also sends the Chinese government the account holder's username, the time and date of transmission, and information about whether the message was sent or received by the user.[18]

Researchers have found that even very high-end videoconferencing systems—the expensive kind, not Skype—can be compromised by man-in-the-middle attacks. That means the signal is routed through someone else before it arrives at your end. The same is true with audio conferences. Unless the moderator has a list of numbers that have dialed in, and unless he has asked to verify any questionable numbers—say, area codes outside the United States—there is no way to prove or determine whether an uninvited party has joined. The moderator should call out any new arrivals and, if they fail to identify themselves, hang up and use a second conference-call number instead.

Say your office has spent big bucks and bought a really expensive videoconferencing system. You'd think it would be more secure than a consumer-grade system. But you'd be wrong.

In looking at these high-end systems, researcher H. D. Moore found that almost all of them default to auto-answer incoming video calls. That makes sense. You set a meeting for 10:00 a.m., and you want participants to dial in. However, it also means that at some other time of day, anyone who knows that number could dial in and, well, literally take a peek at your office.

"The popularity of video conferencing systems among the venture capital and finance industries leads to a small pool of incredibly high-value targets for any attacker intent on industrial espionage or obtaining an unfair business advantage," Moore wrote.[19]

How hard is it to find these systems? Conferencing systems use a unique H.323 protocol. So Moore looked at a sliver of the Internet and identified 250,000 systems using that protocol. He estimates from that number that fewer than five thousand of these were configured to auto-answer—a small percentage of the whole, but still a very large number by itself. And that's not counting the rest of the Internet.

What can an attacker learn from hacking such a system? The conferencing system camera is under the control of the user, so a remote attacker could tilt it up, down, left, or right. In most cases the camera does not have a red light to indicate that it's on, so unless you are watching the camera, you might not be aware that someone has moved it. The camera can also zoom in. Moore said his research team was able to read a six-digit password posted on a wall twenty feet from the camera. They could also read e-mail on a user's screen across the room.

Next time you're at the office, consider what can be seen from the videoconferencing camera. Perhaps the department's organizational chart is on the wall. Perhaps your desktop screen faces the conference room. Perhaps pictures of your kids and spouse are visible as well. That's what a remote attacker could see and possibly use against your company or even you personally.

Some system vendors are aware of this issue. Polycom, for example, provides a multipage hardening (security-strengthening) guide, even limiting the repositioning of the camera.[20] However, IT staffers don't usually have the time to follow guidelines like these, and they often don't even deem security a concern. There are thousands of conferencing systems on the Internet with default settings enabled.

The researchers also discovered that corporate firewalls don't know how to handle the H.323 protocol. They suggest giving the device a public Internet address and setting a rule for it within the corporate firewall.

The biggest risk is that many of the administration consoles for these conferencing systems have little or no security built in. In one example, Moore and his team were able to access a law firm's system, which contained an address-book entry for the boardroom of a well-known investment bank. The researchers had purchased a used videoconferencing device from eBay, and when it arrived its hard drive still had old data on it—including the address book, which listed dozens of private numbers, many of which were configured to auto-answer incoming calls from the Internet at large.[21] As with old printers and copy machines, if it has a hard drive, you need to securely wipe the data from it before you sell it or donate it (see page 220).

Sometimes at work we are tasked with collaborating on a project with a colleague who may be halfway across the planet. Files can be shared back and forth over corporate e-mail, but sometimes they're so large that e-mail systems will simply balk and not accept them as attachments. Increasingly, people have been using file-sharing services to send large files back and forth.

How secure are these cloud-based services? It varies.

The four big players—Apple's iCloud, Google Drive, Microsoft's OneDrive (formerly SkyDrive), and Dropbox—all provide two-step verification. That means you will receive an out-of-band text on your mobile device containing an access code to confirm your identity. And while all four services encrypt the data while it is in transit you must—if you don't want the company or the NSA to read it—encrypt the data before you send it.[22]

There the similarities end.

Two-factor authentication is important, but I can still bypass this by hijacking unused accounts. For example, I recently did a pen test where the client added Google's 2FA to their VPN website using publicly available tools. The way I was able to get in was by obtaining the active directory log-in credentials for a user who didn't sign up to use the VPN portal. Since I was the first to log in to the VPN service, I was prompted to set up 2FA using Google Authenticator. If the employee never accesses the service himself, then the attacker will have continued access.

For data at rest, Dropbox uses 256-bit AES encryption (which is pretty strong). However, it retains the keys, which could lead to unauthorized access by Dropbox or law enforcement. Google Drive and iCloud use a considerably weaker 128-bit encryption for data at rest. The concern here is that the data could potentially be decrypted by strong computational force. Microsoft OneDrive doesn't bother with encryption, which leads one to suspect that this was by design, perhaps at the urging of some governments.

Google Drive has introduced a new information rights management (IRM) feature. In addition to the documents, spreadsheets, and presentations created within Google Docs, Google Drive now accepts PDF and other file formats as well. Useful features include the ability to disable the download, print, and copy capabilities for commenters and viewers. You can also prevent anyone from adding additional people to a shared file. Of course these management features are only available to file owners. That means if someone has invited you to share a file, that person has to set the privacy restrictions, not you.

Microsoft has also introduced a unique per-file encryption feature, which is what it sounds like: a feature that encrypts each individual file with its own key. If one key is compromised, only that individual file will be affected rather than the whole archive. But this is not the default, so users will have to get in the habit of encrypting each file themselves.

Which seems like a good recommendation overall. Employees and users in general should get used to encrypting data before it gets sent to the cloud. That way you retain control of the keys. If a government agency comes knocking at the door of Apple, Google, Dropbox, or Microsoft, those companies won't be able to help—you'll have the individual keys.

You could also choose to use the one cloud service provider that sets itself apart from the rest—SpiderOak, which offers the full benefits of cloud storage and sync capability along with 100 percent data privacy. SpiderOak protects sensitive user data through two-factor password authentication and 256-bit AES encryption so that files and passwords stay private. Users can store and sync sensitive information with complete privacy, because this cloud service has absolutely zero knowledge of passwords and data.

But most users will continue to use other services at their own risk. People love the ease of grabbing data from the cloud, and so do law enforcement agencies. A huge concern about using the cloud is that your data does not have the same Fourth Amendment protections that it would have if it were stored in a desk drawer or even on your desktop computer. Law enforcement agencies are requesting cloud-based data with increasing (and unsettling) frequency. And they can obtain access with relative ease, since everything you upload online—whether to a Web-based e-mail service, Google Drive, or Shutterfly—goes to a server that belongs to the cloud service provider, not to you. The only true protection is to understand that anything you put up there can be accessed by somebody else and to act accordingly by encrypting everything first.

CHAPTER FOURTEEN

Obtaining Anonymity Is Hard Work

A few years ago I was returning to the United States from a trip to Bogota, Colombia, and upon arriving in Atlanta, I was quietly escorted by two US Customs agents into a private room. Having previously been arrested, and having served time in prison, I was perhaps a bit less flustered than the average Joe would have been. Still, it was unsettling. I had not done anything wrong. And I was in that room for four hours—five short of the maximum that I could be held without being arrested.

The trouble started when a US Customs agent swiped my passport and then stared at the screen. "Kevin," the agent said with a big smile on his face. "Guess what? There are some people downstairs who want to have a word with you. But don't worry. Everything will be okay."

I had been in Bogota to give a speech sponsored by the newspaper *El Tiempo*. I was also visiting the woman who was my girlfriend at the time. While I was waiting in that room downstairs, I called my girlfriend back in Bogota. She said the police in Colombia had called asking for her permission to search a package I had put in a FedEx box to the United States. "They found traces of cocaine," she said. I knew they hadn't.

The package contained a 2.5-inch internal hard drive. Apparently the Colombian—or maybe the US—authorities wanted to check the contents of the drive, which was encrypted. The cocaine was a lame excuse to open the package. I never got my hard drive back.

Later I learned that the police had torn open the box, taken the electronic equipment apart, then destroyed my hard drive while trying to open it by drilling a hole in it to check for cocaine. They could have used a special screwdriver to open the drive. They didn't find any drugs.

Meanwhile, back in Atlanta, officials opened my luggage and found my MacBook Pro, a Dell XPS M1210 laptop, an Asus 900 laptop, three or four hard drives, numerous USB storage devices, some Bluetooth dongles, three iPhones, and four Nokia cell phones (each with its own SIM card, so I could avoid roaming charges while speaking in different countries). These are standard tools in my profession.

Also in my luggage was my lock-picking kit and a cloning device that could read and replay any HID proximity card. The latter can be used to retrieve credentials stored on access cards by placing it in close proximity to them. I can, for example, spoof a person's card credentials and enter locked doors without having to make a forged card. I had these because I had given a keynote presentation about security in Bogota. Naturally, the customs agents' eyes lit up when they saw them, thinking I was up to something else—e.g., skimming credit cards, which was impossible with these devices.

Eventually agents from US Immigration and Customs Enforcement (ICE) arrived and asked why I was in Atlanta. I was there to moderate a panel at a security conference sponsored by the American Society for Industrial Security (ASIS). Later an FBI agent on the same panel was able to confirm the reason for my trip.

Things seemed to get worse when I opened my laptop and logged in to show them the e-mail confirming my presence on the panel.

My browser was set to automatically clear my history when started, so when I launched it I was prompted to clear my history. When I confirmed and clicked the OK button to clear my history, the agents freaked out. But then I just pressed the power button to power down the MacBook, so my drive was inaccessible without my PGP passphrase.

Unless I was under arrest, which I was told repeatedly that I was not, I should not have had to give up my password. Even if I had been under arrest, I wouldn't technically have had to give up my password under US law, but whether that right is protected depends on how long one is willing to fight.[1] And different countries have different laws on this. In the UK and Canada, for example, authorities can force you to reveal your password.

After my four hours, both ICE and the customs agents let me go. If an agency like the NSA had targeted me, however, they would have likely succeeded in figuring out the contents of my hard drive. Government agencies can compromise the firmware in your computer or mobile phone, impair the network you use to connect to the Internet, and exploit a variety of vulnerabilities found in your devices.

I can travel to foreign countries that have even more stringent rules and never have the problems I have in the United States because of my criminal record here. So how do you travel abroad with sensitive data? And how do you travel to "hostile" countries such as China?

If you don't want to have any sensitive data available on your hard drive, the choices are:

1. Clean up any sensitive data before you travel and perform a full backup.
2. Leave the data there but encrypt it with a strong key (although some countries may be able to compel you to reveal the key or password). Do not keep the passphrase with you: perhaps give half of the passphrase to a friend outside the United States who cannot be compelled to give it up.

3. Upload the encrypted data to a cloud service, then download and upload as needed.
4. Use a free product such as VeraCrypt to create a hidden encrypted file folder on your hard drive. Again, a foreign government, if it finds the hidden file folder, may be able to force you to reveal the password.
5. Whenever entering your password into your devices, cover yourself and your computer, perhaps with a jacket or other item of clothing, to prevent camera surveillance.
6. Seal your laptop and other devices in a FedEx or other Tyvek envelope and sign it, then put it in the hotel room safe. If the envelope is tampered with, you should notice it. Note, too, that hotel safes aren't really that safe. You should consider buying a camera device that you can put inside the safe to take a photo of anyone opening it and send the photo via cellular in real time.
7. Best of all, don't take any risk. Carry your device with you at all times, and don't let it out of your sight.

According to documents obtained by the American Civil Liberties Union through the Freedom of Information Act, between October of 2008 and June of 2010, more than 6,500 people traveling to and from the United States had their electronic devices searched at the border. This is an average of more than three hundred border searches of electronic devices per month. And almost half of those travelers were US citizens.

Little known fact: Anyone's electronic devices can be searched without a warrant or reasonable suspicion within one hundred air miles of the US border, which likely includes San Diego. Just because you crossed the border doesn't necessarily mean you are safe!

Two government agencies are primarily responsible for inspecting travelers and items entering the United States: the Department of Homeland Security's Customs and Border Protection (CBP) and

Immigration and Customs Enforcement (ICE). In 2008, the Department of Homeland Security announced that it could search any electronic device entering the United States.[2] It also introduced its proprietary Automated Targeting System (ATS), which creates an instant personal dossier about you — a very detailed one — whenever you travel internationally. CBP agents use your ATS file to decide whether you will be subject to an enhanced and sometimes invasive search upon reentering the United States.

The US government can seize an electronic device, search through all the files, and keep it for further scrutiny without any suggestion of wrongdoing whatsoever. CBP agents may search your device, copy its contents, and try to undelete images and video.

So here's what I do.

To protect my privacy and that of my clients, I encrypt the confidential data on my laptops. When I'm in a foreign country, I transmit the encrypted files over the Internet for storage on secure servers anywhere in the world. Then I wipe them physically from the computer before I return home, just in case government officials decide to search or seize my equipment.

Wiping data is not the same as deleting data. Deleting data only changes the master boot record entry for a file (the index used to find parts of the file on the hard drive); the file (or some of its parts) remains on the hard drive until new data is written over that part of the hard drive. This is how digital forensics experts are able to reconstruct deleted data.

Wiping, on the other hand, securely overwrites the data in the file with random data. On solid-state drives, wiping is very difficult, so I carry a laptop that has a standard hard drive and wipe it with at least thirty-five passes. File-shredding software does this by overwriting random data hundreds of times in each pass over a deleted file, making it hard for anyone to recover that data.

I used to make a full image backup of my device onto an external hard drive and encrypt it. I would then send the backup drive to the United States. I wouldn't wipe the data on my end until the drive was confirmed to be received by a colleague in readable condition. Then I'd securely wipe all personal and client files. I wouldn't format the entire drive, and I'd leave the operating system intact. That way, if I was searched, it would be easier to restore my files remotely without having to reinstall the entire operating system.

Since the experience in Atlanta, I've changed my protocol somewhat. I have started to keep an up-to-date "clone" of all my travel computers with a business colleague. My colleague can then just send the cloned systems to me anywhere in the United States, if needed.

My iPhone is another matter. If you ever connect your iPhone to your laptop to charge, and you click "Trust" when it shows you the "Trust This Computer" question, a pairing certificate is stored on the computer that allows the computer to access the entire contents of the iPhone without needing to know the passcode. The pairing certificate will be used whenever the same iPhone is connected to that computer.

For example, if you plug your iPhone into another person's computer and "trust" it, a trusted relationship is created between the computer and the iOS device, which allows the computer to access photos, videos, SMS messages, call logs, WhatsApp messages, and most everything else without needing the passcode. Even more concerning, that person can just make an iTunes backup of your entire phone unless you previously set a password for encrypted iTunes backups (which is a good idea). If you didn't set that password, an attacker could set one for you and simply back up your mobile device to his or her computer without your knowledge.

That means if law enforcement wants to see what's on your passcode-protected iPhone, they can do so easily by connecting it to your laptop, since it likely has a valid pairing certificate with that phone. The rule is: never "trust this computer" unless it's your personal system. What if you want to revoke your entire Apple device's pairing certificates? The good news is that you can reset your pairing certificate on your Apple devices.[3] If you need to share files, and you are using an Apple product, use AirDrop. And if you need to charge your phone, use the lightning cable plugged into your system or an electrical outlet, not into someone else's computer. Or you can buy a USB condom from syncstop.com, which allows you to safely plug into any USB charger or computer.

What if you only have your iPhone and not your computer when traveling?

I have enabled Touch ID on my iPhone so that it recognizes my fingerprint. What I do is reboot my iPhone before approaching immigration control in any country. And when it powers up, I deliberately do not put in my passcode. Even though I have enabled Touch ID, that feature is by default disabled until I first put in my passcode. The US courts are clear that law enforcement cannot demand your password. Traditionally, in the United States, you cannot be compelled to give testimonial evidence; however, you can be compelled to turn over a physical key to a safe. As such, a court can compel you to provide your fingerprints to unlock the device.[4] Simple solution: reboot your phone. That way your fingerprint won't be enabled and you won't have to give up your passcode.

In Canada, however, it's the law; you must, if you are a Canadian citizen, provide your passcode when it's requested. This happened to Alain Philippon, from Sainte-Anne-des-Plaines, Quebec. He was on his way home from Puerto Plata, in the Dominican Republic, when he refused to provide the border agents in Nova Scotia with his mobile phone's passcode. He was charged under section 153.1(b) of the Canadian Customs Act for hindering or preventing border officers from performing their role. The penalty if you're found guilty is $1,000, with a maximum fine of $25,000 and the possibility of one year in jail.[5]

I know firsthand about the Canadian password law. I hired a car service like Uber to take me from Chicago to Toronto in 2015 (I didn't want to fly in severe thunderstorms), and when we crossed the border into Canada from Michigan, we were immediately sent to a secondary inspection site. Maybe it was because a Middle Eastern guy with only a green card was driving. As soon as we arrived at the secondary inspection point, we entered a scene straight out of *CSI*.

A team of customs agents made sure we left the vehicle with all our belongings inside, including our cell phones. The driver and I were separated. One of the agents went to the driver's side of the car and removed his cell phone from the cradle. The agent demanded the driver's passcode and started going through his phone.

I previously had made up my mind never to give out my password. I felt I would have to choose between giving up my password and being allowed to travel into Canada for my gig. So I decided to use a bit of social engineering.

I yelled over to the customs agent searching the driver's phone. "Hey—you aren't going to search my suitcase, right? It's locked so you can't." It immediately got her attention. She said they had every right to search my suitcase.

I replied, "I locked it, so it cannot be searched."

Next thing I know, two agents walked over to me and demanded the key. I started asking them why they needed to search my suitcase, and they explained again that they had the right to search everything. I pulled out my wallet and handed the agent the key to my suitcase.

That was enough. They *completely* forgot about the cell phones and concentrated on my suitcase instead. Mission accomplished through misdirection. I was let go and, thankfully, was never asked for my cell-phone password.

In the confusion of being screened, it is easy to become distracted. Don't let yourself fall victim to circumstance. When going through any security checkpoint, make sure your laptop and electronic devices are the last on the conveyor belt. You don't want your laptop sitting at the other end while someone ahead of you is holding up the line. Also, if you need to step out of the line, make sure you have your laptop and electronic device with you.

Whatever privacy protections we may enjoy at home don't necessarily apply to travelers at the US border. For doctors, lawyers, and many business professionals, an invasive border search might compromise the privacy of sensitive professional information. This information might include trade secrets, attorney–client and doctor–patient communications, and research and business strategies, some of which a traveler has legal and contractual obligations to protect.

For the rest of us, searches on our hard drives and mobile devices might reveal e-mail, health information, and even financial records. If you've recently traveled to certain countries deemed unfriendly to US interests, be aware that this may trigger additional scrutiny from customs agents.

Repressive governments present another challenge. They may insist on looking at your electronic devices more thoroughly—reading your e-mail and checking your Downloads folder. There is also a possibility—especially if they take your laptop from you—that they might attempt to install tracking software on your device.

Many companies issue burner phones and loaner laptops when employees travel abroad. These devices are either thrown away or wiped clean when the employee returns to the United States. But for most of us, uploading encrypted files to the cloud or buying a new device and disposing of it upon return are not practical options.

In general, don't bring electronics that store sensitive information with you unless you absolutely need to. If you do, bring only the bare minimum. And if you need to bring your mobile phone, think about getting a burner phone for the duration of your visit. Especially since voice and data roaming rates are outrageous. Better to bring an unlocked burner phone and purchase a SIM card in the country you are visiting.

* * *

You might think that getting in and out of customs is the most nightmarish part of any trip. But it might not be. Your hotel room can also be searched.

I made several trips to Colombia in 2008—not just the one when I was stopped in Atlanta. On one of the trips I made later that year, something strange happened in my Bogota hotel room. And this was not a questionable hotel; it was one of the hotels where Colombian officials frequently stayed.

Perhaps that was the problem.

I had gone out to dinner with my girlfriend, and when we came back, my door lock displayed yellow when I inserted my room key. Not green. Not red. But yellow, which typically means the door is locked from the inside.

I went down to the front desk and had the clerk issue me a new key card. Again, the lock displayed a yellow light. I did this again. Same result. After the third time, I persuaded the hotel to send someone up with me. The door opened.

Inside, nothing looked immediately wrong. In fact at the time, I chalked the whole thing up to the lock being crappy. It wasn't until I returned to the United States that I realized what had happened.

Before leaving the United States, I had called a former girlfriend, Darci Wood, who used to be the lead technician at TechTV, and asked her to come over to my place and swap out the hard drive in my MacBook Pro laptop. At the time, MacBook Pro hard drives weren't easy to remove. She did it, though. In its place she put a brand-new drive that I had to format and install the OSX operating system on.

Several weeks later, when I returned from that trip to Colombia, I asked Darci to come over to my place in Las Vegas to swap back the drives.

Immediately she noticed something was different. She said someone had tightened the hard-drive screws much more than she had.

Clearly someone in Bogota had removed the drive, perhaps to make an image copy of it when I left my room.

This happened more recently to Stefan Esser, a researcher known for jailbreaking iOS products. He tweeted a picture of his poorly remounted hard drive.

Even a drive with very little data has *some* data on it. Fortunately, I used Symantec's PGP Whole Disk Encryption to encrypt the entire contents of my hard drive. (You could also use WinMagic for Windows or FileVault 2 for OSX; see page 244.) So the clone of my hard drive would be worthless unless the thief could obtain the key to unlock it. It is because of what I think happened in Bogota that I now bring my laptop with me when I travel, even when I'm going out to dinner. If I have to leave my laptop behind, then I never leave it in hibernate mode. Rather, I power it down. If I didn't, an attacker could possibly dump the memory and obtain my PGP Whole Disk encryption keys.[6] So I turn it all the way off.

At the beginning of the book I talked about the many precautions that Edward Snowden took to keep his communication with Laura Poitras private. Once Snowden's secret cache of data was ready to be released to the public, however, he and Poitras needed a place to store it. The most common operating systems — Windows, iOS, Android, and even Linux — contain vulnerabilities. All software does. So they needed a secure operating system, one that is encrypted from day one and requires a key to unlock it.

Hard-disk encryption works like this: when you boot up your computer, you enter a secure password or, rather, a passphrase such as "We don't need no education" (from the famous Pink Floyd song). Then the operating system boots up, and you can access your files and perform your tasks without noticing any time delay, because a driver performs the encryption tasks transparently and on the fly. This does, however, create the possibility that if you get up and leave your device, even for a moment, someone could access your files (since they are unlocked). The important thing to remember is that while your encrypted hard drive is unlocked, you need to take precautions to keep it secure. As soon as you shut down, the encryption key is no longer available to the operating system: that is, it just removes the key from memory so the data on the drive is no longer accessible.[7]

Tails is an operating system that can be booted up on any modern-day computer to avoid leaving any forensically recoverable data on the hard drive, preferably one that can be write-protected.[8] Download Tails onto a DVD or a USB stick, then set your BIOS firmware or EFI (OSX) initial boot sequence for either DVD or USB to boot the Tails distribution. When you boot, it will start up the operating system, which features several privacy tools, including the Tor browser. The privacy tools allow you to encrypt e-mail using PGP, encrypt your USB and hard drives, and secure your messages with OTR (off-the-record messaging).

If you want to encrypt individual files instead of your entire hard drive, there are several choices. One free option, TrueCrypt, still exists but is no longer maintained and doesn't offer full-disk encryption. Because it is no longer maintained, new vulnerabilities will not be addressed. If you continue to use TrueCrypt, be aware of the risks. A replacement for TrueCrypt 7.1a is VeraCrypt, which is a continuation of the TrueCrypt project.

There are several programs for sale, too. One obvious one is Windows BitLocker, which is generally not included in the home editions of the Windows operating system. To enable BitLocker, if installed, open File Explorer, right-click on the C drive, and scroll down to the "Turn on BitLocker" option. BitLocker takes advantage of a special chip on your motherboard known as a trusted platform module, or TPM. It's designed to unlock your encryption key only after confirming that your bootloader program hasn't been modified. This is a perfect defense against evil maid attacks, which I will describe shortly. You can set BitLocker to unlock when you power up or only when there's a PIN or a special USB that you provide. The latter choices are much safer. You also have the option of saving the key to your Microsoft account. Don't do that, because if you do you will have more or less given Microsoft your keys (which, as you will see, it might already have).

There are several issues with BitLocker. First, it uses a pseudorandom number generator (PRNG) called Dual_EC_DRBG, short for dual elliptic curve deterministic random bit generator, which might contain an NSA back door.[9] It is also privately owned, meaning that you just have to take Microsoft's word that it works and that it doesn't have any back doors for the NSA—which may not be the case with open-source software. Another problem with BitLocker is that you must share the key with Microsoft unless you purchase it for $250. Not doing so may allow law enforcement to request the key from Microsoft.

Despite these reservations, the EFF actually does recommend BitLocker for the average consumer looking to protect his or her files.[10] However, be aware there is a way to bypass BitLocker as well.[11]

Another commercial option is PGP Whole Disk Encryption from Symantec. A lot of universities use this, as do many corporations. I have used it in the past as well. PGP Whole Disk Encryption was created by Phil Zimmermann, the man who created PGP for e-mail. Like BitLocker, PGP can support the TPM chip to provide additional authentication when you turn on your PC. A perpetual license sells for around $200.

There is also WinMagic, one of the few options that requires two-factor authentication instead of just a password. WinMagic also doesn't rely on a master password. Rather, encrypted files are grouped, and each group has a password. This can make password recovery harder, so it may not be suitable for everyone.

And for Apple there's FileVault 2. After installation, you can enable FileVault 2 by opening System Preferences, clicking on the "Security

& Privacy" icon, and switching to the FileVault tab. Again, do not save your encryption key to your Apple account. This may give Apple access to it, which they in turn could give to law enforcement. Instead choose "Create a recovery key and do not use my iCloud account," then print out or write down the twenty-four-character key. Protect this key, as anyone who finds it could unlock your hard drive.

If you have iOS 8 or a more recent version of the operating system on your iPhone or iPad, its contents are automatically encrypted. Going a step further, Apple has said that the key remains on the device, with the user. That means that the US government cannot ask Apple for the key: it's unique to each and every device. FBI director James Comey claims that unbreakable encryption ultimately is not a good thing. In a speech he said, "Sophisticated criminals will come to count on these means of evading detection. And my question is, at what cost?"[12] The fear is that bad things will be kept under the cover of encryption.

The same fear delayed my case for months as I languished in jail back in the 1990s. My legal defense team wanted access to the discovery that the government planned to use against me at my trial. The government refused to turn over any encrypted files unless I provided the decryption key. I refused.[13] The court, in turn, refused to order the government to provide the discovery because I wouldn't give them the key.[14]

Android devices, beginning with version 3.0 (Honeycomb), also can be encrypted. Most of us choose not to do so. Beginning with Android 5.0 (Lollipop), encrypted drives are the default on the Nexus line of Android phones but optional on phones from other manufacturers, such as LG, Samsung, and others. If you choose to encrypt your Android phone, note that it could take up to an hour to do so and that your device should be plugged in during the process. Reportedly, encrypting your mobile device does not significantly hinder performance, but once you've made the decision to encrypt, you can't undo it.

In any of these whole-disk encryption programs, there always remains the possibility of a back door. I was once hired by a company to test a USB product that allowed users to store files in an encrypted container. During analysis of the code, we found that the developer had put in a secret back door—the key to unlock the encrypted container was buried in a random location on the USB drive. That meant that anyone with knowledge of the location of the key could unlock the data encrypted by the user.

Worse, companies don't always know what to do with this information. When I completed my security analysis of the encrypted USB device, the CEO called me and asked whether he should leave the back door in or not. He was concerned that law enforcement or the NSA may need to access a user's data. The fact that he needed to ask says a lot.

In its 2014 wiretap report, the US government reported encountering encrypted drives on only twenty-five out of the 3,554 devices that law enforcement had searched for evidence.[15] And they were still able to decrypt the drives on twenty-one of the twenty-five. So while having encryption often is good enough to keep a common thief from accessing your data, for a dedicated government, it might not pose much of a challenge.

Years ago researcher Joanna Rutkowska wrote about what she called an evil maid attack.[16] Say someone leaves a powered-down laptop whose hard drive is encrypted with either TrueCrypt or PGP Whole Disk Encryption in a hotel room. (I had used PGP Whole Disk Encryption in Bogota; I had also powered down the laptop.) Later, someone enters the room and inserts a USB stick containing a malicious bootloader. The target laptop must then be booted off the USB to install the malicious bootloader that steals the user's passphrase. Now the trap is set.

A maid, someone who can frequent a hotel room without too

much suspicion, would be the best candidate to do this—hence the name of the attack. A maid can reenter almost any hotel room the next day and type in a secret key combination that extracts the passphrase that was secretly stored on the disk. Now the attacker can enter the passphrase and obtain access to all your files.

I don't know whether someone did this on my laptop in Bogota. The hard drive itself had been removed and then replaced with the screws turned too tightly. Either way, fortunately, the drive contained no real information.

What about putting your electronics in a hotel safe? Is it better than leaving them out or keeping them in suitcases? Yes, but not much better. When attending a recent Black Hat, I stayed at the Four Seasons in Las Vegas. I placed $4,000 cash in the safe with various credit cards and checks. A few days later, I went and tried to open the safe but the code failed. I called security and they opened it up. I immediately noticed that the pile of $100 bills was much less thick. There was $2,000 left. So where did the other $2,000 go? Hotel security had no idea. A friend of mine who specializes in physical pen testing tried hacking the safe but could not exploit it. Today, it's still a mystery. Ironically, the safe was called a Safe Place.

A German antivirus company, G DATA, found that in hotel rooms where their research staff stayed, "more often than not" the safe had the default password (0000) in place. In cases like that, no matter what private password you select, anyone knowing the default password could also gain access to your valuables inside. G DATA did say that this information was not discovered systematically but anecdotally over several years.[17]

If an attacker doesn't know the default password for a given hotel-room safe, another option for him is to literally brute-force the lock. Although the hotel manager is entrusted with an emergency electronic device that plugs into the USB port and unlocks the safe, a savvy thief can simply unscrew the plate on the front of the safe and use a digital device to open the lock underneath. Or he can short-circuit the safe and initiate a reset, then enter a new code.

If that doesn't bother you, consider this. G DATA also found that the credit card readers on room safes—often the means by which you pay for their use—can be read by a third party who could skim the credit card data and then use or sell that information on the Internet.

Today hotels use NFC or even magnetic-strip swipe cards to lock and unlock your room. The advantage is that the hotel can change these access codes quickly and easily from the front desk. If you lose your card, you can request a new one. A simple code is sent to the lock, and by the time you get to your room, the new key card works. Samy Kamkar's MagSpoof tool can be used to spoof the correct sequences and open a hotel room lock that uses magnetic-strip cards. This tool was used on an episode of the TV show *Mr. Robot.*

The presence of a magnetic strip or an NFC chip has given rise to the idea that personal information might be stored on the hotel key card. It's not. But the urban legend continues. There's even a famous story that originated in San Diego County. Supposedly a sheriff's deputy there issued a warning that a hotel guest's name, home address, and credit card information had been found on a hotel key card. Perhaps you've seen the e-mail. It looks something like this:

> Southern California law enforcement professionals assigned to detect new threats to personal security issues recently discovered what type of information is embedded in the credit card–type hotel room keys used throughout the industry.
>
> Although room keys differ from hotel to hotel, a key obtained from the DoubleTree chain that was being used for a regional identity theft presentation was found to contain the following information:

- Customer's name
- Customer's partial home address
- Hotel room number
- Check-in date and checkout date
- Customer's credit card number and expiration date!

When you turn them in to the front desk, your personal information is there for any employee to access by simply scanning the card in the hotel scanner. An employee can take a handful of cards home and, using a scanning device, access the information onto a laptop computer and go shopping at your expense.

Simply put, hotels do not erase these cards until an employee issues the card to the next hotel guest. It is usually kept in a drawer at the front desk with YOUR INFORMATION ON IT!!!!

The bottom line is, keep the cards or destroy them! NEVER leave them behind and NEVER turn them in to the front desk when you check out of a room. They will not charge you for the card.[18]

The truthfulness of this e-mail has been widely disputed.[19] Frankly, it sounds like bullshit to me.

The information listed certainly could be stored on a key card, but that seems extreme, even to me. Hotels use what can be considered a token, a placeholder number, for each guest. Only with access to the back-end computers that do the billing can the token be connected with personal information.

I don't think you need to collect and destroy your old key cards, but hey—you might want to do so all the same.

Another common question that concerns travel and your data: What's in the bar code on the bottom of your plane ticket? What, if anything, might it reveal? In truth, relatively little personal information, unless you have a frequent flyer number.

Starting in 2005, the International Air Transport Association (IATA) decided to use bar-coded boarding passes for the simple reason that magnetic boarding passes were much more expensive to maintain. The savings have been estimated at $1.5 billion. Furthermore, using bar codes on airline tickets allows passengers to download their tickets from the Internet and print them at home, or they can use a mobile phone at the gate instead.

Needless to say, this change in procedure required some sort of standard. According to researcher Shaun Ewing, the typical boarding-pass bar code contains information that is mostly harmless—name of passenger, name of airline, seat number, departure airport, arrival airport, and flight number.[20] However, the most sensitive part of the bar code is your frequent flyer number.[21] All airline websites now protect their customer accounts with personal passwords. Giving out your frequent flyer number is not like giving out your Social Security number, but it still is a privacy concern.

A bigger privacy concern is the loyalty cards offered at supermarkets, pharmacies, gas stations, and other businesses. Unlike airline tickets, which have to be in your legal name, loyalty cards can be registered under a fake name, address, and phone number (a fake number you can remember), so your purchasing habits cannot be linked back to you.

When you check into your hotel and boot up your computer, you might see a list of available Wi-Fi networks, such as "Hotel Guest," "tmobile123," "Kimberley's iPhone," "attwifi," "Steve's Android," and "Chuck's Hotspot." Which one should you connect to? I hope you know the answer by now!

Most hotel Wi-Fi doesn't use encryption but does require the guest's last name and room number as authentication. There are tricks to get around paywalls, of course.

One trick for getting free Internet at any hotel is to call any other room—perhaps the one across the hall—posing as room service. If the hotel uses caller ID, just use the house phone in the lobby. Tell the party answering the phone that her two burgers are on the way. When the guest says she didn't place an order, you politely ask for her surname to fix the error. Now you have both the room number (you called it) and the surname, which is all that's needed to authenticate you (a nonpaying guest) as a legitimate guest at that hotel.

Let's say you are staying at a five-star hotel with Internet access, free or otherwise. As you log on, perhaps you see a message informing you that Adobe (or some other software maker) has an update available. Being a good citizen of the Internet, you might be tempted to download the update and move on. Except the hotel network should still be considered hostile—even if it has a password. It's not your home network—so the update might not be real, and if you go ahead and download it you may inadvertently install malicious code on your PC.

If you are on the road a lot, as I am, whether to update or not is a tough call. There is little you can do except verify that there is an update available. The problem is, if you use the hotel's Internet to download that update, you might be directed to a spoofed website providing the malicious "update." If you can, use your mobile device to confirm the existence of the update from the vendor's site and, if it's not critical, wait until you're back in a safe environment, such as a corporate office or back home, to download it.[22]

Researchers at Kaspersky Lab, a software security company, discovered a group of criminal hackers they call DarkHotel (also known as Tapaoux) who use this technique. They operate by identifying business executives who might be staying at a particular luxury hotel, then anticipate their arrival by placing malware on the hotel server. When the executives check in and connect to the hotel Wi-Fi, the malware is downloaded and executed on their devices. After the infection is complete, the malware is removed from the hotel server.

Apparently this has been going on for almost a decade, the researchers noted.

Although it primarily affects executives staying at luxury hotels in Asia, it could be common elsewhere. The DarkHotel group in general uses a low-level spear-phishing attack for mass targets and reserves the hotel attacks for high-profile, singular targets—such as executives in the nuclear power and defense industries.

One early analysis suggested that DarkHotel was South Korea–based. A keylogger—malware used to record the keystrokes of compromised systems—used in the attacks contains Korean characters within the code. And the zero-days—vulnerabilities in software that are unknown to the vendor—were very advanced flaws that were previously unknown. Moreover, a South Korean name identified within the keylogger has been traced to other sophisticated keyloggers used by Koreans in the past.

It should be noted, however, that this is not enough to confirm attribution. Software can be cut and pasted from a variety of sources. Also, software can be made to look as though it is created in one country when it is actually created in another.

To get the malware on the laptops, DarkHotel uses forged certificates that appear as though they are issued from the Malaysian government and Deutsche Telekom. Certificates, if you remember from chapter 5, are used to verify the origin of the software or the Web server. To further hide their work, the hackers arranged it so that the malware stays dormant for up to six months before becoming active. This is to throw off IT departments that might link a visit with an infection.

Kaspersky only learned of this attack when a group of its customers became infected after staying at certain luxury hotels in Asia. The researchers turned to a third-party Wi-Fi host common to both, and the Wi-Fi host partnered with the antivirus company to find out what was happening on its networks. Although the files used to infect the guests were long gone, file deletion records were left behind that corresponded to the dates of the guests' stays.

The easiest way to protect yourself against this kind of attack is to connect to a VPN service as soon as you connect to the Internet at the hotel. The one I use is cheap—only six dollars per month. However, that's not a good choice if you want to be invisible, since it won't allow anonymous setup.

If you want to be invisible, don't trust the VPN provider with your real information. This requires setting up a fake e-mail address in advance (see page 37) and using an open wireless network. Once you have that fake e-mail address, use Tor to set up a Bitcoin wallet, find a Bitcoin ATM to fund the wallet, and then use a tumbler to essentially launder the Bitcoin so it cannot be traced back to you on the blockchain. This laundering process requires setting up two Bitcoin wallets using different Tor circuits. The first wallet is used to send the Bitcoin to the laundering service, and the second is set up to receive the laundered Bitcoin.

Once you have achieved true anonymity by using open Wi-Fi out of camera view plus Tor, find a VPN service that accepts Bitcoin for payment. Pay with the laundered Bitcoin. Some VPN providers, including WiTopia, block Tor, so you need to find one that doesn't—preferably with a VPN provider that doesn't log connections.

In this case, we are not "trusting" the VPN provider with our real IP address or name. However, when using the newly set-up VPN, you must be careful not to use any of the services connected to your real name and not to connect to the VPN from an IP address that can be tied back to you. You might consider tethering to an anonymously acquired burner phone, see page 48.

It's best to purchase a portable hotspot—purchased in such a way that it would be very difficult to identify you. For example, you can hire someone to purchase it for you so your face does not appear on a surveillance camera in a store. When you're using the anonymous hotspot, you should turn off any of your personal devices that use cellular signals to prevent the pattern of your personal devices registering in the same place as the anonymous device.

To summarize, here's what you need to do to use the Internet privately while traveling:

1. Purchase prepaid gift cards anonymously (see page 98). In the EU, you can purchase prepaid credit cards anonymously at viabuy.com.
2. Use open Wi-Fi after changing your MAC address (see page 117).
3. Find an e-mail provider that allows you to sign up without SMS validation. Or you can sign up for a Skype-in number using Tor and a prepaid gift card. With Skype-in, you can receive voice calls to verify your identity. Make sure you are out of camera view (i.e., not in a Starbucks or anywhere else with camera surveillance). Use Tor to mask your location when you sign up for this e-mail service.
4. Using your new anonymous e-mail address, sign up at a site such as paxful.com, again using Tor, to sign up for a Bitcoin wallet and buy a supply of Bitcoin. Pay for them using the prepaid gift cards.
5. Set up a second anonymous e-mail address and new secondary Bitcoin wallet after closing and establishing a new Tor circuit to prevent any association with the first e-mail account and wallet.
6. Use a Bitcoin laundering service such as bitlaunder.com to make it hard to trace the currency's origin. Have the laundered Bitcoin sent to the second Bitcoin address.[23]
7. Sign up for a VPN service using the laundered Bitcoin that does not log traffic or IP connections. You can usually find

out what is logged by reviewing the VPN provider's privacy policy (e.g., TorGuard).

8. Have a cutout obtain a burner portable hotspot device on your behalf. Give the cutout cash to purchase it.
9. To access the Internet, use the burner hotspot device away from home, work, and your other cellular devices.
10. Once powered up, connect to VPN through the burner hotspot device.
11. Use Tor to browse the Internet.

CHAPTER FIFTEEN

The FBI Always Gets Its Man

In the science fiction section of the Glen Park branch of the San Francisco Public Library, not far from his apartment, Ross William Ulbricht was engaged in an online customer-support chat for the company he owned. At the time—October of 2013—the person on the other end of the Internet chat thought he was talking to the site's admin, who went by the Internet name of Dread Pirate Roberts, a name taken from the movie *The Princess Bride*. Roberts, also known as DPR, was in fact Ross Ulbricht—not only the admin but also the owner of Silk Road, an online drug emporium, and as such was the subject of a federal manhunt.[1] Ulbricht frequently used public Wi-Fi locations such as the library for his work, perhaps under the mistaken impression that the FBI, should it ever identify him as DPR, would never conduct a raid in a public place. On that day, however, the person with whom Ulbricht was chatting happened to be an undercover FBI agent.

Running an online drug emporium, in which customers could order cocaine and heroin and a wide range of designer drugs anonymously, required a certain moxie. The site was hosted on the Dark Web (see page 47) and was only accessible through Tor. The site only took Bitcoin as payment. And the creator of Silk Road had been careful, but not careful enough.

A few months before Ulbricht sat in the San Francisco Public Library with the FBI circling him, an unlikely hero connected with the federal manhunt came forward with evidence tying Ulbricht to DPR. The hero, an IRS agent named Gary Alford, had been reading up on Silk Road and its origins, and in the evenings he had been running advanced Google searches to see what he could find. One of the earliest mentions of Silk Road he found was from 2011. Someone who went by the name "altoid" had been talking it up in a chat group. Since Silk Road had not yet launched, Alford figured that altoid most likely had inside knowledge of the operation. Naturally Alford started a search for other references.

He struck gold.

Apparently altoid had posted a question to another chat group—but had deleted the original message. Alford pulled up a response to the now deleted query that contained the original message. In that message, altoid said that if anyone could answer his question, that person could contact him at rossulbricht@gmail.com.[2]

It was not the last time that slipup would be made. There were other posted questions, one to a site called Stack Overflow: the original question had been sent in from rossulbricht@gmail.com, but then, remarkably, the sender's name had been changed to DPR.

Rule number 1 about being invisible: you can't ever link your anonymous online persona with your real-world persona. You just can't.

There were other linkages established after that. Ulbricht, like DPR, espoused Ron Paul–free market–libertarian philosophies. And at one point Ulbricht had even ordered a set of false IDs—driver's licenses in different names from various states—which drew federal authorities to his doorstep in San Francisco in July of 2013, but at that time the authorities had no idea they were talking with DPR.

Slowly the evidence grew so compelling that one morning in October of 2013, as soon as DPR's customer-support chat began, federal agents began quietly entering the Glen Park library. Then, in a surgical strike, they seized Ulbricht before he could shut down his laptop. Had he shut it down, certain key evidence would have been destroyed. As it was, they were able to photograph the system administration screens for a site called Silk Road moments after the arrest and thereby establish a concrete link between Ulbricht, Dread Pirate Roberts, and Silk Road, thus ending any future hope of anonymity.

On that October morning in Glen Park, Ulbricht was logged in to Silk Road as an administrator. And the FBI knew that because they had been observing his machine logging on to the Internet. But what if he could have faked his location? What if he wasn't in the library at all but using a proxy server instead?

In the summer of 2015, researcher Ben Caudill of Rhino Security announced that not only would he be speaking at DEF CON 23 about his new device, ProxyHam, he would also be selling it at cost—around $200—in the DEF CON vendors' room. Then, approximately one week later, Caudill announced that his talk was canceled and that all existing ProxyHam units would be destroyed. He offered no further explanation.[3]

Talks at major security conferences get pulled for various reasons. Either the companies whose products are being discussed or the federal government puts pressure on researchers to not go public. In this case, Caudill wasn't pointing out a particular flaw; he had built something new.

Funny thing about the Internet: once an idea is out there, it tends to remain out there. So even if the feds or someone else convinced Caudill that his talk was not in the interests of national security, it seemed likely that someone else would create a new device. And that's exactly what happened.

ProxyHam is a very remote access point. Using it is much like putting a Wi-Fi transmitter in your home or office. Except that the person using and controlling ProxyHam could be up to a mile away. The Wi-Fi transmitter uses a 900 MHz radio to connect to an antenna dongle on a computer as far as 2.5 miles away. So in the case of Ross Ulbricht, the FBI could have been amassing outside the Glen Park library while he was in someone's basement doing laundry several blocks away.

The need for such devices is clear if you live in an oppressed country. Contacting the outside world through Tor is a risk many take. This kind of device would add another layer of security by masking the geolocation of the requester.

Except someone didn't want Caudill to speak about it at DEF CON.

In interviews Caudill denied that the Federal Communications Commission had discouraged him. *Wired* speculated that secretly planting a ProxyHam on someone else's network might be interpreted as unauthorized access under America's draconian and vague Computer Fraud and Abuse Act. Caudill refuses to comment on any of the speculation.

As I said, once an idea is out there, anyone can run with it. So security researcher Samy Kamkar created ProxyGambit, a device that essentially replaces ProxyHam.[4] Except it uses reverse cellular traffic, meaning that instead of your being only a few miles from the device when you use it, you could be halfway across the world. Cool!

ProxyGambit and devices like it will of course create headaches for law enforcement when criminals decide to use them.

Ulbricht's Silk Road was an online drug emporium. It was not something you could search for on Google; it was not on what's called the Surface Web, which can easily be indexed and searched. The Surface Web, containing familiar sites like Amazon and YouTube, represents only 5 percent of the entire Internet. All the websites most of you have been to or know about make up a trivial number compared to the actual number of sites out there. The vast majority of Internet sites are actually hidden from most search engines.

After the Surface Web, the next biggest chunk of the Internet is what's called the Deep Web. This is the part of the Web that is hidden behind password access—for example, the contents of the card catalog for the Glen Park branch of the San Francisco Public Library. The Deep Web also includes most subscription-only sites and corporate intranet sites. Netflix. Pandora. You get the idea.

Finally, there is a much smaller piece of the Internet known as the Dark Web. This part of the Internet is not accessible through an ordinary browser, nor is it searchable on sites such as Google, Bing, and Yahoo.

The Dark Web is where Silk Road lived, alongside sites where you can hire an assassin and acquire child pornography. Sites like these live on the Dark Web because it is virtually anonymous. I say "virtually" because nothing truly ever is.

Access to the Dark Web can be gained only through a Tor browser. In fact Dark Web sites, with complicated alphanumeric URLs, all end with .onion. As I mentioned earlier, the onion router was created by the US Naval Research Laboratory to give oppressed people a way to contact each other as well as the outside world. I've also explained that Tor does not connect your browser directly to a site; rather, it establishes a link to another server, which then attaches to *another* server to finally reach the destination site. The multiple hops make it harder to trace. And sites such as Silk Road are the products of hidden services within the Tor network. Their URLs are generated from an algorithm, and lists of Dark Web sites change frequently. Tor can access both the Surface Web and the Dark Web. Another Dark Web browser, I2P, can also access the Surface Web and Dark Web.

Even before the takedown of Silk Road, people speculated that the NSA or others had a way to identify users on the Dark Web. One way for the NSA to do that would be to plant and control what are called exit nodes, the points at which an Internet request is passed to one of these hidden services, though that still wouldn't allow identification of the initial requester.

To do that the government observer would have to see that a request was made to access site X and that a few seconds earlier, someone in New Hampshire fired up the Tor browser. The observer might suspect that the two events were related. Over time, access to the site and repeated access to Tor around the same time could establish a pattern. One way to avoid creating that pattern is to keep your Tor browser connected at all times.

In Ulbricht's case—he got sloppy. Ulbricht apparently didn't have a plan early on. In his initial discussions of Silk Road, he alternated between using his real e-mail address and a pseudonymous one.

As you can see, it is very hard to operate in the world today without leaving traces of your true identity somewhere on the Internet. But as I said at the outset, with a little bit of care, you, too, can master the art of invisibility. In the following pages, I will show you how.

CHAPTER SIXTEEN

Mastering the Art of Invisibility

After reading this far, you might be thinking about your level of experience and how easy (or hard) it will be for you to disappear online. Or you might be asking yourself how far you should go or whether any of this is for you. After all, you may not have state secrets to share! You might, however, be fighting your ex in a legal dispute. Or you might be in a disagreement with your boss. You might be contacting a friend who is still in touch with an abusive family member. Or you might want to keep some activities private and unobservable by a lawyer. There are a variety of legitimate reasons why you might need to communicate with others online or to use the Web and other technology anonymously. So...

What steps do you really need to take to go all-in? How long will it take? And how much will it cost?

If it's not abundantly clear by now, to be invisible online you more or less need to create a separate identity, one that is completely unrelated to you. That is the meaning of being anonymous. When you're not being anonymous, you must also rigorously defend the separation of your life from that anonymous identity. What I mean by that is that you need to purchase a few separate devices that are only used when you are anonymous. And this could get costly.

You could, for example, use your current laptop and create what's called a virtual machine (VM) on your desktop. A virtual machine is a software computer. It is contained within a virtual machine application, such a VMware Fusion. You can load a licensed copy of Windows 10 inside a VM and tell it how much RAM you want, how much disk space you need, and so on. To someone observing you on the other side of the Internet, it would appear that you are using a Windows 10 machine even if in fact you are using a Mac.

Professional security researchers use VMs all the time—creating and destroying them easily. But even among professionals there exists the possibility of leakage. For example, you might be in your VM version of Windows 10 and, for some reason, log in to your personal e-mail account. Now that VM can be associated with you.

So the first step of being anonymous is purchasing a stand-alone laptop that you will only use for your anonymous online activities. As we have seen, the nanosecond that you lapse and, say, check your personal e-mail account on that machine, the anonymity game is over. So I recommend a low-priced Windows laptop (Linux is better, if you know how to use it). The reason I'm not recommending a MacBook Pro is that it's much more expensive than a Windows laptop.

Previously I recommended that you buy a second laptop, specifically, a Chromebook, to use only for online banking. Another option for online banking would be to use an iPad. You must sign up for an Apple ID using your e-mail address and a credit card, or by purchasing an iTunes gift card. But since this device is only used for your secure personal banking, invisibility is not the goal.

But if your objective here is invisibility, a Chromebook is not the best solution because you don't have the same flexibility as using a laptop with Windows or a Linux-based operating system like Ubuntu. Windows 10 is okay as long as you skip the option that asks you to sign up for a Microsoft account. You do not want to create any links from your computer to Microsoft whatsoever.

You should purchase the new laptop with cash in person, not online—that way the purchase cannot easily be traced to you. Remember, your new laptop has a wireless network card with a unique MAC address. You do not want anyone possibly tracing the equipment to you—in the event your real MAC address is somehow leaked. For example, if you're at a Starbucks and power up the laptop, the system will probe for any previously "connected to" wireless networks. If there is monitoring equipment in the area that logs the probe request, it could possibly result in revealing your real MAC address. One concern is that the government may have a way of tracing the purchase of your laptop if any link exists between the MAC address of your network card and the serial number of your computer. If so, the feds would only need to find who purchased the specific computer to identify you, which probably isn't so difficult.

You should install both Tails (see page 243) and Tor (see page 46) and use those instead of the native operating system and browser.

Do not log in to any sites or applications under your real identity. You already learned the risks based on how easy it is to track people and computers on the Internet. As we have discussed, using sites or accounts under your real identify is a very bad idea—banks and other sites routinely use device fingerprinting to minimize fraud, and this leaves a huge footprint that can identify your computer if you ever access the same sites anonymously.

In fact, it's best to turn your wireless router off before you boot your anonymous laptop at home. Your service provider could obtain your anonymous laptop's MAC address if you connect to your home router (assuming the provider owns and manages the router in your home). It's always best to purchase your own home router that you have full control over, so the service provider cannot obtain the MAC addresses assigned to your computers on your local network. As such, the service provider will only see the MAC address of your router, which is no risk to you.

What you want is plausible deniability. You want to proxy your connections through multiple layers so that it would very, very hard for an investigator to ever tie them back to a single person, let alone you. I made a mistake while still a fugitive. I repeatedly dialed up to modems at Netcom—a ghost of Internet service providers past—using a cellular phone modem to mask my physical location. Since I was at a fixed location it was child's play to use radio direction-finding techniques to find me—once they knew what cellular tower my mobile phone was using for data connections. This allowed my adversary (Tsutomu Shimomura) to find the general location and pass it along to the FBI.[1]

What this means is that you can't ever use your anonymous laptop at home or work. Ever. So get a laptop and commit to never using it to check your personal e-mail, Facebook, or even the local weather.[2]

Another way you can be traced online is through the tried-and-true method of following the money. You will need to pay for a few things, so prior to taking your anonymous laptop out and finding an open wireless network, the first step is to anonymously purchase some gift cards. Since every store that sells gift cards most likely has surveillance cameras at the kiosk or counter, you must exercise extreme caution. You should not purchase these yourself. You should hire a randomly chosen person off the street to purchase the gift cards while you wait a safe distance away.

But how do you do that? You might approach, as I did, someone in a parking lot and say that your ex works in that store over there and you don't want a confrontation—or offer some other excuse that sounds plausible. Perhaps you add that she has a restraining order against you. For $100 in cash, making a purchase for you might sound very reasonable to someone.

Now that we've set up our cutout to go inside the store and purchase a handful of prepaid cards, which cards should he or she purchase? I recommend purchasing a few prepaid, preset $100 cards. Don't purchase any of the refillable credit cards, as you have to provide your real identity under the Patriot Act when you activate them. These purchases require your real name, address, birth date, and a Social Security number that will match the information about you on file with the credit bureaus. Providing a made-up name or someone else's Social Security number is against the law and is probably not worth the risk.

We're trying to be invisible online, not break the law.

I recommend having the cutout purchase Vanilla Visa or Vanilla MasterCard $100 gift cards from a chain pharmacy, 7-Eleven, Walmart, or big box store. These are often given out as gifts and can be used just as regular credit cards would be. For these you do not have to provide any identifying information. And you can purchase them anonymously, with cash. If you live in the EU, you should anonymously order a physical credit card using viabuy.com. In Europe they can ship the cards to the post office, which requires no ID to pick up. My understanding is that they send you a PIN code, and you can open up the drop box with the PIN to anonymously pick up the cards (assuming there is no camera).

So where can you use your new laptop and anonymously purchased prepaid cards?

With the advent of inexpensive optical storage devices, businesses providing free wireless access can store surveillance camera footage for years. For an investigator it is relatively easy to get that footage and look for potential suspects. During the time of your visit, the investigator can analyze the logs—searching for MAC addresses authenticated on the wireless network that match your MAC address. That's why it's important to change your MAC address each time you connect to a free wireless network. So you need to find a location near or adjacent to one that offers free Wi-Fi. For example, there may be a Chinese restaurant next door to a Starbucks or other establishment that offers free wireless access. Sit at a table near the wall adjoining the service provider. You might experience slightly slower connection speeds, but you will have relative anonymity (at least until the investigator starts looking at all the surveillance footage from the surrounding area).

Your MAC address will likely be logged and stored once you authenticate on the free wireless network. Remember General David Petraeus's mistress? Remember that the times and dates of her hotel registrations matched the times and dates of her MAC address's appearance on the hotel's network? You don't want simple mistakes like these to compromise your anonymity. So remember to change your MAC address each time you access public Wi-Fi (see page 117).

So far this seems pretty straightforward. You want to buy a separate laptop from which you will do your anonymous activity. You want to anonymously purchase some gift cards. You want to find a Wi-Fi network that you can access from a near or adjacent site to avoid being seen on camera. And you want to change your MAC address every time you connect to a free wireless network.

Of course there's more. Much more. We're only getting started.

You might also want to hire a second cutout, this time to make a more important purchase: a personal hotspot. As I mentioned before, the FBI caught me because I was dialing up to systems around the world using my cellular phone and modem, and over time my fixed location was compromised because my mobile phone was connected to the same cellular tower. At that point it was easy to use radio-direction finding to locate the transceiver (my cell phone). You can avoid that by hiring someone to go into a Verizon store (or AT&T or T-Mobile) and purchase a personal hotspot that allows you to connect to the Internet using cellular data. That means you have your own local access to the Internet, so you don't have to go through a public Wi-Fi network. Most important, you should never use a personal hotspot in a fixed location for too long when you need to maintain your anonymity.

Ideally the person you hire won't see your license plate or have any way to identify you. Give the person cash: $200 for the hotspot and another $100 when the person returns with the hotspot. The mobile operator will sell the cutout a personal hotspot that carries no identifying information. And while you're at it, why not purchase a few refill cards to add more data? Hopefully the cutout won't abscond with your money, but it's a worthwhile risk for anonymity. Later you can refill the burner device using Bitcoin.[3]

Once you have anonymously purchased a portable hotspot, it is very important that, as with the laptop, you never, never, *never* turn the device on at home. Every time the hotspot is turned on, it registers with the closest cellular tower. You don't want your home or office or anyplace you frequent to show up in the mobile operator's log files.

And never turn on your personal phone or personal laptop in the same location where you turn on your anonymous laptop or burner phone or anonymous hotspot. The separation is really important. Any record that links you to your anonymous self at a later date and time negates the whole operation.

Now, armed with prepaid gift cards and a personal hotspot with a prepaid data plan—both purchased anonymously by two very different people who wouldn't have any information about you to identify you to the police—we're almost set. Almost.

From this point on, the Tor browser should always be used to create and access all online accounts because it constantly changes your IP address.

One of the first steps is to set up a couple of anonymous e-mail accounts using Tor. This was something that Ross Ulbricht neglected to do. As we saw in the previous chapter, he used his personal e-mail account more than once while conducting his Silk Road business on the Dark Web. These unintentional crossovers from Dread Pirate Roberts to Ross Ulbricht and back again helped investigators confirm that the two names were associated with one person.

To prevent abuse, most e-mail providers—such as Gmail, Hotmail, Outlook, and Yahoo—require mobile phone verification. That means you have to provide your mobile number and, immediately during the sign-up process, a text message is sent to that device to confirm your identity.

You can still use a commercial service like the ones mentioned above if you use a burner phone. However, that burner phone and any refill cards must be obtained securely—i.e., purchased in cash by a third party who cannot be traced back to you. Also, once you have a burner phone, you cannot use it when you're close to any other cellular devices you own. Again, leave your personal phone at home.

In order to purchase Bitcoin online, you are going to need at least two anonymously created e-mail addresses and Bitcoin wallets. So how do you create anonymous e-mail addresses like those created by Edward Snowden and Laura Poitras?

In my research, I found I was able to create an e-mail account on protonmail.com and one on tutanota.com using Tor, both without any requests to verify my identity. Neither of these two e-mail providers asked me for verification upon setup. You can conduct your own research by searching for e-mail providers and checking to see whether they require your mobile phone number during the sign-up process. You can also see how much information they need to create the new accounts. Another e-mail option is fastmail.com, which is not nearly as feature rich as Gmail, but because it is a paid service, there is no mining of user data or displaying of ads.

So now we have a laptop, with Tor and Tails loaded, a burner phone, a handful of anonymous prepaid gift cards, and an anonymous hotspot with an anonymously purchased data plan. We're still not ready. To maintain this anonymity, we need to convert our anonymously purchased prepaid gift cards to Bitcoin.

In chapter 6 I talked about Bitcoin, virtual currency. By itself Bitcoin is not anonymous. They can be traced through what's called a blockchain back to the source of the purchase; similarly, all subsequent purchases can be traced as well. So Bitcoin by itself is not going to hide your identity. We will have to run the funds through an anonymity mechanism: converting prepaid gift cards into Bitcoin, then running the Bitcoin through a laundering service. This process will result in anonymized Bitcoin to be used for future payments. We will need the laundered Bitcoin, for example, to pay for our VPN service and any future purchases of data usage on our portable hotspot or burner phone.

Using Tor, you can set up an initial Bitcoin wallet at paxful.com or other Bitcoin wallet sites. Some sites broker deals in which you can buy Bitcoin with prepaid gift cards, such as those preset Vanilla Visa and Vanilla MasterCard gift cards I mentioned earlier. The downside is that you will pay a huge premium for this service, at least 50 percent. Paxful.com is more like an eBay auction site where you find Bitcoin sellers—the site just connects you with buyers and sellers.

Apparently anonymity has a high cost. The less identity information you provide in a transaction, the more you'll pay. That makes sense: the people selling the Bitcoin are taking a huge risk by not verifying your identity. I was able to purchase Bitcoin in exchange for my anonymously purchased Vanilla Visa gift cards at a rate of $1.70 per dollar, which is outrageous but necessary to ensure anonymity.

I mentioned that Bitcoin by itself is not anonymous. For example, there is a record that I exchanged certain prepaid gift cards for Bitcoin. An investigator could trace my Bitcoin back to the gift cards.

But there are ways to launder Bitcoin, obscuring any link back to me.

Money laundering is something that criminals do all the time. It is most often used in drug trafficking, but it also plays a role in white-collar financial crime. Laundering means that you disguise the original ownership of the funds, often by sending the money out of the country, to multiple banks in countries that have strict privacy laws. Turns out you can do something similar with virtual currency.

There are services called tumblers that will take Bitcoin from a variety of sources and mix—or tumble—them together so that the resulting Bitcoin retains its value but carries traces of many owners. This makes it hard for someone to say later which owner made a certain purchase. But you have to be extremely careful, because there are tons of scams out there.

I took a chance. I found a laundering service online and they took an extra fee out of the transaction. I actually got the Bitcoin value that I wanted. But think about this: that laundering service now has one of my anonymous e-mail addresses and both Bitcoin addresses that were used in the transaction. So to further mix things up, I had the Bitcoin delivered to a second Bitcoin wallet that was set up by opening a new Tor circuit, which established new hops between me and the site I wanted to visit. Now the transaction is thoroughly obfuscated, making it very hard for someone to come along later and figure out that the two Bitcoin addresses are owned by the same person. Of course, the Bitcoin laundering service could cooperate with third parties by providing both Bitcoin addresses. That's why it's so important to securely purchase the prepaid gift cards.

After using the gift cards to purchase Bitcoin, remember to securely dispose of the plastic cards (not in your trash at home). I recommend using a cross-cut shredder that's rated for plastic cards, then disposing of the shreds in a random dumpster away from your home or office.

Once the laundered Bitcoin has been received, you can sign up for a VPN service that makes your privacy a priority. The best policy when you are trying to be anonymous is simply not to trust any VPN provider, especially those that claim not to retain any logs. Chances are they'll still cough up your details if contacted by law enforcement or the NSA.

For example, I cannot imagine any VPN provider not being able to troubleshoot issues within its own network. And troubleshooting requires keeping some logs—e.g., connection logs that could be used to match customers to their originating IP addresses.

So because even the best of these providers cannot be trusted, we will purchase a VPN service using laundered Bitcoin through the Tor browser. I suggest reviewing a VPN provider's terms of service and privacy policies and find the one that seems the best of the bunch. You're not going to find a perfect match, only a good one. Remember that you cannot trust any provider to maintain your anonymity. You have to do it yourself with the understanding that a single error can reveal your true identity.

Now, with a stand-alone laptop, running either Tor or Tails, using a VPN provider purchased with laundered Bitcoin, over an anonymously purchased hotspot, and with a supply of even more laundered Bitcoin, you have completed the easy part: the setup. This will cost you a couple of hundred bucks, perhaps five hundred, but all the pieces have been randomized so that they can't easily be connected back to you. Now comes the hard part—maintaining that anonymity.

All the setup and processes we've just gone through can be lost in a second if you use the anonymous hotspot at home, or if you power on your personal cell phone, tablet, or any other cellular device linked to your real identity at the physical location where you are using your anonymous identity. It only takes one slip by you for a forensic investigator to be able to correlate your presence to a location by analyzing the cellular provider's logs. If there is a pattern of anonymous access at the same time your cellular device is registered in the same cell site, it could lead to unmasking your true identity.

I've already given a number of examples of this.

Now, should your anonymity be compromised and should you decide to engage in another anonymous activity, you might need to go through this process once again—wiping and reinstalling the operating system on your anonymous laptop and creating another set of anonymous e-mail accounts with Bitcoin wallets and purchasing another anonymous hotspot. Remember that Edward Snowden and Laura Poitras, both of whom already had anonymous e-mail accounts, set up additional anonymous e-mail accounts so they could communicate specifically with each other. This is only necessary if you suspect that the original anonymity you've established is compromised. Otherwise you could use the Tor browser (after establishing a new Tor circuit) through the anonymous hotspot and VPN to access the Internet using a different persona.

Of course, how much or how little you choose to follow these recommendations is up to you.

Even if you follow my recommendations, it is still possible for someone on the other end to recognize you. How? By the way you type.

There is a considerable body of research that has focused on the specific word choices people make when writing e-mails and commenting on social media posts. By looking at those words, researchers can often identify sex and ethnicity. But beyond that they cannot be more specific.

Or can they?

In World War II the British government set up a number of listening stations around the country to intercept signals from the German military. The advances that led to the Allies decrypting these messages came a bit later—at Bletchley Park, the site of the Government

Code and Cypher School, where the German Enigma code was broken. Early on, the people at Bletchley Park intercepting the German telegraph messages could identify certain unique characteristics of a sender based on the intervals between the dots and the dashes. For example, they could recognize when a new telegraph operator came on, and they even started giving the operators names.

How could mere dots and dashes reveal the people behind them?

Well, the time interval between the sender's tapping of a key and the tapping of the key again can be measured. This method of differentiation later became known as the Fist of the Sender. Various Morse code key operators could be identified by their unique "fists." It wasn't what the telegraph was designed to do (who cares who sent the message; what *was* the message?), but in this case the unique tapping was an interesting by-product.

Today, with advances in digital technology, electronic devices can measure the nanosecond differences in the way each person presses keys on computer keyboards—not only the length of time a given key is held but also how quickly the next key follows. It can tell the difference between someone who types normally and someone who hunts and pecks at the keyboard. That, coupled with the words chosen, can reveal a lot about an anonymous communication.

This is a problem if you've gone through the trouble of anonymizing your IP address. The site on the other side can still recognize you—not because of something technical but because of something uniquely human. This is also known as behavioral analysis.

Let's say a Tor-anonymized website decides to track your keystroke profile. Maybe the people behind it are malicious and just want to know more about you. Or maybe they work with law enforcement.

Many financial institutions already use keystroke analysis to further authenticate account holders. That way if someone does have your username and password, he or she can't really fake the cadence of your typing. That's reassuring when you want to be authenticated online. But what if you don't?

Because keystroke analysis is so disturbingly easy to deploy, researchers Per Thorsheim and Paul Moore created a Chrome browser plug-in called Keyboard Privacy. The plug-in caches your individual keystrokes and then plays them out at different intervals. The idea is to introduce randomness in your normal keystroke cadence as a means of achieving anonymity online. The plug-in might further mask your anonymous Internet activities.[4]

As we have seen, maintaining the separation between your real life and your anonymous life online is possible, but it requires constant vigilance. In the previous chapter I talked about some spectacular failures at being invisible. These were glorious but short-term attempts at invisibility.

In the case of Ross Ulbricht, he didn't really plan his alter ego very carefully, occasionally using his real e-mail address instead of an anonymous one, particularly in the beginning. Through the use of a Google advanced search, an investigator was able to piece together enough information to reveal the mysterious owner of Silk Road.

So what about Edward Snowden and others like him who are concerned about their surveillance by one or more government agencies? Snowden, for example, has a Twitter account. As do quite a few other privacy folks—how else might I engage them in a round of feisty conversation online? There are a couple of possibilities to explain how these people remain "invisible."

They're not under active surveillance. Perhaps a government or government agency knows exactly where its targets are but doesn't care. In that case, if the targets aren't breaking any laws, who's to say they haven't let their guard down at some point? They might claim to only use Tor for their anonymous e-mails, but then again they might be using that account for their Netflix purchases as well.

They're under surveillance, but they can't be arrested. I think that might very well describe Snowden. It is possible he has slipped regarding his anonymity at some point and that he is now being actively tracked wherever he goes—except he's living in Russia. Russia has no real reason to arrest him and return him to the United States.

You'll notice I said "slipped": unless you have amazing attention to detail, it's really hard to live two lives. I know. I've done it. I let my guard down by using a fixed location when accessing computers through a cellular phone network.

There's a truism in the security business that a persistent attacker will succeed given enough time and resources. I succeed all the time when testing my client's security controls. All you are really doing by trying to make yourself anonymous is putting up so many obstacles that an attacker will give up and move on to another target.

Most of us only have to hide for a little while. To avoid that boss who is out to get you fired. To avoid that ex whose lawyers are looking for something, anything, to hold against you. To evade that creepy stalker who saw your picture on Facebook and is determined to harass you. Whatever your reason for being invisible, the steps I've outlined will work long enough to get you out from under a bad situation.

Being anonymous in today's digital world requires a lot of work and constant vigilance. Each person's requirements for anonymity differ—do you need to protect your passwords and keep private documents away from your coworkers? Do you need to hide from a fan who is stalking you? Do you need to evade law enforcement because you're a whistleblower?

Your individual requirements will dictate the necessary steps you need to take to maintain your desired level of anonymity—from setting strong passwords and realizing that your office printer is out to get you all the way to going through the steps detailed here to make it extremely difficult for a forensic investigator to discover your true identity.

In general, though, we can all learn something about how to minimize our fingerprints in the digital world. We can think before posting that photo with a home address visible in the background. Or before providing a real birth date and other personal information on our social media profiles. Or before browsing the Internet without using the HTTPS Everywhere extension. Or before making confidential calls or sending texts without using an end-to-end encryption tool such as Signal. Or before messaging a doctor through AOL, MSN Messenger, or Google Talk without OTR. Or before sending a confidential e-mail without using PGP or GPG.

We can think proactively about our information and realize that even if what we're doing with it *feels* benign—sharing a photograph, forgetting to change default log-ins and passwords, using a work phone for a personal message, or setting up a Facebook account for our kids—we're actually making decisions that carry a lifetime of ramifications. So we need to act.

This book is all about staying online while retaining our precious privacy. Everyone—from the most technologically challenged to professional security experts—should make a committed practice of mastering this art, which becomes more essential with each passing day: the art of invisibility.

Acknowledgments

This book is dedicated to my loving mother, Shelly Jaffe, and my grandmother Reba Vartanian, who both sacrificed a great deal for me all my life. No matter what situation I got myself into, my mom and Gram were always there for me, especially in my times of need. This book would not have been possible without my wonderful family, who has given me so much unconditional love and support throughout my life.

On April 15, 2013, my mother passed away after a long struggle with lung cancer. It came after years of hardship and struggling to deal with the effects of chemotherapy. There were few good days after the terrible treatments used in modern medicine to fight off these types of cancers. Usually patients have a very short time—typically it is only months before they succumb to the disease. I feel very fortunate for the time I was able to spend with her while she was fighting this horrible battle. I am so grateful to have been raised by such a loving and dedicated mother, whom I also consider my best friend. My mom is such an amazing person and I miss her incredibly so.

On March 7, 2012, my grandmother passed away unexpectedly while being treated at Sunrise Hospital in Las Vegas. Our family was expecting her to return home, but it never happened. For the past several years leading up to my grandmother passing away, her heart was in constant sadness because of my mother's battle with cancer. She is missed terribly and I wish she were here to enjoy this accomplishment.

I hope this book will bring much happiness to my mother's and grandmother's hearts and make them proud that I'm helping to protect people's right to privacy.

I wish my dad, Alan Mitnick, and my brother, Adam Mitnick, were here to celebrate the publication of this important book on becoming invisible when spying and surveillance is now the norm.

I have had the good fortune of being teamed up with security and privacy expert Robert Vamosi to write this book. Rob's notable knowledge in security and skills as a writer include his ability to find compelling stories, research these topics, and take information provided by me and write it up in such a style and manner that any nontechnical person could understand it. I must tip my hat to Rob, who did a tremendous amount of hard work on this project. Truthfully, I couldn't have done it without him.

I'm eager to thank those people who represent my professional career and are dedicated in extraordinary ways. My literary agent, David Fugate of LaunchBooks, negotiated the book contract and acted as a liaison with the publisher, Little, Brown. The concept of *The Art of Invisibility* was created by John Rafuse of 121 Minds, who is my agent for speaking engagements and endorsements, and he also performs strategic business development for my company. Entirely upon his own initiative, John gave me an intriguing book proposal, along with a mock-up of the cover. He strongly encouraged me to write this book to help educate the world's population on how to protect their personal privacy rights from the overstepping of Big Brother and Big Data. John is awesome.

I'm grateful to have had the opportunity to work with Little, Brown on developing this exciting project. I wish to thank my editor,

John Parsley, for all his hard work and great advice on this project. Thank you, John.

I wish to thank my friend Mikko Hypponen, chief research officer of F-Secure, for spending his valuable time penning the foreword for this book. Mikko is a highly respected security and privacy expert who has focused on malware research for over twenty-five years.

I would also like to thank Tomi Tuominen of F-Secure for taking time out of his busy schedule to do a technical review of the manuscript and help spot any errors and catch anything that was overlooked.

Notes

All source URLs cited below were accurate as of the original writing of this book, July 2016.

Introduction: Time to Disappear

1. https://www.youtube.com/watch?t=33&v=XEVlyP4_11M.
2. Snowden first went to Hong Kong before receiving permission to live in Russia. He has since applied to live in Brazil and other nations and has not ruled out a return to the United States if he were to receive a fair trial.
3. http://www.reuters.com/article/2011/02/24/idUSN2427826420110224.
4. https://www.law.cornell.edu/supct/html/98-93.ZD.html.
5. https://www.law.cornell.edu/uscode/text/16/3372.
6. http://www.wired.com/2013/06/why-i-have-nothing-to-hide-is-the-wrong-way-to-think-about-surveillance/.

Chapter One: Your Password Can Be Cracked!

1. https://www.apple.com/pr/library/2014/09/02Apple-Media-Advisory.html.
2. http://anon-ib.com/. Please note this site is not safe for work and may also contain disturbing images as well.
3. http://www.wired.com/2014/09/eppb-icloud/.
4. https://www.justice.gov/usao-mdpa/pr/lancaster-county-man-sentenced-18-months-federal-prison-hacking-apple-and-google-e-mail.
5. http://arstechnica.com/security/2015/09/new-stats-show-ashley-madison-passwords-are-just-as-weak-as-all-the-rest/.
6. http://www.openwall.com/john/.
7. "MaryHadALittleLamb123$" as rendered by http://www.danstools.com/md5-hash-generator/.
8. http://news.bbc.co.uk/2/hi/technology/3639679.stm.

9. http://www.consumerreports.org/cro/news/2014/04/smart-phone-thefts-rose-to-3-1-million-last-year/index.htm.
10. http://www.mercurynews.com/california/ci_26793089/warrant-chp-officer-says-stealing-nude-photos-from.
11. http://arstechnica.com/security/2015/08/new-data-uncovers-the-surprising-predictability-of-android-lock-patterns/.
12. http://www.knoxnews.com/news/local/official-explains-placing-david-kernell-at-ky-facility-ep-406501153-358133611.html.
13. http://www.wired.com/2008/09/palin-e-mail-ha/.
14. http://fusion.net/story/62076/mothers-maiden-name-security-question/.
15. http://web.archive.org/web/20110514200839/http://latimesblogs.latimes.com/webscout/2008/09/4chans-half-hac.html.
16. http://www.commercialappeal.com/news/david-kernell-ut-student-in-palin-email-case-is-released-from-supervision-ep-361319081-326647571.html; http://edition.cnn.com/2010/CRIME/11/12/tennessee.palin.hacking.case/.
17. http://www.symantec.com/connect/blogs/password-recovery-scam-tricks-users-handing-over-email-account-access.
18. https://techcrunch.com/2016/06/10/how-activist-deray-mckessons-twitter-account-was-hacked/.

Chapter Two: Who Else Is Reading Your E-mail?

1. In case you're wondering, images of child sexual abuse are identified and tagged by the National Center for Missing and Exploited Children, which is how Google and other search engine companies' automated scanning system distinguishes those images from the nonpornographic images on their networks. See http://www.dailymail.co.uk/news/article-2715396/Google-s-email-scan-helps-catch-sex-offender-tips-police-indecent-images-children-Gmail-account.html.
2. http://www.braingle.com/brainteasers/codes/caesar.php.
3. https://theintercept.com/2014/10/28/smuggling-snowden-secrets/.
4. For example, see the list here: https://en.wikipedia.org/wiki/Category:Cryptographic_algorithms.
5. Mailvelope works with Outlook, Gmail, Yahoo Mail, and several other Web-based e-mail services. See https://www.mailvelope.com/.
6. To see the metadata on your Gmail account, choose a message, open it, then click the down arrow in the upper right corner of the message. Among the choices ("Reply," "Reply All," "Forward," and so on) is "Show Original." In Apple Mail, select the message, then choose View>Message>All Headers. In Yahoo, click "More," then "View Full Header." Similar options appear in other mail programs.

7. http://www.bbc.com/future/story/20150206-biggest-myth-about-phone-privacy.
8. https://immersion.media.mit.edu/.
9. http://www.npr.org/2013/06/13/191226106/fisa-court-appears-to-be-rubberstamp-for-government-requests.
10. You can type "IP Address" into the Google search window to see your own IP address at the time of the request.
11. https://play.google.com/store/apps/details?id=org.torproject.android.
12. http://www.wired.com/threatlevel/2014/01/tormail/.
13. https://www.theguardian.com/technology/2014/oct/28/tor-users-advised-check-computers-malware.
14. http://arstechnica.com/security/2014/07/active-attack-on-tor-network-tried-to-decloak-users-for-five-months/.
15. For the Tor box on a Raspberry Pi, you can use something like Portal: https://github.com/grugq/PORTALofPi.
16. https://www.skype.com/en/features/online-number/.
17. http://www.newyorker.com/magazine/2007/02/19/the-kona-files.
18. Again, it's probably best not to use Google or large e-mail providers, but for the sake of illustration I'm using it here.

Chapter Three: Wiretapping 101

1. You can opt out of sharing your personal data with commuting services on the Android. Go to Settings>Search & Now>Accounts & privacy>Commute sharing. Apple does not provide a similar service, but future versions of iOS may help you plan trips based on where your phone is at a given moment.
2. http://www.abc.net.au/news/2015-07-06/nick-mckenzie-speaks-out-about-his-brush-with-the-mafia/6596098.
3. You would actually purchase a refill card that you would use with the phone itself. Best to use Bitcoin to do it.
4. https://www.washingtonpost.com/news/the-switch/wp/2014/12/18/german-researchers-discover-a-flaw-that-could-let-anyone-listen-to-your-cell-calls-and-read-your-texts/.
5. http://arstechnica.com/gadgets/2010/12/15-phone-3-minutes-all-thats-needed-to-eavesdrop-on-gsm-call/.
6. http://www.latimes.com/local/la-me-pellicano5mar05-story.html#navtype=storygallery.
7. http://www.nytimes.com/2008/03/24/business/media/24pellicano.html?pagewanted=all.
8. https://www.hollywoodreporter.com/thr-esq/anthony-pellicanos-prison-sentence-vacated-817558.

9. http://www.cryptophone.de/en/products/landline/.
10. https://www.kickstarter.com/projects/620001568/jackpair-safeguard-your-phone-conversation/posts/1654032.
11. http://spectrum.ieee.org/telecom/security/the-athens-affair.
12. http://bits.blogs.nytimes.com/2007/07/10/engineers-as-counterspys-how-the-greek-cellphone-system-was-bugged/.
13. https://play.google.com/store/apps/details?id=org.thoughtcrime.redphone.

Chapter Four: If You Don't Encrypt, You're Unequipped

1. http://caselaw.findlaw.com/wa-supreme-court/1658742.html.
2. http://courts.mrsc.org/mc/courts/zsupreme/179wn2d/179wn2d0862.htm.
3. http://www.komonews.com/news/local/Justices-People-have-right-to-privacy-in-text-messages-247583351.html.
4. http://www.democracynow.org/2016/10/26/headlines/project_hemisphere_at_ts_secret_program_to_spy_on_americans_for_profit.
5. http://www.wired.com/2015/08/know-nsa-atts-spying-pact/.
6. http://espn.go.com/nfl/story/_/id/13570716/tom-brady-new-england-patriots-wins-appeal-nfl-deflategate.
7. https://www.bostonglobe.com/sports/2015/07/28/tom-brady-destroyed-his-cellphone-and-texts-along-with/ZuIYu0he05XxEeOmHzwTSK/story.html.
8. DES was cracked partly because it only encrypted the data once. AES uses three layers of encryption and is therefore much stronger, even independent of the number of bits.
9. Diskreet is no longer available.
10. https://twitter.com/kevinmitnick/status/346065664592711680. This link provides a more technical explanation of the thirty-two-bit DES used: https://www.cs.auckland.ac.nz/~pgut001/pubs/norton.txt.
11. http://www.theatlantic.com/technology/archive/2014/06/facebook-texting-teens-instagram-snapchat-most-popular-social-network/373043/.
12. http://www.pewinternet.org/2015/04/09/teens-social-media-technology-2015.
13. http://www.forbes.com/sites/andygreenberg/2014/02/21/whatsapp-comes-under-new-scrutiny-for-privacy-policy-encryption-gaffs/.
14. https://www.wired.com/2016/10/facebook-completely-encrypted-messenger-update-now/.
15. https://community.skype.com/t5/Security-Privacy-Trust-and/Skype-to-Skype-call-recording/td-p/2064587.
16. https://www.eff.org/deeplinks/2011/12/effs-raises-concerns-about-new-aol-instant-messenger-0.

17. http://www.wired.com/2007/05/always_two_ther/.
18. http://venturebeat.com/2016/08/02/hackers-break-into-telegram-revealing-15-million-users-phone-numbers/.
19. http://www.csmonitor.com/World/Passcode/2015/0224/Private-chat-app-Telegram-may-not-be-as-secretive-as-advertised.
20. https://otr.cypherpunks.ca/.
21. https://chatsecure.org/.
22. https://guardianproject.info/apps/chatsecure/.
23. https://crypto.cat/.
24. https://getconfide.com/.

Chapter Five: Now You See Me, Now You Don't

1. https://www.techdirt.com/articles/20150606/16191831259/according-to-government-clearing-your-browser-history-is-felony.shtml.
2. http://www.cbc.ca/news/trending/clearing-your-browser-history-can-be-deemed-obstruction-of-justice-in-the-u-s-1.3105222.
3. http://ftpcontent2.worldnow.com/whdh/pdf/Matanov-Khairullozhon-indictment.pdf.
4. https://www.eff.org/https-everywhere%20.
5. http://www.tekrevue.com/safari-sync-browser-history/.
6. http://www.theguardian.com/commentisfree/2013/aug/01/government-tracking-google-searches.
7. https://myaccount.google.com/intro/privacy.
8. http://www.fastcompany.com/3026698/inside-duckduckgo-googles-tiniest-fiercest-competitor.

Chapter Six: Every Mouse Click You Make, I'll Be Watching You

1. https://timlibert.me/pdf/Libert-2015-Health_Privacy_on_Web.pdf.
2. An informal test conducted while writing this book showed that the Ghostery plug-in on Chrome blocked up to twenty-one requests from partners of the Mayo Clinic and twelve requests from partners of WebMD when returning results for "athlete's foot."
3. For a more detailed look at what information your browser leaks, check out http://browserspy.dk/.
4. https://noscript.net/.
5. https://chrome.google.com/webstore/detail/scriptblock/hcdjknjpbnhdoabbngpmfekaecnpajba?hl=en.
6. https://www.ghostery.com/en/download?src=external-ghostery.com.

7. By "mail drop" I mean commercial mailbox outfits such as the UPS Store, although many do require a photo ID before you can obtain one.
8. http://www.wired.com/2014/10/verizons-perma-cookie/.
9. http://www.pcworld.com/article/2848026/att-kills-the-permacookie-stops-tracking-customers-internet-usage-for-now.html.
10. http://www.verizonwireless.com/support/unique-identifier-header-faqs/.
11. http://www.reputation.com/blog/privacy/how-disable-and-delete-flash-cookies; http://www.brighthub.com/computing/smb-security/articles/59530.aspx.
12. http://en.wikipedia.org/wiki/Samy_Kamkar.
13. https://github.com/samyk/evercookie.
14. http://venturebeat.com/2015/07/14/consumers-want-privacy-yet-demand-personalization/.
15. http://www.businessinsider.com/facebook-will-not-honor-do-not-track-2014-6.
16. https://chrome.google.com/webstore/detail/facebook-disconnect/ejpepffjfmamnambagiibghpglaidiec?hl=en.
17. https://facebook.adblockplus.me/.
18. https://zephoria.com/top-15-valuable-facebook-statistics/.
19. http://www.latimes.com/business/la-fi-lazarus-20150417-column.html.
20. https://www.propublica.org/article/meet-the-online-tracking-device-that-is-virtually-impossible-to-block#.
21. https://addons.mozilla.org/en-us/firefox/addon/canvasblocker/.
22. https://chrome.google.com/webstore/detail/canvasfingerprintblock/ipmjngkmngdcdpmgmiebdmfbkcecdndc?hl=en-US.
23. https://trac.torproject.org/projects/tor/ticket/6253.
24. https://www.technologyreview.com/s/538731/how-ads-follow-you-from-phone-to-desktop-to-tablet/.
25. https://theintercept.com/2014/10/28/smuggling-snowden-secrets/.

Chapter Seven: Pay Up or Else!

1. http://www.computerworld.com/article/2511814/security0/man-used-neighbor-s-wi-fi-to-threaten-vice-president-biden.html.
2. http://www.computerworld.com/article/2476444/mobile-security-comcast-xfinity-wifi-just-say-no.html.
3. http://customer.xfinity.com/help-and-support/internet/disable-xfinity-wifi-home-hotspot/.
4. BitTorrent is a streaming video service for movies, some of which are provided by sources other than the copyright holders.

5. http://blog.privatewifi.com/why-six-strikes-could-be-a-nightmare-for-your-internet-privacy/.
6. There is also the basic service set (BSS), which provides the basic building block of an 802.11 wireless LAN (local area network). Each BSS or ESS (extended service set) is identified by a service set identifier (SSID).
7. http://www.techspot.com/guides/287-default-router-ip-addresses/.
8. http://www.routeripaddress.com/.
9. It's easy to figure out the MAC address of authorized devices by using a penetration-test tool known as Wireshark.
10. https://www.pwnieexpress.com/blog/wps-cracking-with-reaver.
11. http://www.wired.com/2010/10/webcam-spy-settlement/.
12. http://www.telegraph.co.uk/technology/internet-security/11153381/How-hackers-took-over-my-computer.html.
13. https://www.blackhat.com/docs/us-16/materials/us-16-Seymour-Tully-Weaponizing-Data-Science-For-Social-Engineering-Automated-E2E-Spear-Phishing-On-Twitter.pdf.
14. http://www.wired.com/2010/01/operation-aurora/.
15. http://www.nytimes.com/2015/01/04/opinion/sunday/how-my-mom-got-hacked.html.
16. http://arstechnica.com/security/2013/10/youre-infected-if-you-want-to-see-your-data-again-pay-us-300-in-bitcoins/.
17. https://securityledger.com/2015/10/fbis-advice-on-cryptolocker-just-pay-the-ransom/.

Chapter Eight: Believe Everything, Trust Nothing

1. It's important to note that public Wi-Fi is not open in all parts of the world. For example, in Singapore, to use public Wi-Fi outside your hotel or a McDonald's restaurant, you will need to register. Locals must have a Singapore cell-phone number, and tourists must present their passports to a local authority before getting approval.
2. https://business.f-secure.com/the-dangers-of-public-wifi-and-crazy-things-people-do-to-use-it/.
3. http://dnlongen.blogspot.com/2015/05/is-your-home-router-spying-on-you.html.
4. There are lots of considerations a user should know about when choosing a VPN provider. See https://torrentfreak.com/anonymous-vpn-service-provider-review-2015-150228/3/.
5. One commercial VPN choice is TunnelBear, a Canadian VPN company. They state: "TunnelBear does NOT store users originating IP addresses

when connected to our service and thus cannot identify users when provided IP addresses of our servers. Additionally, we cannot disclose information about the applications, services or websites our users consume while connected to our Services; as TunnelBear does NOT store this information." https://www.tunnelbear.com/privacy-policy/.

6. http://www.howtogeek.com/215730/how-to-connect-to-a-vpn-from-your-iphone-or-ipad/.
7. http://www.howtogeek.com/135036/how-to-connect-to-a-vpn-on-android/?PageSpeed=noscript.
8. http://www.cbc.ca/news/politics/csec-used-airport-wi-fi-to-track-canadian-travellers-edward-snowden-documents-1.2517881.
9. http://www.telegraph.co.uk/news/worldnews/northamerica/usa/9673429/David-Petraeus-ordered-lover-Paula-Broadwell-to-stop-emailing-Jill-Kelley.html.
10. http://www.nytimes.com/2012/11/12/us/us-officials-say-petraeuss-affair-known-in-summer.html.
11. https://www.wired.com/2012/11/gmail-location-data-petraeus/.
12. http://www.howtogeek.com/192173/how-and-why-to-change-your-mac-address-on-windows-linux-and-mac/?PageSpeed=noscript.

Chapter Nine: You Have No Privacy? Get Over It!

1. http://www.wired.com/2012/12/ff-john-mcafees-last-stand/.
2. http://defensetech.org/2015/06/03/us-air-force-targets-and-destroys-isis-hq-building-using-social-media/.
3. http://www.bbc.com/future/story/20150206-biggest-myth-about-phone-privacy.
4. http://www.dailymail.co.uk/news/article-3222298/Is-El-Chapo-hiding-Costa-Rica-Net-closes-world-s-wanted-drug-lord-hapless-son-forgets-switch-location-data-Twitter-picture.html.
5. https://threatpost.com/how-facebook-and-facial-recognition-are-creating-minority-report-style-privacy-meltdown-080511/75514.
6. http://www.forbes.com/sites/kashmirhill/2011/08/01/how-face-recognition-can-be-used-to-get-your-social-security-number/2/.
7. http://searchengineland.com/with-mobile-face-recognition-google-crosses-the-creepy-line-70978.
8. Robert Vamosi, *When Gadgets Betray Us: The Dark Side of Our Infatuation with New Technologies* (New York: Basic Books, 2011).
9. http://www.forbes.com/sites/kashmirhill/2011/08/01/how-face-recognition-can-be-used-to-get-your-social-security-number/.

10. https://techcrunch.com/2015/07/13/yes-google-photos-can-still-sync-your-photos-after-you-delete-the-app/.
11. https://www.facebook.com/legal/terms.
12. http://www.consumerreports.org/cro/news/2014/03/how-to-beat-facebook-s-biggest-privacy-risk/index.htm.
13. http://www.forbes.com/sites/amitchowdhry/2015/05/28/facebook-security-checkup/.
14. http://www.consumerreports.org/cro/magazine/2012/06/facebook-your-privacy/index.htm.
15. http://www.cnet.com/news/facebook-will-the-real-kevin-mitnick-please-stand-up/.
16. http://www.eff.org/files/filenode/social_network/training_course.pdf.
17. http://bits.blogs.nytimes.com/2015/03/17/pearson-under-fire-for-monitoring-students-twitter-posts/.
18. http://www.washingtonpost.com/blogs/answer-sheet/wp/2015/03/14/pearson-monitoring-social-media-for-security-breaches-during-parcc-testing/.
19. http://www.csmonitor.com/World/Passcode/Passcode-Voices/2015/0513/Is-student-privacy-erased-as-classrooms-turn-digital.
20. https://motherboard.vice.com/blog/so-were-sharing-our-social-security-numbers-on-social-media-now.
21. http://pix11.com/2013/03/14/snapchat-sexting-scandal-at-nj-high-school-could-result-in-child-porn-charges/.
22. http://www.bbc.co.uk/news/uk-34136388.
23. https://www.ftc.gov/news-events/press-releases/2014/05/snapchat-settles-ftc-charges-promises-disappearing-messages-were.
24. http://www.informationweek.com/software/social/5-ways-snapchat-violated-your-privacy-security/d/d-id/1251175.
25. http://fusion.net/story/192877/teens-face-criminal-charges-for-taking-keeping-naked-photos-of-themselves/.
26. http://www.bbc.com/future/story/20150206-biggest-myth-about-phone-privacy.
27. http://fusion.net/story/141446/a-little-known-yelp-setting-tells-businesses-your-gender-age-and-hometown/?utm_source=rss&utm_medium=feed&utm_campaign=/author/kashmir-hill/feed/.
28. On the iPhone or iPad, go to Settings>Privacy>Location Services, where you find a list of all of your location-aware apps. For example, it is possible to disable the geolocation for the Facebook Messenger app by itself. Scroll to "Facebook Messenger" and ensure that its location services are set to "Never." On Android devices, Open the Facebook Messenger app, click the "Settings"

icon (shaped like a gear) in the upper right corner, scroll to "New messages include your location by default," and uncheck it. On Android devices in general you will have to individually disable geolocation (if it's offered as a choice); there is no one-size-fits-all setting.

29. https://blog.lookout.com/blog/2016/08/25/trident-pegasus/.

Chapter Ten: You Can Run but Not Hide

1. You can turn off GPS in later verions of iOS as described here: http://smallbusiness.chron.com/disable-gps-tracking-iphone-30007.html.
2. https://gigaom.com/2013/07/08/your-metadata-can-show-snoops-a-whole-lot-just-look-at-mine/.
3. http://www.zeit.de/datenschutz/malte-spitz-data-retention.
4. https://www.washingtonpost.com/local/public-safety/federal-appeals-court-that-includes-va-md-allows-warrantless-tracking-of-historical-cell-site-records/2016/05/31/353950d2-2755-11e6-a3c4-0724e8e24f3f_story.html.
5. http://fusion.net/story/177721/phone-location-tracking-google-feds/?utm_source=rss&utm_medium=feed&utm_campaign=/author/kashmir-hill/feed/.
6. http://www.forbes.com/sites/andyrobertson/2015/05/19/strava-flyby/?ss=future-tech.
7. http://fusion.net/story/119745/in-the-future-your-insurance-company-will-know-when-youre-having-sex/?utm_source=rss&utm_medium=feed&utm_campaign=/author/kashmir-hill/feed/.
8. http://thenextweb.com/insider/2011/07/04/details-of-fitbit-users-sex-lives-removed-from-search-engine-results/.
9. http://fusion.net/story/119745/in-the-future-your-insurance-company-will-know-when-youre-having-sex/?utm_source=rss&utm_medium=feed&utm_campaign=/author/kashmir-hill/feed/.
10. http://www.engadget.com/2015/06/28/fitbit-data-used-by-police/.
11. http://abc27.com/2015/06/19/police-womans-fitness-watch-disproved-rape-report/.
12. http://www.theguardian.com/technology/2014/nov/18/court-accepts-data-fitbit-health-tracker.
13. http://www.smithsonianmag.com/innovation/invention-snapshot-changed-way-we-viewed-world-180952435/?all&no-ist.
14. https://books.google.com/books?id=SlMEAAAAMBAJ&pg=PA158&lpg=PA158&dq=%22The+kodak+has+added+a+new+terror+to+the+picnic%22&source=bl&ots=FLtKbYGv6Y&sig=YzE2BisTYejb1pT3vYhR2QBPAYM

&hl=en&sa=X&ei=BhUwT7fVBOTgiALv2-S3Cg&ved=0CCAQ6AEwAA#v=onepage&q=%22The%20koda&f=false.
15. http://www.smithsonianmag.com/innovation/invention-snapshot-changed-way-we-viewed-world-180952435/?no-ist=&page=2.
16. https://www.faa.gov/uas/media/Part_107_Summary.pdf.
17. https://www.faa.gov/uas/where_to_fly/b4ufly/.
18. http://www.slate.com/articles/technology/future_tense/2015/06/facial_recognition_privacy_talks_why_i_walked_out.html.
19. http://www.extremetech.com/mobile/208815-how-facial-recognition-will-change-shopping-in-stores.
20. http://www.retail-week.com/innovation/seven-in-ten-uk-shoppers-find-facial-recognition-technology-creepy/5077039.article.
21. http://www.ilga.gov/legislation/ilcs/ilcs3.asp?ActID=3004&ChapterID=57.
22. http://arstechnica.com/business/2015/06/retailers-want-to-be-able-to-scan-your-face-without-your-permission/.
23. http://fusion.net/story/154199/facial-recognition-no-rules/?utm_source=rss&utm_medium=feed&utm_campaign=/author/kashmir-hill/feed/.
24. https://www.youtube.com/watch?v=NEsmw7jpODc.
25. http://motherboard.vice.com/read/glasses-that-confuse-facial-recognition-systems-are-coming-to-japan.

Chapter Eleven: Hey, KITT, Don't Share My Location

1. http://www.wired.com/2015/07/hackers-remotely-kill-jeep-highway/.
2. This is silly. Just because something is prohibited doesn't mean it won't happen. And this creates a dangerous scenario in which hacked cars can still affect the driving public. Zero-days for automobiles, anyone?
3. http://keenlab.tencent.com/en/2016/06/19/Keen-Security-Lab-of-Tencent-Car-Hacking-Research-Remote-Attack-to-Tesla-Cars/.
4. http://www.buzzfeed.com/johanabhuiyan/uber-is-investigating-its-top-new-york-executive-for-privacy.
5. http://www.theregister.co.uk/2015/06/22/epic_uber_ftc/.
6. http://nypost.com/2014/11/20/uber-reportedly-tracking-riders-without-permission/.
7. https://www.uber.com/legal/usa/privacy.
8. http://fortune.com/2015/06/23/uber-privacy-epic-ftc/.
9. http://www.bbc.com/future/story/20150206-biggest-myth-about-phone-privacy.
10. http://tech.vijay.ca/of-taxis-and-rainbows-f6bc289679a1.

11. http://arstechnica.com/tech-policy/2014/06/poorly-anonymized-logs-reveal-nyc-cab-drivers-detailed-whereabouts/.
12. You can walk into a transit authority office and request to pay cash for an NFC card, but this requires extra time and will undoubtedly result in a lecture about tying your bank or credit card to the card instead.
13. http://www.wsj.com/articles/SB10000872396390443995604578004723603576296.
14. https://www.aclu.org/blog/free-future/internal-documents-show-fbi-was-wrestling-license-plate-scanner-privacy-issues.
15. http://www.wired.com/2015/05/even-fbi-privacy-concerns-license-plate-readers/.
16. Five of the sources were the St. Tammany Parish Sheriff's Office, the Jefferson Parish Sheriff's Office, and the Kenner Police Department, in Louisiana; the Hialeah Police Department, in Florida; and the University of Southern California Department of Public Safety.
17. http://www.forbes.com/sites/robertvamosi/2015/05/04/dont-sell-that-connected-car-or-home-just-yet/.
18. https://www.washingtonpost.com/blogs/the-switch/wp/2015/06/24/tesla-says-its-drivers-have-traveled-a-billion-miles-and-tesla-knows-how-many-miles-youve-driven/.
19. http://www.dhanjani.com/blog/2014/03/curosry-evaluation-of-the-tesla-model-s-we-cant-protect-our-cars-like-we-protect-our-workstations.html.
20. http://www.teslamotors.com/blog/most-peculiar-test-drive.
21. http://www.forbes.com/sites/kashmirhill/2013/02/19/the-big-privacy-takeaway-from-tesla-vs-the-new-york-times/.
22. http://www.wired.com/2015/07/gadget-hacks-gm-cars-locate-unlock-start/.
23. http://spectrum.ieee.org/cars-that-think/transportation/advanced-cars/researchers-prove-connected-cars-can-be-tracked.
24. http://www.wired.com/2015/10/cars-that-talk-to-each-other-are-much-easier-to-spy-on/.
25. https://grahamcluley.com/2013/07/volkswagen-security-flaws/.
26. https://grahamcluley.com/2015/07/land-rover-cars-bug/.
27. http://www.wired.com/2015/07/hackers-remotely-kill-jeep-highway/.
28. http://www.forbes.com/sites/robertvamosi/2015/03/24/securing-connected-cars-one-chip-at-a-time/.
29. http://www.nytimes.com/2016/07/30/business/tesla-faults-teslas-brakes-but-not-autopilot-in-fatal-crash.html.

Chapter Twelve: The Internet of Surveillance

1. http://www.amazon.com/review/R3IMEYJFO6YWHD.

2. https://www.blackhat.com/docs/us-14/materials/us-14-Jin-Smart-Nest-Thermostat-A-Smart-Spy-In-Your-Home.pdf.
3. http://venturebeat.com/2014/08/10/hello-dave-i-control-your-thermostat-googles-nest-gets-hacked/.
4. http://www.forbes.com/sites/kashmirhill/2014/07/16/nest-hack-privacy-tool/.
5. http://venturebeat.com/2014/08/10/hello-dave-i-control-your-thermostat-googles-nest-gets-hacked/.
6. http://www.networkworld.com/article/2909212/security0/schneier-on-really-bad-iot-security-it-s-going-to-come-crashing-down.html.
7. http://www.forbes.com/sites/kashmirhill/2013/07/26/smart-homes-hack/.
8. http://www.dhanjani.com/blog/2013/08/hacking-lightbulbs.html.
9. http://www.wired.com/2009/11/baby-monitor/.
10. http://www.bbc.com/news/technology-31523497.
11. http://mashable.com/2012/05/29/sensory-galaxy-s-iii/.
12. http://www.forbes.com/sites/marcwebertobias/2014/01/26/heres-how-easy-it-is-for-google-chrome-to-eavesdrop-on-your-pc-microphone/.
13. http://www.theguardian.com/technology/2015/jun/23/google-eavesdropping-tool-installed-computers-without-permission.
14. Perhaps the easiest way is to open the Amazon Echo app. Go to your settings, then go to History>Tap Individual Recording>Delete.
15. Log in to your account on Amazon, then from "Account Settings," click on Your Devices>Amazon Echo>Delete.
16. http://www.theregister.co.uk/2015/08/24/smart_fridge_security_fubar/.
17. www.shodan.io.

Chapter Thirteen: Things Your Boss Doesn't Want You to Know

1. http://www.wsj.com/articles/SB10001424052702303672404579151440488919138.
2. http://theweek.com/articles/564263/rise-workplace-spying.
3. https://olin.wustl.edu/docs/Faculty/Pierce_Cleaning_House.pdf.
4. http://harpers.org/archive/2015/03/the-spy-who-fired-me/.
5. https://room362.com/post/2016/snagging-creds-from-locked-machines/.
6. Normally document metadata is hidden from view. You can see the metadata included with your document by clicking File>Info, then viewing the properties on the right side of the window.
7. If you use Document Inspector, first make a copy of your document, because changes made cannot be undone. In the copy of your original document, click the "File" tab, then click "Info." Under "Prepare for Sharing," click "Check for Issues," then click "Inspect Document." In the Document Inspector

dialog box, select the check boxes for the content that you want to be inspected. Click "Inspect." Review the results of the inspection in the Document Inspector dialog box. Click "Remove All" next to the inspection results for the types of hidden content that you want to remove from your document.

8. http://www.infosecurity-magazine.com/news/printer-related-security-breaches-affect-63-of/.
9. http://www.wired.com/2014/08/gyroscope-listening-hack/.
10. http://ossmann.blogspot.com/2013/01/funtenna.html.
11. http://cs229.stanford.edu/proj2013/Chavez-ReconstructingNon-IntrusivelyCollectedKeystrokeDataUsingCellphoneSensors.pdf.
12. http://www.cc.gatech.edu/~traynor/papers/traynor-ccs11.pdf.
13. http://samy.pl/keysweeper/.
14. http://www.wired.com/2015/10/stingray-government-spy-tools-can-record-calls-new-documents-confirm/.
15. http://phys.org/news/2013-07-femtocell-hackers-isec-smartphone-content.html.
16. http://arstechnica.com/information-technology/2015/04/this-machine-catches-stingrays-pwnie-express-demos-cellular-threat-detector/.
17. http://www.guardian.co.uk/world/2013/jul/11/microsoft-nsa-collaboration-user-data.
18. http://www.computerworld.com/article/2474090/data-privacy/new-snowden-revelation-shows-skype-may-be-privacy-s-biggest-enemy.html.
19. https://community.rapid7.com/community/metasploit/blog/2012/01/23/video-conferencing-and-self-selecting-targets.
20. http://www.polycom.com/global/documents/solutions/industry_solutions/government/max_security/uc-deployment-for-maximum-security.pdf.
21. https://community.rapid7.com/community/metasploit/blog/2012/01/23/video-conferencing-and-self-selecting-targets.
22. For example, https://www.boxcryptor.com/en.

Chapter Fourteen: Obtaining Anonymity Is Hard Work

1. That this is a border search and arrest is not really relevant. U.S. courts have not settled whether a person of interest has to give up their passwords—so far not. However, a court has ruled that a person of interest can be forced into authenticating his or her iPhone by using Touch ID (fingerprint). To eliminate the risk, whenever you pass through customs in any country, reboot your iPhone or any other Apple device with Touch ID and do not put in your passcode. As long as you don't enter your passcode, Touch ID will fail.
2. http://www.computerweekly.com/Articles/2008/03/13/229840/us-department-of-homeland-security-holds-biggest-ever-cybersecurity.htm.

3. In iOS 8 or more recent versions of the operating system, you can reset all pairing relationships by going to Settings>General>Reset>Reset Location & Privacy or Reset Network Settings. Researcher Jonathan Zdziarski has published a number of blog posts on the topic. The instructions are beyond the scope of this book, but if you are serious about removing these, he offers a way. See http://www.zdziarski.com/blog/?p=2589.
4. http://www.engadget.com/2014/10/31/court-rules-touch-id-is-not-protected-by-the-fifth-amendment-bu/.
5. http://www.cbc.ca/news/canada/nova-scotia/quebec-resident-alain-philippon-to-fight-charge-for-not-giving-up-phone-password-at-airport-1.2982236.
6. http://www.ghacks.net/2013/02/07/forensic-tool-to-decrypt-truecrypt-bitlocker-and-pgp-contains-and-disks-released/.
7. https://www.symantec.com/content/en/us/enterprise/white_papers/b-pgp_how_wholedisk_encryption_works_WP_21158817.en-us.pdf.
8. http://www.kanguru.com/storage-accessories/kanguru-ss3.shtml.
9. https://www.schneier.com/blog/archives/2007/11/the_strange_sto.html.
10. https://theintercept.com/2015/04/27/encrypting-laptop-like-mean/.
11. http://www.securityweek.com/researcher-demonstrates-simple-bitlocker-bypass.
12. https://www.fbi.gov/news/speeches/going-dark-are-technology-privacy-and-public-safety-on-a-collision-course.
13. http://www.nytimes.com/library/tech/00/01/cyber/cyberlaw/28law.html.
14. https://partners.nytimes.com/library/tech/00/01/cyber/cyberlaw/28law.html.
15. https://www.wired.com/2015/10/cops-dont-need-encryption-backdoor-to-hack-iphones/.
16. http://theinvisiblethings.blogspot.com/2009/10/evil-maid-goes-after-truecrypt.html.
17. https://blog.gdatasoftware.com/blog/article/hotel-safes-are-they-really-safe.html.
18. http://www.snopes.com/crime/warnings/hotelkey.asp.
19. http://www.themarysue.com/hotel-key-myth/.
20. https://shaun.net/posts/whats-contained-in-a-boarding-pass-barcode.
21. Apparently United is one of the few airlines that only gives a partial frequent flyer mile number. Most other airlines do put the full number in the bar code.
22. http://www.wired.com/2014/11/darkhotel-malware/.
23. https://bitlaunder.com/launder-bitcoin.

Chapter Fifteen: The FBI Always Gets Its Man

1. https://www.wired.com/2015/05/silk-road-creator-ross-ulbricht-sentenced-life-prison/.

2. http://www.nytimes.com/2015/12/27/business/dealbook/the-unsung-tax-agent-who-put-a-face-on-the-silk-road.html?_r=0.
3. http://www.wired.com/2015/07/online-anonymity-box-puts-mile-away-ip-address/.
4. https://samy.pl/proxygambit/.

Chapter Sixteen: Mastering the Art of Invisibility

1. There's more. Even though the FBI identified my apartment complex, they didn't know where I was. That changed when I stepped outside one night. This story can be found in my book *Ghost in the Wires*.
2. Sites like Weather Underground put the longitude and latitude of the visitor in the URL.
3. For example, https://www.bitrefill.com.
4. https://nakedsecurity.sophos.com/2015/07/30/websites-can-track-us-by-the-way-we-type-heres-how-to-stop-it/.

Index

Index

About the Authors

KEVIN MITNICK, the world's most famous (former) hacker, is now a security consultant. He is the founder and CEO of Mitnick Security Consulting, a world-class penetration-testing company, and the chief hacking officer of KnowBe4, a company that trains employees to make smarter security decisions. Mitnick has been the subject of countless news and magazine articles and has appeared on numerous television and radio programs offering expert commentary on information security. He has testified before the US Senate and written for the *Harvard Business Review*. Mitnick is the author, with William L. Simon, of the bestselling books *The Art of Deception, The Art of Intrusion,* and *Ghost in the Wires*. He lives in Las Vegas, Nevada, and travels the world as the top keynote speaker on cybersecurity.

ROBERT VAMOSI is a CISSP, an award-winning journalist, and the author of *When Gadgets Betray Us: The Dark Side of our Infatuation with New Technologies*. He is featured in the history-of-hacking documentary *Code2600*. Vamosi has been writing about information security for more than fifteen years for publications including Forbes.com, *ZDNet, CNET,* CBS News, *PC World,* and *Security Ledger.*